THE KNIGHTS TEMPLAR

CRUSADE, MYTH AND HOLLYWOOD

PATRICK MASTERS

The History Press

For my wife and daughters

First published 2025

The History Press
97 St George's Place, Cheltenham,
Gloucestershire, GL50 3QB
www.thehistorypress.co.uk

British Library Cataloguing in Publication Data.
A catalogue record for this book is available from the British Library.

ISBN 978 1 80399 316 4

Typesetting and origination by The History Press
Printed and bound in Great Britain by TJ Books Limited, Padstow, Cornwall.

EU Authorised Representative: Easy Access System Europe
Mustamäe tee 50, 10621 Tallinn, Estonia
gpst.request@easproject.com

MIX
Paper | Supporting responsible forestry
FSC® C013056

Trees for Life

CONTENTS

ACKNOWLEDGEMENTS

I would like to express my gratitude to Chris Course for providing me with the maps to use in the book and patiently making the minor changes I requested. I would also like to thank Professor Geraghty for his mentorship and encouragement to continue my research into the Knights Templar. I am grateful to Sarah, who was supportive with flexible working to enable me to research and draft the book.

I would also like to thank my family: first, my parents, Brian and Nicky, sister Felicity and Grandad Doug, who have supported me throughout all my research projects. I would like to offer a special thank you to my wife, Charlotte, and my daughters, who continue to be my inspiration; without their support, the book would not have been possible.

MAPS

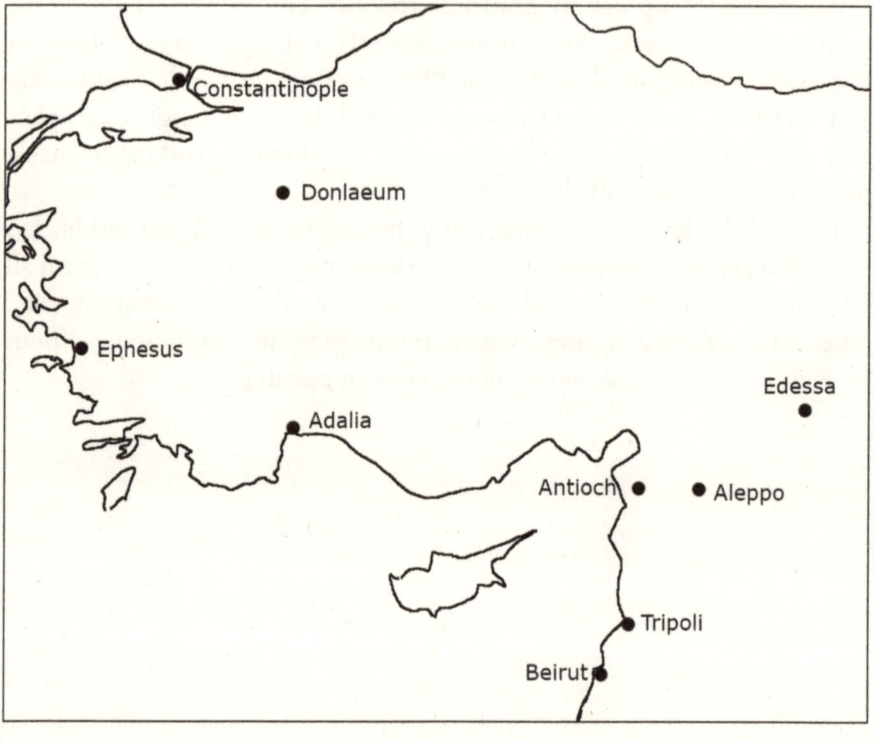
Constantinople
Donlaeum
Ephesus
Edessa
Adalia
Antioch
Aleppo
Tripoli
Beirut

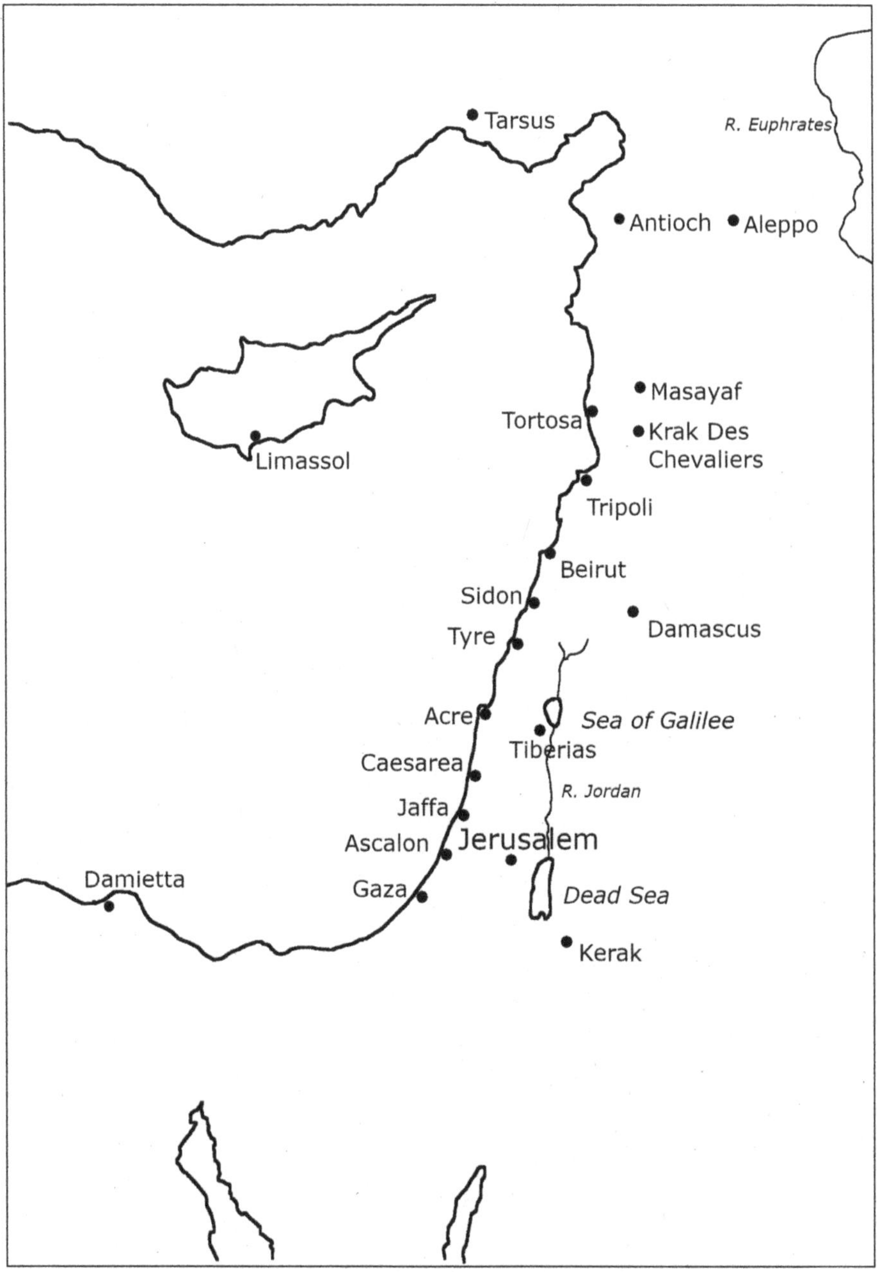
Tarsus
R. Euphrates
Antioch
Aleppo
Masayaf
Tortosa
Krak Des Chevaliers
Limassol
Tripoli
Beirut
Sidon
Damascus
Tyre
Acre
Sea of Galilee
Tiberias
Caesarea
R. Jordan
Jaffa
Ascalon
Jerusalem
Damietta
Gaza
Dead Sea
Kerak

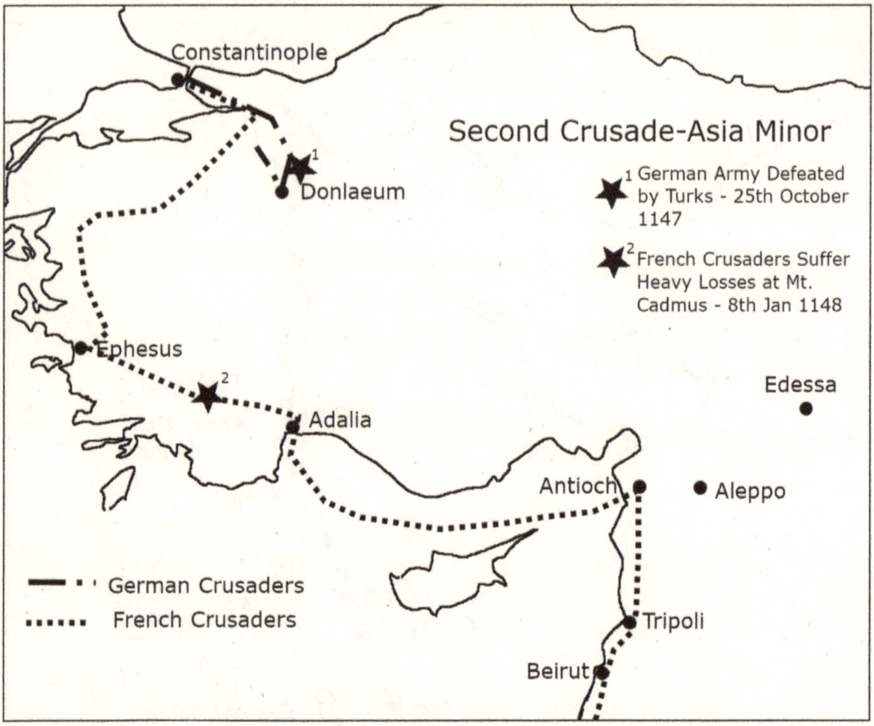
Second Crusade-Asia Minor
1 German Army Defeated by Turks - 25th October 1147
2 French Crusaders Suffer Heavy Losses at Mt. Cadmus - 8th Jan 1148
Constantinople
Donlaeum
Ephesus
Adalia
Edessa
Antioch
Aleppo
Tripoli
Beirut
German Crusaders
French Crusaders

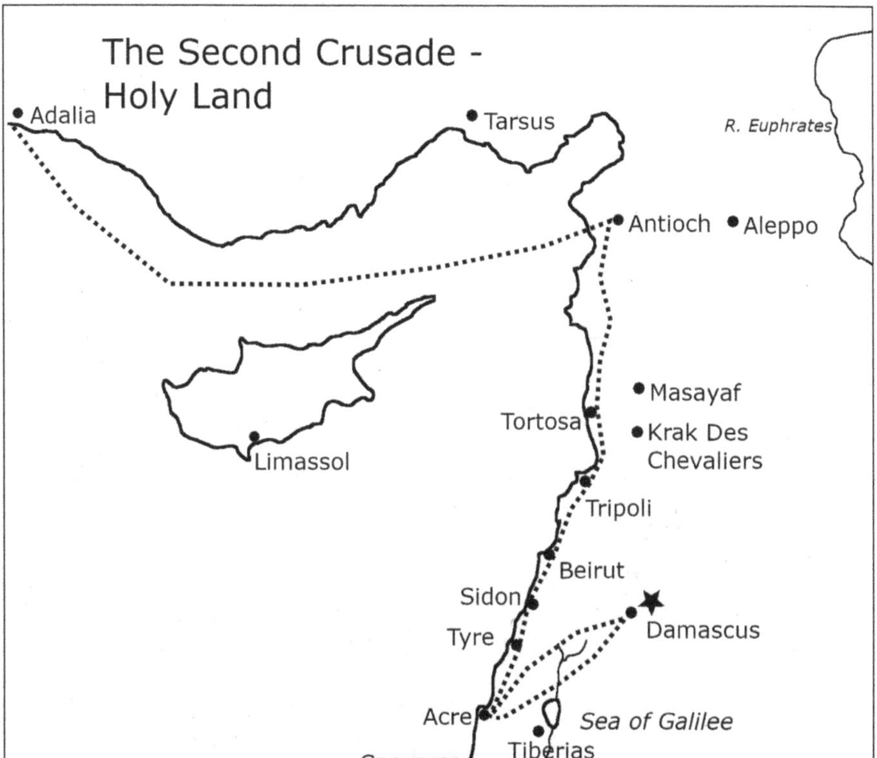
The Second Crusade -
Holy Land
Adalia
Tarsus
R. Euphrates
Antioch
Aleppo
Masayaf
Tortosa
Krak Des
Chevaliers
Limassol
Tripoli
Beirut
Sidon
Damascus
Tyre
Acre
Sea of Galilee
Tiberias
Caesarea
R. Jordan
Jaffa
Ascalon
Jerusalem
Damietta
Gaza
Dead Sea
Kerak
Combined French and German
Crusade Army
Unsuccessful Siege of
Damascus - 1148

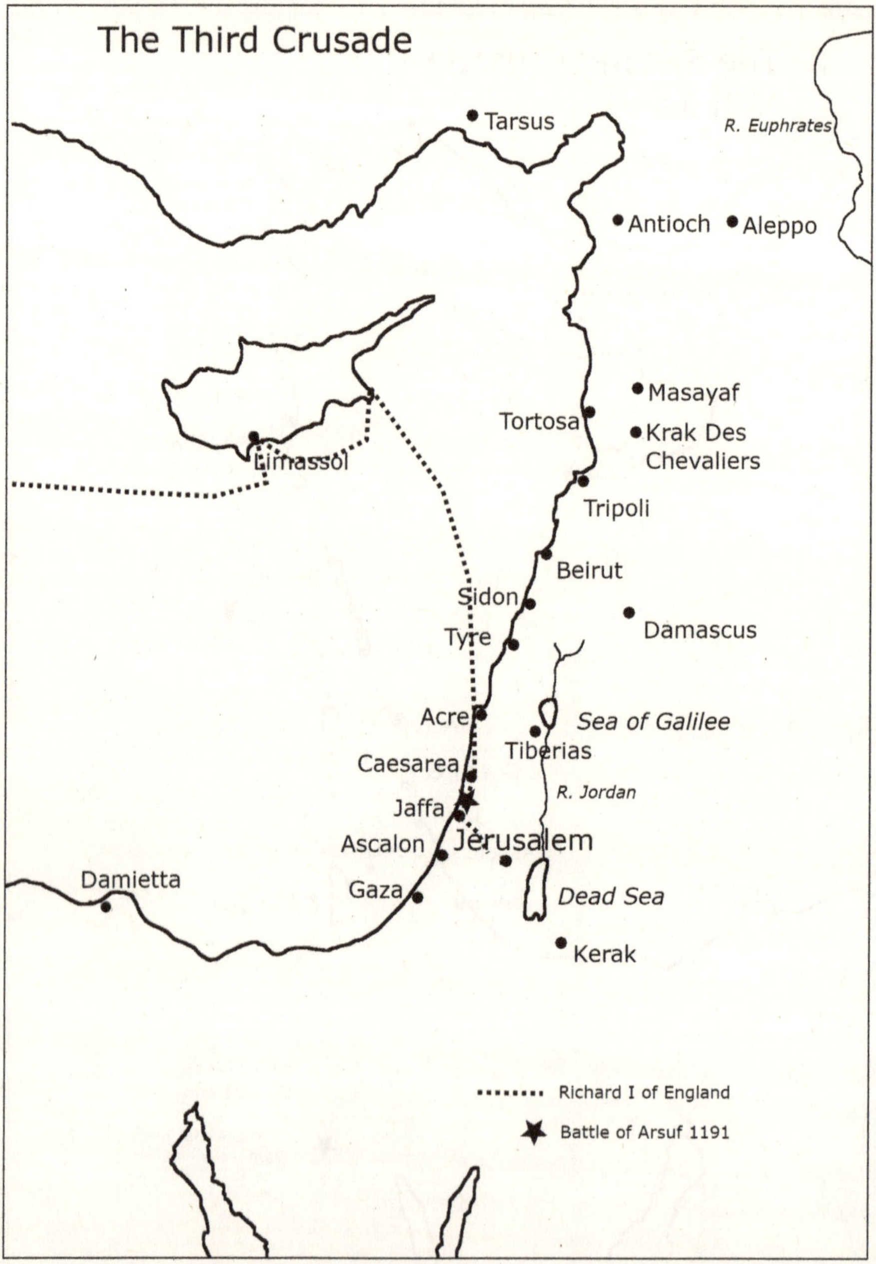
The Third Crusade
Tarsus
R. Euphrates
Antioch
Aleppo
Masayaf
Tortosa
Krak Des Chevaliers
Limassol
Tripoli
Beirut
Sidon
Damascus
Tyre
Acre
Sea of Galilee
Tiberias
Caesarea
R. Jordan
Jaffa
Ascalon
Jerusalem
Damietta
Gaza
Dead Sea
Kerak
Richard I of England
Battle of Arsuf 1191

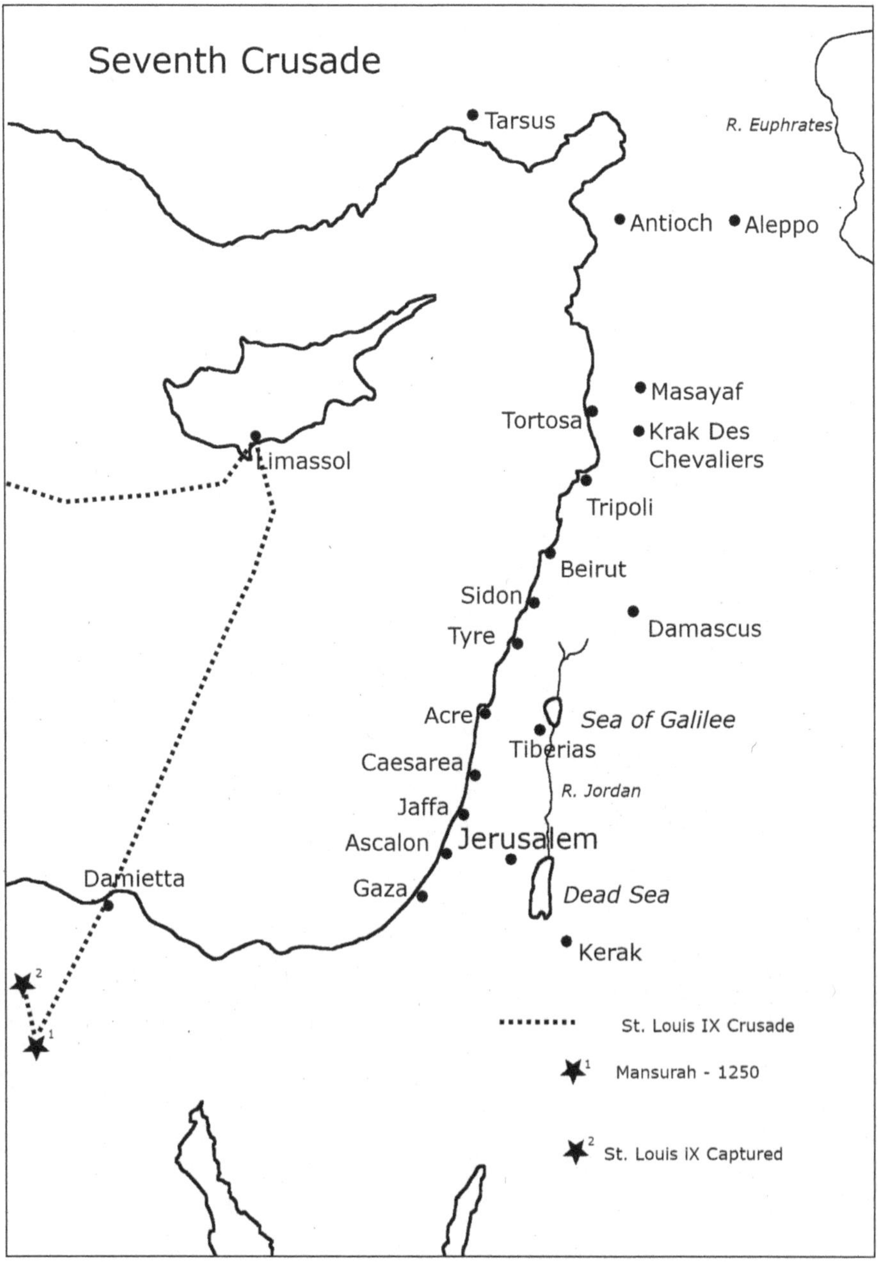
Seventh Crusade
Tarsus
R. Euphrates
Antioch
Aleppo
Masayaf
Tortosa
Krak Des Chevaliers
Limassol
Tripoli
Beirut
Sidon
Damascus
Tyre
Acre
Sea of Galilee
Tiberias
Caesarea
R. Jordan
Jaffa
Ascalon
Jerusalem
Damietta
Gaza
Dead Sea
Kerak
St. Louis IX Crusade
Mansurah - 1250
St. Louis IX Captured

INTRODUCTION

THE HOLY LAND BEFORE THE TEMPLARS

The infamous Order of the Knights Templar was established early in the twelfth century but still captures the popular imagination 900 years later. The Knights Templar were formed to patrol the roads of the Holy Land but became a premier military force of the Crusades. The Templars' abolishment in 1312 has fuelled the continuing presence of myths and false claims, such as links to the occult, the Freemasons and secret treasure. In the modern era, they have been depicted in fiction with contradicting roles, such as guardians of the Holy Grail, undead monsters and knights, both heroic and villainous. The Templars became most known by their association with the nineteenth-century novels of Sir Walter Scott and their part in a centuries-old conspiracy in Dan Brown's 2003 bestseller *The Da Vinci Code*.

This book examines the 900-year story of the Knights Templar, examining the Order's origin, detailing the Templars as an organisation, their increasing influence in the Crusader states and their role in the Crusades. The Knights Templar fought alongside figures such as Richard the Lionheart and St Louis IX and were involved in some of the Crusaders' most significant victories, such as the Battle of Montgisard, and their most devastating defeats, such as the Battle of Hattin. The Templars held a vast amount of land in Europe before their sudden arrest by King Philip IV in 1307.

To examine the legacy of these warrior monks, this book will look beyond the myths that followed the Templars' demise and explore how they came to be and how these myths influenced artistic imagination and further embedded them within popular culture through literature, film and even computer games.

For the history of the Knights Templar, this book uses primary sources from both Christian and Muslim chroniclers of the period to attempt to provide a balanced perspective on the Templars. To supplement the primary accounts, this book draws upon the work of other historians' accounts of the Crusades, which may give this narrative a subtle Western bias. However, this is the story of the Templars and, therefore, their victories and losses will be described as such, but it is without the intention of partiality.

By providing a detailed history of the Templars, this book aims to ascertain the truth behind the myths and perceptions by comparing the fantastical associations with the historical reality. The book will tell the entire 900-year story of the Knights Templar, from the history to the myths that followed and how these are perceived in the modern era through fiction.

In examining the history of the Templars, it is vital to provide the context of not only the First Crusade, which preceded their creation, but also to establish the political make-up of the Holy Land prior to the First Crusade and the radical transformation left in its wake.

BYZANTINE DECLINE AND ISLAMIC DOMINANCE

Throughout almost all of the eleventh century, there were no Latin states in the Holy Land because they were created following the titanic shift in Western and Eastern politics at the end of the eleventh century. This saw European Christians invade the Holy Land as an armed pilgrimage and led to countless deaths and genocidal slaughter.

The war between Christians and Muslims over control of the Holy Land began centuries before the First Crusade. The Byzantines held Jerusalem before the Muslim conquest of the city in AD 638.

Damascus was the first Byzantine city to be lost after the Arabic forces laid siege to it in 634. Despite putting up fierce resistance, the city fell, and the Christian inhabitants were given three days of safe passage, but after the third day passed the escaping Christians were hunted down and killed. Knowing the fate of those at Damascus, Jerusalem resisted, with its defences led by the elderly Greek Orthodox patriarch, Sophronius, and they held out for two years before surrendering due to starvation.

The Christians at Jerusalem did not share the horrific fate of the Damascenes and they were allowed to remain within the city unharmed and their property intact as long as they paid *Jizya*, a tax for non-Muslims.[1] Jerusalem remained under Muslim control for 400 years before the arrival of the First Crusaders, who did not allow the Muslim citizens the same clemency.

By the end of the eleventh century, the Byzantines had been pushed back to Constantinople, having lost their territories in the Holy Land, Syria and almost all of Asia Minor. Following the Muslim conquest of the Holy Land, the Muslim territory would stretch from the Indus River and the borders of China across North Africa and into Spain and southern France.[2] The empire would become fragmented and split into independent states.

In 661, following the death of Ali (the Prophet's cousin and son-in-law), power was seized by the Umayyad dynasty, who moved the Muslim capital from Arabia to Damascus. The rise of the Umayyad dynasty saw the emergence of the Shia branch of Islam, which believed that only a descendant of Ali and his wife Fatima, the daughter of Muhammad, could rule as caliph.

In 750, the Umayyads' rule came to a violent end and another Arab dynasty seized control, the Abbasids. The Abbasids moved the centre of Sunni Islam to Baghdad as the new capital, which would remain the centre of the religious denomination for 500 years.[3]

Although Spain had been independent from the empire since the eighth century, there was further division when, in 969, a Shi'ite faction known as the Fatimids, who claimed descent from Muhammad's daughter, took control of north Africa and established a rival caliphate that rejected Sunni Baghdad's authority. The Fatimids soon captured Jerusalem and Damascus, bringing several coastal territories into the Shi'ite caliphate. Eventually, the rival caliph's influence would dwindle and become a figurehead, while the actual power was wielded by the lieutenants, the sultan in Baghdad and the vizier in Cairo.[4]

Despite the continual decline of Byzantine power in Asia Minor and the Holy Land, the tenth century saw the Byzantines recapture lost territory. In 934, Byzantine general John Curcuas captured the city of Melitene, which the Arabs had held since 638. The shocking loss and further Byzantine victories caused an outbreak of violence against Christians, such as the sacking of the Holy Sepulchre on Palm Sunday in 937, when the church was looted and set alight. This caused sections of the building to collapse, including the Anastasis that was thought to enclose the Tomb of Christ.[5]

Throughout much of the tenth century, the Byzantines retook a large number of territories, such as Crete and Cyprus, before capturing the lost coastal territories of Antioch and Latakia and much of northern Syria, eventually retaking Damascus. By the eleventh century, the reinvigorated Byzantines were on the back foot as a new force appeared in the Holy Land, the Seljuq Turks, and their dominance would be one of the catalysts for the First Crusade.

In 1040, the Turks arrived. Nomadic tribesmen from Central Asia and a clan known as the Seljuq adopted Sunni Islam as their religion and pledged allegiance to the Abbasid caliph. The Seljuqs would gain dominance, as by 1045 the warlord Tughril had been appointed Sultan of Baghdad, which not only gave control of Sunni Islam to the Seljuqs, but they soon dominated the region, taking back Damascus and the coastal territories, driving the Fatimids back and retaking Jerusalem.

Following the gains from the Byzantines, a splinter group established an independent sultanate in Asia Minor.[6] The power of the Seljuk Empire would be split when the Seljuk Sultan Malik-Shah died in 1092; his sons fought over their inheritance, and Malik-Shah's brother Tutush seized Syria for himself. After Tutush died in 1095, his sons fought over the succession and took control of Aleppo and Damascus separately.

The state of the Holy Land at the dawn of the First Crusade was not a unified Islamic power, and Sunni Islam was in disarray, while the Fatimids were contending with the appointment of a new vizier following the sudden death of the Fatimid Caliph in 1094 and his vizier a year later. Crusades historian Thomas Ashbridge notes that despite the challenges facing the Muslim states in the Holy Land, there is no evidence that the Latin Christians were aware of this, but the timing was extremely advantageous.[7]

The catalyst for the launch of the First Crusade was not the loss of Jerusalem, as the Christians had lost control of the city in the seventh century, nor was it due to the suffering of Christians, even though there were cases of violence as mentioned previously. The Christians had been second-class citizens since the seventh century, but they were free to practise their religion as long as they paid the *Jizya*.

Christians and Muslims had been at war in the Holy Land for hundreds of years, and although there had been outbreaks of violence and intolerance at the end of the eleventh century, there was little indication of the seismic events that would follow.

THE LAUNCH OF THE FIRST CRUSADE

On 27 November 1095, in a field outside Clermont, Pope Urban II delivered a sermon that would change European society and see a mass exodus of Europeans pouring into Asia Minor. The sermon delivered by Urban was the result of months of development as, in March of that year, he received ambassadors from the Byzantine Emperor Alexius I, who sought aid from the European Christians to help repel the Seljuk Turks. Urban may have been moved by Constantinople's plight, but since becoming pope in 1088 he had worked tirelessly to rebuild the influence of the papacy, so the appeal from Alexius I offered a chance to extend his authority and direct the warring European nobles towards a new goal.

After visiting several monasteries to gather support, in November, Urban held a Great Council at Clermont in France, attended by twelve archbishops, eighty bishops and ninety abbots. After nine days of discussion, Urban delivered the infamous sermon at Clermont to hundreds of spectators.[8]

Urban spoke of the need to aid the Byzantines and warned that the Turks would invade Europe if nothing were done. Although Fulcher of Chartres' chronicle was written after the First Crusade, it gives an account of the specifics of Urban's speech. In the sermon, Urban called on those assembled to carry out genocide against the Muslims and liberate the local Christians, which would quickly descend into acts of violence and mass slaughter against non-Christians. Those taking part in the armed pilgrimage were promised the remission of their sins, with Urban proclaiming:

> Those going thither there will be remission of sins if they come to the end of this fettered life while either marching by land or crossing by sea, or in fighting the pagans. This I grant to all who go, through the power vested in me by God.[9]

Although the Byzantine Emperor had called for aid in pushing back against the Seljuk Turks, retaking Jerusalem soon became the primary goal.

Bishop Adhemar of Le Puy was the first to take the cross, followed by many others, who took a small piece of cloth torn from garments and shaped it into a cross that was fixed to their shoulder. The act of taking the cross is how Urban's armed pilgrimage came to be known as a crusade. Originally, the First Crusade was known as a journey or pilgrimage. It wasn't until the end of the twelfth century that the term *crucesignatus* ('one signed with the cross') was used to describe a crusader, with the wars eventually being known by the French term *croisade*, which meant 'the way of the cross'.[10]

Count Raymond of Toulouse was the next significant figure to take the cross, followed by prominent senior nobles from France, western Germany and Italy. Adhemar of Le Puy was appointed the Papal Legate to act as Pope Urban's representative. However, given the gradual waves of participants, there was no fixed leader for the Crusade. The number of First Crusaders is estimated to have involved between 60,000 and 100,000

European Christians who undertook the journey, of which 7,000 to 10,000 were knights and between 35,000 and 50,000 infantry.[11]

The other senior leaders of the First Crusade included Bohemond of Taranto and his nephew, the young Tancred of Hauteville. Duke Godfrey of Bouillon and his brother, Baldwin of Boulogne, led a contingent of troops from Lorraine, Lotharingia and Germany. The other prominent leaders were Duke Robert of Normandy, the eldest son of William the Conqueror, Count Stephen of Blois and Count Robert II of Flanders.

However, the First Crusade was not a purely military venture, it was also spiritual, and it involved tens of thousands of non-combatants who took the cross after Urban's call was echoed across Europe by the bishops in attendance. Urban's call to retake Jerusalem was so popular that unofficial preachers took up the cause and preached for the Crusade.

The most infamous of these was Peter the Hermit. Peter is described as an austere wanderer with a repellent appearance, but to the poorest, he was regarded as a living saint. Peter soon raised a rabble numbering around 15,000, which was the first wave to reach Asia Minor and became known as the People's Crusade.[12] The rabble was poorly armed and lacked the funds needed to finance the long journey, which demonstrates how Urban's message captivated those from across the classes of medieval society.

However, the first wave also consisted of fighting men and knights such as Walter Sansavoir. The armies of the First Crusade departed periodically and made their way to Constantinople in their separate hosts.

While en route to Constantinople, the Crusaders carried out atrocities against the Jewish communities in Germany, the most horrific taking place in Worms and Mainz. The acts of antisemitism in relation to the First Crusade began in December 1095 with antisemitic riots in Rouen, and in 1096 the violence spread to the Rhineland at Speyer, Trier, Metz, Regensburg and Cologne.[13] An account of the atrocities was written after 1140 by Solomon Bar Simson, a member of the Mainz Jewish community.

In Speyer, the Crusaders killed several members of the Jewish community who refused to convert to Christianity. The Crusaders set upon the Worms Jewish community in their homes, sparing none found within and looting and plundering what they could. Some were temporarily saved by the Bishop of Worms, who sheltered those he could, but ultimately he could not prevent the horde from killing those hiding inside. The account also details how some of the Jews sheltering there killed themselves for fear of the Crusaders' brutality.[14]

The leader of this mass murder was Count Emicho of Leiningen, who Solomon Bar Simson describes as 'the oppressor of all the Jews' and adds, 'may his bones be ground to dust between iron millstones'.[15] However, it must be mentioned that Godfrey of Bouillon extorted 500 pieces of silver from the Jews of Cologne and Mainz for protection, which he failed to honour.[16]

Terrified of Emicho's hordes, the Jewish community of Mainz paid a considerable sum of money to the archbishop to shelter them from the murderous Crusaders. Sadly, he could not protect them; Emicho's army massacred those sheltered and, as at Worms, entire families committed suicide to escape the Crusaders.[17]

Crusades historian Hans Mayer proposes that the atrocities carried out by Count Emicho and others were to procure means of finance for their journey to the Holy Land, although such was his reputation for brutality that Emicho's forces were destroyed at the Hungarian border by the King of Hungary's army.[18] The atrocities committed against the Jewish communities showed the violent nature awoken by Urban's call and they would be inflicted on the inhabitants of Muslim-controlled cities and, most infamously, at Jerusalem.

After travelling to Constantinople, the first wave of Crusaders, known as the People's Crusade, reached Asia Minor near Nicaea around 7 August 1096. Here, they committed terrible atrocities against the local populace until they were defeated in battle by a Turkish army in October 1097. Here, Walter Sansavoir met his end, and with the army destroyed, the Turks fell upon the helpless non-combatants at the camp, killing or enslaving them all. The People's Crusade ended in complete annihilation, but Peter the Hermit was in Constantinople when the massacre occurred and joined the second wave, led by the senior nobles of Europe.[19]

TO JERUSALEM

The second wave also ventured to the Holy Land via Constantinople, however, the leaders were pressured to swear an oath to Emperor Alexius that all territories captured that the Byzantines had lost to the Turks would be restored to Byzantine control. In February 1097, Godfrey of Bouillon and his army crossed the Gulf of Nicomedia and were joined on the coast of Asia Minor by the other Crusader armies throughout spring and into the summer.

At first, the Crusaders and Byzantine coalition held firm as the city of Nicaea, the capital city of the Seljuk Sultan Kilij Arslan, was captured after a short siege on 18 June. After the ease with which Kilij Arslan had destroyed the People's Crusade, the sultan underestimated the second wave and was defeated by the Crusaders in a pitched battle before Nicaea on 21 May.

Nicaea was returned to Byzantine control, and the Crusaders were forbidden from entering for fear of looting. Although the emperor gave the leaders generous gifts, despite their oath, they were underwhelmed and wished to receive more spoils.[20] Even so, the Crusaders' mood following the victory at Nicaea was positive, with Stephen of Blois writing to his wife, Adelaide, 'I tell you, my love, that five weeks after leaving the oft-mentioned Nicaea we will reach Jerusalem if Antioch does not hold us up.'[21]

The naïve optimism of Stephen of Blois would not last, and the Crusaders had to endure a brutal march through Anatolia to Antioch during the height of the summer with little food or water. On the long march, the Crusaders were attacked by Kilij Arslan, whose forces ambushed them at the Battle of Dorylaeum on 1 July 1097. The Crusader army decisively defeated the sultan and took much plunder to aid with their harsh journey.

This victory for the Crusaders would not be repeated during the Second Crusade, but it opened the way for them to reach Antioch. They arrived before the walled city in October, which stalled the momentum and gains seen since crossing the Gulf of Nicomedia. The sheer size of the walls meant that the Crusaders could not storm them, and scale of the city made it impossible for them to surround it and starve the inhabitants into submission.

The siege of Antioch lasted almost a year, and along with the constant fighting between the Crusaders and the defenders, the Crusaders were pushed to almost starvation. Fulcher of Chartres described how the starving Crusaders were forced to eat the beanstalks, herbs and thistles they found.[22]

In 1098, an army led by Kerbogha of Mosul was marching on Antioch to destroy the Crusaders before its great walls. At this dire news, Bohemond of Taranto revealed he had reached an agreement with Firouz, a captain of the Antioch guard, to help them climb the walls, but in return Bohemond wanted control of Antioch. The leaders of the Crusade were forced to forsake their vows and promise Bohemond the city. On 3 June, Firouz left rope ladders for a small force of Crusaders to climb and capture the city and slaughter the Turks within.

Although they had captured the city, they found themselves trapped with no food as Kerbogha's army reached Antioch. Faced with starvation or the sword, the Crusaders attempted a desperate attack on 28 June 1098 at the Battle of Antioch, and they achieved a resounding victory. This unlikely event occurred due to a lack of unity in Kerbogha's army, which included a coalition of forces from Syria. This led to a disorganised army and needed a unifying leader, but according to the Muslim chronicler Ibn al-Athīr, Kerbogha was not the leader needed, and he had 'treated the Muslims with such contempt and scorn'.[23]

The Crusaders saw their victory as a miracle, which coincided with the supposed discovery of the Holy Lance after capturing Antioch. Reputed to be the spear that pierced Christ at the Crucifixion, the alleged lance was found under the Basilica of St Peter by Peter Bartholomew. Historian Thomas Ashbridge proposes that religious devotion played a factor in the victory – a less-devout army might have broken under dire circumstances, but the Crusader army held out with steadfast resolve.[24]

The Crusaders reached the walls of Jerusalem on 7 June 1099, which was now under the control of the Fatimids, who retook the city from the Seljuks in July 1098. Although the Crusaders were within reach of their goal, they were in a highly vulnerable position. In their haste, they had not taken control of the port of Jaffa and were cut off from any support as they were hundreds of miles from Antioch. The Crusader army had massively dwindled due to disease, starvation and warfare, now numbering around 1,200 knights and 15,000 able-bodied men.

The Fatimid governor, Iftikhar ad-Daulah, was well prepared for the Crusaders' arrival. He had brought additional troops and reinforced Jerusalem's defensive walls. He also brought the Muslims from the surrounding villages inside the city and poisoned the wells before expelling the Christians from the city to ensure they could not aid the Crusaders. The governor had prepared Jerusalem well to hold out against the Crusaders while awaiting the arrival of an army from Egypt to finally destroy the Europeans.[25]

After a week camped outside the city, on 13 June, the Crusaders launched their first attack on the huge walls of Jerusalem via ladders. Although the direct assault failed, the Crusaders' spirits were lifted on 17 June by the arrival of a fleet of ships from Genoa, who landed at Jaffa unopposed and brought supplies and craftsmen to the siege camp.[26] Camped outside the city, the Crusaders were supplied with food but lacked water, so this had to be brought into the camp from miles away.[27] The Crusaders could not remain outside the city and needed to capture Jerusalem before a relief army arrived.

On 15 July, Godfrey of Bouillon captured the northern battlements, and the defence collapsed, forcing the Muslim garrison to flee for their lives. After three years of tremendous struggle, the Crusaders had captured Jerusalem, but at the cost of tens of thousands of lives.

After achieving their Holy goal, the Crusaders began to sack the city and unleashed a bloody ferocity upon the inhabitants. No one was spared, and the Crusaders slaughtered through the streets to Solomon's Temple. Here, Fulcher of Chartres gives a chilling account, writing, 'Nearly ten thousand were beheaded in this Temple. If you had been there your feet would have been stained to the ankles in the blood of the slain. What shall I say? None of them were left alive. Neither women or children were spared.'[28]

Pope Urban could not have envisioned the monster he would create following his sermon in 1095, yet four years later, the armed pilgrimage, against overwhelming odds and by causing immeasurable human suffering, liberated the Holy Land for Christianity. What followed was the creation of the Latin Crusader states, known collectively as Outremer, in the newly conquered land; controlling these would require an enormous amount of manpower.

This led to the formation of the Order of the Knights Templar. It is in the context of the suffering and genocide caused by the First Crusade that the Templars must be discussed, as they were created to protect the gains that had been won by mass slaughter.

The remainder of this book examines the history of the Knights Templar and their prominent role in the Crusades. Part 1 examines the Templars' origin, the organisation and their involvement with politics at the height of the Crusader states. Part 2 visits the rise of Saladin and the Templars' role in the disasters that befell the Kingdom of Jerusalem. Part 3 analyses the loss of the Crusader states and the shadowy nature that led to the demise of the Templars. The final section explores various articles of popular fiction such as Hollywood films, literature, and even *Star Wars*, to determine how the Templar myths such as the Holy Grail, their role in the Freemasons and the occult have flourished for centuries after the Order's abolishment.

PART 1

THE CRUSADER STATES OF OUTREMER

1

THE CRUSADERS AND THE ORIGIN OF THE TEMPLARS

OUTREMER IS BORN

On 15 July 1099, the city of Jerusalem fell to the Crusaders. Two days after the massacre of the city's population, the leaders of the First Crusade met to elect a new King of Jerusalem.

There would be three claimants to the rule of Jerusalem before the end of the next year: Godfrey, Baldwin and Daimbert. Initially, and after days of deliberation, the crown was offered to French Duke Godfrey of Bouillon, who accepted the honour but refused the title of king, preferring to be *Advocatus Sancti Sepulchri* (the Defender of the Holy Sepulchre).

However, Godfrey was dead within a year, succumbing to an illness akin to typhoid in July 1100.[1] His successor would be his younger brother, Baldwin of Boulogne, who was currently the count in the newly acquired territory of Edessa. He would not be so shy about the title king, becoming King Baldwin I. Unfortunately, a coronation would have to wait – Jerusalem's new king would not be crowned until Christmas Day, as another claimed rulership of the holy city.

The Patriarch of Jerusalem, Daimbert of Pisa, had his own vision for the new Christian Kingdom of Jerusalem as an ecclesiastical state with the Patriarch (himself) as head of state. Daimbert's ambition would fail though, because he was absent from Godfrey during his final moments, besieging the port of Haifa with Tancred of Hauteville, who became Prince of Galilee after Jerusalem's conquest. He had failed to seize the initiative.

Daimbert's absence enabled Baldwin's supporters to occupy the Tower of David, the city's key fortification, then send messengers to Baldwin at Edessa. By September, the news had reached Baldwin, who was in his thirties, and although he was an ambitious man, he was reportedly grieved at the death of his brother but celebrated the news of his inheritance.[2]

In October, Baldwin set out south for Jerusalem with a force numbering almost 1,000, consisting of 700 infantry and 200 knights.[3] The future king sent a trusted knight on ahead to liaise with his allies in the Tower of David and arrange for Baldwin's arrival in early November to be met with crowds of cheering Christians. There could be no doubt who was to be Jerusalem's next ruler.

Baldwin granted the County of Edessa to his cousin, Baldwin of Bourcq, and was crowned as the first King of Jerusalem in the Church of the Nativity at Bethlehem on 25 December 1100 by none other than Daimbert himself. With his dream of Jerusalem as an ecclesiastical state unfulfilled, Daimbert most likely chose to serve in order to keep his position as the Patriarch of Jerusalem.

With Baldwin I's coronation, the threat of civil war was averted. Tancred left the region shortly after in early 1101 to rule Antioch as regent during his uncle Bohemond's imprisonment (he was captured while on an expedition against the Danishmend Turks). Daimbert would lose his position that year as Patriarch after he was caught embezzling funds sent for use in defending the new Crusader lands.

Jerusalem became the capital city of the newly created Kingdom of Jerusalem. This territory resembled the extent of modern-day Israel and Palestine, including across from the eastern shore of the River Jordan, stretching down from southern Lebanon to south-western Syria. At the border to the north of the kingdom was Beirut and Gaza sat to the south, with the royal-controlled cities of Jerusalem, Acre and Tyre somewhat spread out as the spine of the kingdom. The cities and castles were mostly populated by the new immigrants from Europe, while the population of the surrounding countryside was made up of the native Syrians who were both Christian and Muslim.[4]

The Kingdom of Jerusalem was administered with the feudalistic model used in Europe. The kingdom was fragmented into lordships that varied in size from the smaller territory lordship of Ibelin in the east of Jerusalem to the larger lordships, such as Sidon, in the north. The lords of these territories were the king's vassals and, as tenants-in-chief, were obligated to provide military service. However, the lords had control over the administration of their lands and jurisdiction over their vassals, who were known as rear-vassals.[5]

To the north of the Kingdom of Jerusalem were several newly created Crusader feudal states. They consisted of two Latin Christian territories formed in 1098, prior to the capture of Jerusalem – the Principality of Antioch and the County of Edessa. The Principality of Antioch was a coastal territory around the north-eastern edge of the Mediterranean. The principality was established after the city fell to the First Crusaders, with Bohemond, the Norman Prince of Taranto, becoming the first Prince of Antioch. The County of Edessa was east of Antioch. Unlike the other Crusader states, it was landlocked, with half of its territory east of the Euphrates, making the county isolated and vulnerable.

The territory became part of the Crusader states when the future King of Jerusalem, Baldwin of Boulogne, married Arda of Armenia (future first Queen of Jerusalem) and became the heir to her father, Lord Thoros of Edessa. How Baldwin ascended to the lordship is open to debate, with claims that he had a hand in his father-in-law's murder when the unpopular lord was thrown from the battlements by a ferocious mob.[6] Either way, Baldwin succeeded his father-in-law as ruler of Edessa in March 1098 and established the Crusader state with the city of Edessa as the new count's seat.

The County of Tripoli was the smallest of the Crusader states, formed after years of campaigning from 1102 by the First Crusader Raymond of Toulouse, who died in 1105. In 1109, the city of Tripoli fell and Raymond's son, Bertrand of Toulouse, became the first count of the newly conquered territory. The tiny state was located on the edge of the Mediterranean, sandwiched between the Kingdom of Jerusalem and the Principality of Antioch.

DANGER ON THE ROADS

With their crusading vows fulfilled, most of the First Crusaders returned home to Europe, leaving behind the new European states carved out in the Holy Land. Although the Crusaders had successfully captured these new Christian states, it would still require significant manpower to hold on to them successfully. With a lack of fighting men immigrating from Europe, the towns and cities were fortified with the remaining Christian forces, leaving the lands outside the settlements vulnerable and impossible to control. Furthermore, the roads outside these Christian strongholds were hazardous and deadly for many pilgrims and travellers, who were vulnerable to bandits and murderers.

Saewulf of Canterbury describes the dangers and horrors seen on the roads of Outremer during his pilgrimage in 1102. On the mountain road journey to Jerusalem, Saewulf claimed, 'the Saracens, who are continually plotting an ambush against Christians, were hiding in the caves of the hills and among rocky caverns'. Saewulf recorded the grizzly details of the unfortunate travellers whose bodies were abandoned on the road:

> Anyone who has taken that road can see how many human bodies there are in the road and next to the road, and there are countless corpses which have been torn up by wild beasts. It might be questioned why so many Christian corpses should lie there unburied, but it is in fact no surprise. There is little soil there, and the rocks are not easy to move. Even if the soil were there, who would be stupid enough to leave his brethren and be alone digging a grave! Anybody who did this would dig a grave not for his fellow Christian but for himself![7]

Daniel, a Russian abbot, described the dangers of travelling the Holy Land on a pilgrimage. When near the town of Basham in Galilee, he wrote, 'This place is terrible and difficult of access for here live fierce pagan Saracens who attack travellers at the fords on these rivers.'[8]

The most shocking attack on pilgrims came in 1119, during Easter, when armed Fatimids from Ascalon attacked a huge party of 700 Christian men and women. The Christians had planned to venture from Jerusalem to the baptismal site of Jesus Christ on the River Jordan, when they were set upon, and 300 pilgrims were killed, with sixty captured to be sold into slavery.[9]

The massacre at Easter was the third in a triumvirate of disasters to befall the Christian states at the end of the decade. The first came in the death of King Baldwin I, who died in 1118 while campaigning against the Fatimids in north-eastern Egypt. Jerusalem's first king had died from an infection in an old wound that had never truly healed. The king's body was taken to Jerusalem to be buried next to his brother, Godfrey.

Baldwin I died without an heir, and although he had a younger brother, Eustace of Boulogne, bringing Eustace from Europe would take time and potentially leave the kingdom vulnerable to attack. The second prominent candidate was Baldwin's cousin, Baldwin of Bourcq, who had succeeded Baldwin I as Count of Edessa. He accepted the offer and declared Jocelyn of Courtenay (who supported the choice of Baldwin as king) to succeed him as Count of Edessa.

The second disaster was that the Principality of Antioch suffered a heavy defeat in a battle that stripped the Crusader state of its military strength.

THE FIELD OF BLOOD

The first Prince of Antioch and leader of the First Crusade, Bohemond I, died in 1111. He was succeeded by his infant son, Bohemond II, with his uncle Tancred, the Prince of Galilee and veteran of the First Crusade, acting as Regent of Antioch. Tancred died in a typhoid epidemic in 1112, having named his cousin Roger of Salerno as successor to the regency of the principality.

The Principality of Antioch was in a constant state of war with nearby Aleppo and initially the principality gained the upper hand following Roger's victory over General Bursuq ibn Bursuq at the Battle of Sarmin in 1115. For the battle, Roger's troops allied with Count Baldwin's forces from Edessa and the future King Baldwin II carried out a surprise attack on the Bursuq army, which was camped near Sarmin. Although the Frankish losses were light, the number of Turkish casualties was estimated at 3,000.

The Frankish victory would give the region a short period of stability. Unfortunately, this ended in June 1119 when Roger and the entire Antioch army was massacred at the Battle of *Ager Sanguinis* (Latin for the 'Field of Blood').

Four years after the victory at Battle of Sarmin, the principality was invaded by the Atabeg Llghazi, who took control of Aleppo in 1117; an attack launched after Roger captured the city of Azaz in 1118. However, the capture of Azaz left Aleppo vulnerable, and Llghazi invaded the principality in 1119 with a large army of at least 10,000.[10]

Perhaps Roger was overconfident after his victory in 1115. He chose not to wait for reinforcements from the now King Baldwin II and instead left the relative safety of the fortress at Artah to pursue the invading army. Roger rode out with a force of 700 knights and 3,000 infantry troops.[11]

However, on 27 June, the Frankish troops woke to find that Llghazi's larger army had surrounded their camp. In the battle that followed, despite Roger trying to mount a desperate defence, the outnumbered Franks were slaughtered, Roger himself was killed and the few who were taken prisoner were later executed.

Despite the loss of Antioch's army, Llghazi hesitated and would later retreat from the forces of King Baldwin II (who had taken over as regent) at the Battle of Hab in August. There would be a greater misfortune for the principality when Prince Bohemond II, who had reached his early twenties, was killed in 1130 while raiding Cilicia. Bohemond II had been married to Baldwin II's daughter, Alice, and his sudden death left their infant daughter Constance as the rightful heir to the principality.

NINE FRENCH KNIGHTS

The creation of the Templars resulted from the significant setbacks Outremer faced after the veterans of the First Crusade returned to Europe and created a serious lack of manpower. The Frankish leaders were short on soldiers to protect the Crusader states' vulnerable borders. But, as the Easter massacre showed, neither could they provide troops to protect the travellers on roads inside their territories. It was out of this need to guard the roads of Outremer that a revolutionary form of knighthood was born. This comprised knights who would live as monks and dedicate themselves to protecting civilians travelling the dangerous roads of these new Christian territories in the Holy Land.

A group of nine French knights had come to Jerusalem intending to live a monastic lifestyle to atone for their sins. William of Tyre gave an account of the Templars' origin in his chronicle *Historia rerum partibus transmarinis gestarum* (*A History of Deeds Done Beyond the Sea*) in the late twelfth century. Tyre wrote that in the year 1119:

> Some noblemen of knightly rank, devoted to God, pious and God fearing, placed themselves in the hands of the lord patriarch for the service of Christ, professing the wish to live perpetually in the manner of regular canons in chastity, and obedience, without personal belongings. The leading and most eminent of these men were the venerable Hugh de Payns [Hugues de Paynes] and Godfrey de Saint Omer. As they had neither church nor fixed abode, the king gave them a temporary home in his palace which was on the south side of the Temple of the Lord, [...] Their main duty, imposed on them by the patriarch and the other bishops for the remission of their sins, was that they should maintain the safety of the roads and the highways to the best of their ability, for the benefit of pilgrims in particular, against attacks of bandits and marauders.[12]

King Baldwin proposed this revolutionary monastic lifestyle to Hugues and his companions in this radical format.

The new order of knights was formed on Christmas Day 1119, with Hugues de Paynes and the other knights taking their vows in the Church of the Holy Sepulchre. The order was called the Poor Fellow-Soldiers of Christ. They were officially recognised in January 1120 when the nine Knights of the Poor Fellow-Soldiers of Christ were introduced to an assembly of Frankish leaders in Nablus. Due to their vows of poverty, they had relinquished all they owned and had to rely on donations.

Hugues was the first grand master of the Templars and came from Payns, a town in the county of Champagne in France. Before taking his vows in Jerusalem, he served as a knight in the company of Hugh, Count of Champagne. The second most prominent member of the Templar founders was Godfrey de Saint Omer, a Flemish knight. Although he was not the grand master, his mention in William of Tyre's account of the origin suggests his prominence in the order's founding.

Although in 1120 the order attracted the interest of Fulk V, Count of Anjou, on his visit to the Holy Land and he gifted them an annual revenue, they still were considerably poor and had no distinct uniform but wore donated clothes.[13] The original seal of the order exemplified this vow of poverty as it depicted two knights riding a single horse.

It was this poverty that led to the order's change of name when Baldwin II gave them quarters in his palace in Jerusalem. This was the al-Aqsa Mosque, located in the south-east of the city, close to the Tanners Gate. Bernard of Clairvaux describes the headquarters, writing, 'The façade of the temple is decorated, but with arms not jewels, and in lieu of ancient crowns of gold are hung shields. In place of candelabras, censors, and ewers are bridles, saddles, and lances.'[14] The section that the order was using as its headquarters was supposed to have been built upon the foundations of the Temple of Solomon, which led to the order becoming known as the Poor Fellow-Soldiers of Christ and the Temple of Solomon – eventually the Knights Templar.

THE COUNCIL OF TROYES AND THE LATIN RULE

The Knights Templar did not see significant growth or investment until the end of the decade, when Hugues had the opportunity to travel to Europe to raise the order's profile and attract donations and recruits.

The survival of the Crusader states was always of the utmost importance, so first Baldwin II needed to secure the future of his lineage. As he had no sons but four daughters, the Kingdom of Jerusalem would adopt cognatic succession, which meant that all blood relatives could inherit, in contrast to the more conventional agnatic succession when only male heirs had a claim.[15] The king was to be succeeded by his eldest daughter Melisende, and in 1127, Baldwin II sent an embassy to France to offer Melisende's hand to Count Fulk of Anjou. Hugues and Godfrey were part of the party as this was an opportunity to promote the Templars to Europe's most prominent noblemen.

The king's objectives were successful. The Templars were given many donations and Fulk married Melisende in 1129, a union that would give birth to the future King of Jerusalem, Baldwin III. Fulk and Melisende would be co-rulers until Baldwin came of age.

The senior Templars' promotional tour of Europe proved fruitful. This new type of knighthood found validation among the European nobility and they were gifted land, money, horses and equipment. Hugues de Paynes visited the court of Henry I of England in 1128, where he was granted gifts of money. It was then that Hugues established the first Templar house in London on Chancery Lane, before travelling to Scotland to receive yet more generous donations.[16]

Hugues' and Godfrey's most significant gain came from the Council of Troyes in January 1129. The council convened to grant official monastic recognition to the Knights Templar and was hosted by Count Hugh of Champagne, whom Hugues de Paynes had served as a knight. Also in attendance was the Papal Legate, Cardinal Bishop Matthew, two archbishops and several abbots. Among them was Bernard of Clairvaux, who promoted the Templars by writing the influential piece *In Praise of the New Knighthood* and would one day be a prominent preacher of the Second Crusade.

At the council, Hugues de Paynes told the religious leaders the story of the Templars' origin and their mission in the Holy Land, asking for the assembly to grant them an official habit for their dual life as monk-knight, as well as a Rule so that they could live as other monks did in their day-to-day life. This Rule would become known as the Primitive Rule – as the Rule would later be greatly expanded.

The Primitive Rule required the Templars to attend masses, eat communal meals and wear simple clothing, and contact with women would be forbidden. Originally, it is possible there were women members of the Templars, but the Rule put an end to that. Bernard felt that women members were a threat to the men's 'flower of chastity' and it was 'dangerous to add more sisters to the order because the ancient enemy has expelled many men from the straight path of paradise on account of their consorting with women'.[17]

The Rule outlined how the Templars would dress, explaining that Templar brothers were to wear a white habit, similar to the Cistercian monks (the red cross would come later), symbolising their purity. In addition, their sergeants and servants were required to wear a black or brown cloak and it was only the knights themselves who could don the white cloak.[18] Shoelaces and pointed shoes were forbidden because it was believed that they were associated with paganism. However, a brother was entitled to wear a linen shirt from Easter to All Saints in the intense heat of the Holy Land, should a brother request it.[19]

The Rule offers great insight into how the Templar knights lived their lives while carrying out their duties. Templar knights were provided with three horses each and a squire to assist them, but they were forbidden from having gold, silver or anything ornate on their bridles, stirrups or spurs. There was an exception, though – if such items were given in charity and any gold was tarnished so that the brother took no pride in such ornate equipment, it would be permitted.[20] The ownership of horses and armour remained under the house commander's control. He could reissue the horse and equipment to any serving brother, and the brother being so relieved was expected to avoid being angry as the Rule explained that this would be going against God.[21]

The everyday life of the Templar knights was highly controlled. For example, they were forbidden from keeping a lockable purse or bag, although this did not apply to the senior members, such as house commanders or masters. Templar brothers were not allowed to receive any letters sent to them, even if it was from their own family. It was down to the master or house commander to decide if the brother should have the letter read to him.[22]

The Rule gave strict rules for mealtimes: brothers were to eat together but must do so in silence while the Bible was read aloud. At the end of the meal, the brother must give thanks to God, but it must be given in silence. Even though the brothers lived as monks, they also carried out martial duties, and therefore the Templar brothers could eat red meat three times a week to sustain them for the physical toll their knightly duties took, whereas normally a monk was permitted only fish and eggs.[23]

The Templar brothers were also expected to retire to their sleeping quarters in silence. After Compline (end-of-day prayers), the brothers were expected to go to bed without speaking unless there was an emergency or serious problem that needed to be dealt with before the morning; even then, there must be no idle chat or laughter.[24]

Hugues de Paynes returned to the Holy Land in 1131 with donations, manpower and a Latin Rule for the Templar members to live by. The revolutionary Templar knighthood was now firmly established in both the Holy Land and Europe.

IN PRAISE OF THE NEW KNIGHTHOOD

To further promote the Knights Templar in Europe, Bernard of Clairvaux wrote a letter to Hugues de Paynes in 1135 as a model for current members, to attract potential members and as a means to justify the new type of order of warrior monks within a Christian context.[25] In it, Bernard promotes the Templars as a new type of knighthood, exemplifying the morality of those knights taking up arms for the Templar cause and the piety of the life of a Templar.

He begins by exclaiming that the Templars are a new type of knightly order that was previously unknown, a knighthood that fights in 'two wars, one against adversaries of flesh and blood, and another against a spiritual army of wickedness in the heavens'.[26] He then points to the ethics of knightly combat, arguing that knights who kill their enemies are sinners. Speaking to the knightly class, Bernard proposes that 'as worldly knights, you must have feared that the death of an enemy in the flesh should cause the death of your soul', but even killing with justification in self-defence 'is not good, since the death of the body is a lesser evil than death of the soul' as 'the soul that sins will die'.[27]

The letter poses the question to the knightly class: what can guilty knights do about their eternal soul after so much violence? The answer he gives is for them to join the Templars because, as a Templar, 'either to bring about death, or to die for Christ, you have not sin but an abundant right to glory'. Bernard argues that fighting for the Templars sidesteps the sinful dilemma of killing in warfare – if a knight serving Christ 'kills wicked men, he is not a murderer under these circumstances. I say that he is murderer of wickedness and a champion of Christ.'[28]

Bernard then praises the pious lifestyle of the Templar brothers, with the letter echoing the conduct laid out in the Rule. He writes, 'When they are not on duty, they eat their bread with care, repair either their armour or their torn vestments, or put order to the disordered,' and highlights the recreational activities that are abhorrent to the Templar brothers, which include gaming, gambling, jousting, jesters and falconry.[29] Bernard's examples of Templar daily activities and those they do not participate in gives insight into the hard work that was the daily life of a Templar knight.

Hugues de Paynes, the first grand master and founder of the Knights Templar, died in 1136. The end of his leadership would also see the end to Hugues' vision of a pious knighthood that protected Christian pilgrims, and soon the order would be escorting Crusader armies across the

Holy Land, although the Templars still protected pilgrims on the road to Jerusalem, as the Commander of Jerusalem dedicated ten knights to this duty.[30]

The order greatly expanded under the leadership of Grand Master Robert of Craon. To increase the Templars' influence and their physical and financial strength, he sought closer ties with the papacy, and in 1139 Pope Innocent showed his support for the Templars with the bull, *Omne datum optimum*. This declaration meant that priests could join the Templars as Templar chaplains. The chaplain could hear their brothers' confessions and absolve sins.

Omne datum optimum put the Templar order under the direct control of the papacy, meaning that they were no longer under the influence of the Patriarch of Jerusalem, before whom the order had previously taken their vows. The declaration gave the Knights Templar the total autonomy needed to control their international lands and houses.

The Templars' gradual refocusing away from policing the roads to military campaigns is evident in the later expansion to the Primitive Rule, the Hierarchical Statutes, written in 1165.[31] These detailed the hierarchal ranks with the order as well as its military protocols.

The grand master was the most senior figure. The seneschal was the second in command; he carried the order's battle standard. Third in command was the marshal, who commanded the Templars' military. The Commander of the Kingdom of Jerusalem was the order's treasurer. Then there was the draper, a senior official in charge of clothing and linen to ensure that expectations for dress were upheld. This was an important position in the order, according to the Rule, 'After the Master and the Marshal, the Draper is superior to all the other brothers'.[32]

Below these offices were the regional commanders: Commander of the City of Jerusalem, Commander of the Land of Antioch and Commander of the Land of Tripoli. Then there were the regional masters, who managed the endeavours of these areas, followed by the Commanders of the Houses, who manage the order's farms, houses and castles in the territories overseen by the regional masters.[33]

The long list of ranks demonstrates the growth of the order from Hugues de Paynes' vision of pilgrim protectors to depict a transnational military power. This would soon take centre stage in the Crusader campaigns and become a vital martial presence in the Holy Land. The Crusader territories would soon need the Templars' greater military strength because in 1144, Edessa, the first Crusader state, had fallen to the Seljuk atabeg, Zengi.

2

THE LAUNCH OF THE SECOND CRUSADE

THE RULE OF THE REGENCY

In August 1131, Jerusalem's King Baldwin II - the man who was instrumental to the founding of the Templars – died. Twelfth Century historian Ibn al-Qalānisi described the late king as 'an old man, rich in experiences and inured to every trial and hardship of life'. He was critical of Baldwin's successor, however, writing, 'He was succeeded by a man who lacked his good sense and gift for kingship.'[1]

Nevertheless, the late king's wishes for his succession were to be followed and his son-in-law, Fulk V of Anjou, and his eldest daughter, Melisende, were to succeed until their son, also Baldwin, came of age. However, on his deathbed, Baldwin II declared that his 2-year-old grandson was also named in the succession,[2] so, on 14 September 1131, husband, wife and son were crowned together in Jerusalem's Holy Sepulchre.

Baldwin's hope of King Fulk and Queen Melisende ruling together through cooperation was quickly in danger of collapse as the Kingdom of Jerusalem split into two factions when Antioch, Tripoli and Edessa attempted to state their independence from the kingdom's overlordship. After the coronation, Fulk was needed in Antioch because Princess Alice – following the death of her father, who was Regent of Antioch – attempted to install herself as the new ruler of Antioch with the backing of the Counts of Edessa and Tripoli. King Fulk exerted his authority by taking over the regency of the principality.[3]

Despite politically defeating the Crusader states' leaders' opportunism in the north, a civil war in the kingdom threatened. A faction led by Count Hugh of Jaffa rebelled against Fulk, accusing the king of ignoring the rights of Queen Melisende and disrespecting the wishes of the late

Baldwin II and cognatic succession by acting as sole ruler of the kingdom. There is some doubt over the precise year that Hugh's rebellion took place, with Mayer explaining it took place between 1132, at the earliest, and the more likely date of 1134.[4]

The crisis came to a conclusion when Fulk accepted his position as co-ruler, but the rebellion's leader, Hugh, was to be banished for three years with the understanding that his land and properties be reinstated to him upon his return. Unfortunately for Hugh, an assassination attempt was made on his life, and he died from his wounds in exile. Public suspicion as to who ordered the assassination attempt was solely directed towards Fulk.[5]

However, after subduing the threat of civil war, Fulk faced a greater threat in the form of war with the Seljuk Turk, Zengi (or Zangi), the Atabeg of Mosul and Aleppo.

ZENGI AND THE FALL OF EDESSA

Thirteenth Century historian Ibn al-Athīr bestowed upon Zengi the title of 'martyr for the faith' and described him as 'a handsome man, with a swarthy complexion, fine eyes, and hair that was beginning to go grey'.[6] He also noted that he 'was the bravest man in the world'.[7]

Zengi was born around 1085 to a Turkish warlord and rose to power as the governor of Mosul in 1127 and Aleppo in 1128. Although he was a fierce enemy of the Franks and the instigator of the Muslim counter-offensive, his primary objective was subjugating the Muslim state of Damascus. He attempted to take Damascus by force in both 1130 and 1135, but failed.

In 1137, Zengi besieged the Frankish castle of Montferrand, also known as Ba'rīn. King Fulk led his army to relieve the city but was defeated by Zengi. Ibn al-Athīr describes Zengi's victory, writing, 'He stood firm to await them, and when they arrived he faced them in a battle which after some bitter fighting resolved itself into a rout of the Franks, who fled, closely pursued by the Muslims.'[8] King Fulk fled inside the castle and found himself trapped by the besieging army.

Unbeknown to Fulk, a relief force from Jerusalem, Edessa and Antioch was marching on Montferrand, but Zengi had cut off all communication. Fulk asked for terms and the castle was surrendered to Zengi and their lives spared with a ransom of 50,000 dinars. Only when they left the castle did they learn of the huge relief force that was on its way.[9] Zengi had humiliated the King of Jerusalem and proved himself to be a highly intelligent and dangerous enemy to the Franks.

The atabeg extended his influence and control by capturing Damascene territories to the south, taking the city of Baalbek in 1139. After a heavy assault, the inhabitants of Baalbek surrendered on the promise that the troops would be spared. What followed gives a clear example of how Zengi got his reputation for his brutality.

Zengi went back on his promise and crucified the garrison to a man – all to send a message to those who would resist his authority. He appointed a new governor from his entourage to ensure the city's continued cooperation. He was a Kurdish man named Ayyūb ibn Shādi, whose family would one day shape the power structure in the Holy Land.[10]

Given Zengi's fearsome reputation, when his army laid siege to Damascus in 1139 the Damascene ruler, Unur, refused to submit to him, and in 1140 chose to appeal to the Franks to build a Damascus and Jerusalem alliance against him. To join an alliance with Damascus, the Kingdom of Jerusalem was to receive a monthly sum of 20,000 gold pieces and the return of Banyas, which had been captured in 1132.[11] At first, the alliance proved successful, as Zengi retreated from Damascus at the sight of the relief force led by King Fulk, suggesting that allying with neighbouring powers would be enough to halt Zengi's advance.

For the moment, Damascus was safe from Zengi's forces. However, the smaller territories to the north were under threat from his ever-growing control. To counter the aggression from Zengi, Qara Arslan, the ruler of Hisn Kaifa, sought an alliance with Count Joscelin II of Edessa against Zengi. In autumn 1144, with the promise of territory in payment for military aid, Count Joscelin marched from Edessa with a large army to aid his ally, Qara Arslan.

Ibn al-Athīr describes Joscelin as 'the most famous of the franks' and praises the count, stating he was 'the leader of their army by virtue of his valour and command strategy'.[12] However, Joscelin was to be outmanoeuvred by Zengi when the small number of troops left to guard the city were horrified to see a hostile army appear outside Edessa. Ibn al-Qalānisi explained, 'Zangi had always coveted Edessa and watched for a chance to achieve his ambition.'[13]

Zengi utilised a vast network of spies, and his masses of information presented him with an opportunity to strike a huge blow against the Crusaders. Once he received word that the count had left Edessa vulnerable, he switched targets from Diyar Bakr and marched on the Crusader state's capital, arriving in late November.[14]

For four weeks, the city held out under the constant bombardment, assaults on the walls and sappers from underneath. Count Joscelin hastily tried to organise a relief force, but before he could attack the besiegers, he learnt the terrible news that the city had fallen. On 24 December 1144, Zengi's sappers managed to collapse a huge section of the city's wall, and now his army could pour in through the breach. Ibn al-Qalānisi described the approach used by Zengi's besiegers and its effectiveness, writing:

> Special detachments of sappers from Khurasān and Aleppo began work at several suitable places, digging into bowels of the earth until their tunnels, propped up with beams and special equipment, reached under the towers of the city wall. The next step was to light the fires, and they applied to Zangi for permission. This was given after he had been into the tunnels to inspect them and had admired their imposing work. The wooden supports were fired, flames spread and devoured the beams, the walls above the tunnels crumbled, and the Muslims took the city by storm. Many men of both sides were killed when the walls collapsed, and many more Franks and Armenians were killed, wounded or put to flight.[15]

Those who could leave the city fled towards the citadel, though many were crushed in the panic, including the Latin archbishop. However, those who made it inside the citadel could only hold out until 26 December, and then Zengi had complete control over the city.

Although the capital city fell, the county would endure for a while longer as Count Joscelin made Turnbessel, to the west, his capital and managed to hold onto his territory up to the River Euphrates. However, in 1150 he was captured, and he died in prison in 1159.

Zengi would not live to see the end of the county. In 1146, he was murdered in his tent while besieging the fortress of Jabar. The culprit or reasons behind the murder are unclear, as accounts vary, but one version recounts that Zengi was killed by his Frankish slave.[16] Following Zengi's death, control over his land was shared between his sons. His eldest son, Saif al-Dīn, took control in Mosul, while the second son, Nūr ad-Dīn, succeeded his father in ruling Aleppo.

CALLS FOR A NEW CRUSADE

Edessa was the first established Crusader state and the first to be lost. Most of the city's population was eastern Christian, as it had been when Baldwin established the County of Edessa in 1098. The loss of Edessa would be the catalyst for the launching of the Second Crusade when, in 1145, messengers from the Holy Land travelled to Europe to deliver the devastating news of Edessa's loss and that the Christian lands stood on the brink of being lost.

The European nobility and peasantry were shocked at the news, and Crusading frenzy would once again take hold of the European popular and political climate. After hearing the news of Edessa's loss, Pope Eugenius III, who had only become pope that year, issued the crusading bull, *Quantum Praedecessores*, on 1 December 1145. The bull echoed the memories of Pope Urban's original call to Crusade in 1095, stating:

> For our predecessor of blessed memory, pope Urban, did sound, as it were, a celestial trump and did take care to arouse for its deliverance the sons of the holy Roman church from the different parts of the earth.[17]

However, in looking back to the First Crusade for inspiration, Eugenius would also attract non-combatants, which would be a huge hindrance to the logistics of such a large military campaign to the Holy Land. The majority of the First Crusaders were non-combatants, as the First Crusade was preached as a large-scale pilgrimage for which anyone could volunteer. The participants of the Second Crusade would be granted spiritual rewards such as absolution from sins. However, the Pope truly wanted to attract the nobility, so he also promised that the Church would protect the families and possessions of those who took the cross.[18] This bull did not have the intended effect and appeared to attract little, if any, interest in Crusading.

While the Pope was calling for a Crusade that Christmas, the young French King Louis VII, who was in his mid-twenties, announced his intention to travel to the Holy Land on an armed pilgrimage while holding court at Bourges. Even though King Louis' plan was significantly less than what Pope Eugenius called for, his vassals received his plans with little interest. It is uncertain whether King Louis knew of the Pope's intentions beforehand. However, he made no mention of it when addressing the court.[19] Instead, Louis appealed to the most prominent Christian philosopher of the times, Bernard of Clairvaux, who had supported and helped legitimise the Templars.

The king looked to Bernard because he was a leading figure in the Latin Church, seen as an excellent speaker and helped Pope Innocent II win over his rival, Anacletus.[20] Bernard, though, felt this was a matter for the Pope and would not advise the king without consulting Pope Eugenius.

After a slow start, the fires of Crusading frenzy ignited in 1146 when the Pope reissued the *Quantum Praedecessores* bull, and Bernard of Clairvaux began to preach of a new Crusade to the Holy Land. In a field outside the town of Vézelay in France on 1 March 1146, which was fifty-one years after Pope Urban had preached what would become known as the First Crusade, Bernard called on the masses in attendance to take up the cross. Similar to Urban's call to Crusade, the crowd gathered was too large to fit inside the town's abbey as planned, so a stage was set up for Bernard outside the town in a field.

The first to take the cross was King Louis, then his lords, the Queen of France, Eleanor of Aquitaine, bishops and other nobles from Flanders and England followed suit. Bernard's preaching created such a frenzy for Crusading that he and his monks had to cut up their own habits into crosses to satisfy the desire for the participants to take the cross.

To avoid the atrocities that had been committed against the Jewish communities in the First Crusade, Bernard preached through France and along the Rhine, emphasising that the Jewish people 'are not to be persecuted, killed or even put to flight' and arguing that the Jewish people had been placed in Europe to 'be witnesses of our [European Christians'] redemption'. Although antisemitic crimes were carried out in the new Crusader frenzy, they were not on the same horrific scale as the First Crusade, which can be accredited to Bernard's preaching.[21]

Redemption was the major theme of the Second Crusades' call to arms as, aside from the loss of Edessa, the Holy Land was in the control of the Franks, and the call to Crusade could not copy the First Crusade's theme of liberating Christians. The focus on the redemption of Christian souls can be seen in the letter Bernard sent to the English, 'Now is the accepted time, the day of abundant salvation'. Bernard preached that all participants' souls would be redeemed, even those with the greatest sins. He wrote:

> What is it but a unique and wonderful act of divine generosity when Almighty God treats murderers, thieves, adulterers, perjurors [*sic*], and criminals of all kinds as though they were men of righteousness and worthy to be called to his service. Do not hesitate.[22]

Bernard aimed to recruit another Prince of Europe following the King of France taking the cross. He also hoped to convince King Conrad III of Germany to take the cross. However, his first attempt at recruiting the German king in November was a failure and Conrad rejected his call to Crusade. Then at Christmas, after Bernard delivered a sermon to Conrad and his court, the king appeared unexpectedly to have a change of heart. He described the German king facing Christ at the last judgement as Christ said to Conrad, 'Man, what ought I have done for you that I have not done?'[23] Bernard's words seemed to move Conrad to take the cross, followed by his nobles.

Powerful European nobles had led the First Crusade, but the Second would be led by mighty European kings, so it seemed that an even greater success would be achieved. It was believed that the miraculous successes of the First Crusade would be bestowed upon the Crusaders by God and a Crusade led by kings would be greater than that led by lords.

King Louis, the first of the royal leaders of the Second Crusade, had a significant Crusader pedigree. His great-uncle Hugh had been one of the First Crusaders and Louis' wife, Queen Eleanor, was the niece of Prince Raymond of Antioch. This Crusader lineage, through both blood and marriage, made him the ideal man to lead the Second Crusade. While Conrad appears to have had a change of heart following Bernard's sermon, he had, in fact, been engaging in diplomatic talks with the Byzantine Emperor Manuel I since 1146, who pleaded with Conrad for help with combating the threat of Turkish aggression.[24]

The Second Crusade would also introduce the Knights Templar as a major military force that would dominate the Christian struggle for power in the Holy Land.

THE TEMPLARS AS A MILITARY FORCE

Although the Second Crusade was to be led by kings, the significance of the Knights Templar began to emerge when it was at their European headquarters in Paris that a preparation meeting was held with King Louis and Pope Eugenius in attendance. On 27 April 1147, at the Paris Temple, Everard des Barres, the Master of the Temple in France, met with the Pope and the French king. Everard brought with him 130 Templar knights, with sergeants and squires to accompany them. Previously, the Templars had policed the roads of Outremer; now, they stood with the elite Christians of Europe as a military force.

It was at this meeting that the Pope granted the Templars the right to bear a red cross of martyrdom upon their white mantle of purity. Thus, the Templars would adopt the iconography they would forever be associated with.

The Templars were also granted a second benefit during this meeting. They were to receive the taxes on Church goods to fund the Crusade. This benefit is perhaps more significant because it sowed the seeds of the Templars' financial relationship with the French Crown, one that would prove disastrous.

The German army marched through Hungary unopposed and reached the Byzantine capital Constantinople in September. However, their journey was not without incident; there is a story of a drunken disagreement with a snake charmer that turned violent at Philippopolis. More concerning, though, was Frederick of Swabia's attempt to burn down a monastery in revenge for the Greeks' robbery of a German noble at a monastery in Adrianople. Fortunately, this was prevented by troops led by Byzantine Commander Prosuch.[25]

To ensure loyalty, Conrad III was required to swear an oath to the Byzantine Emperor Manuel I to acknowledge the Byzantine claims over lands in Syria. Manuel I was the grandson of Emperor Alexius I, who had also required a similar oath from the First Crusaders en route to Asia Minor. Although Manuel I had good relations with Conrad III, he was keen to assist with transporting the German Crusaders to Asia Minor before the French Crusader army arrived.

At the end of September, the German Crusaders were shipped across the Bosporus Strait to muster at the city of Nicaea in Asia Minor, where Conrad gathered provisions to march south. It was here that the German contingent of the Second Crusade made a fatal error. Conrad decided against waiting for the French Crusaders and, without their numbers, began the long march across Asia Minor. He split his forces into two parts. He was to lead the armed forces and his half-brother, Bishop Otto of Freising, whose section consisted of non-combatants, was instructed to take the longer coastal road.

In October, Conrad III marched his army out from Nicaea and away from the relative safety of the Greek-controlled northern coast to follow the path the First Crusaders had taken some fifty years prior. Echoing the events of the First Crusade, the German Crusaders were attacked near Dorylaeum by a Seljuq army. The battle did not evoke the success of the First Crusaders and the German army was utterly defeated.

Ashbridge proposes that the Germans' defeat came about due to their inexperience and inability to cope with the Seljuq horsemen's speedy battle tactics.[26] The survivors limped back to the safety of Nicaea, where most abandoned the Crusade and returned home. The contingent led by Otto did not fare any better, and they would eventually march inland and suffer a devastating attack from the Seljuk Turks at Laodicea. Otto and the few survivors fled for the coast and took a ship the rest of the way to Outremer. Neither of Conrad's Crusader sections was able to successfully replicate the First Crusade's long, arduous march across Asia Minor.

Louis VII and the French army arrived and camped outside Constantinople on 4 October. The French king's chaplain, Odo of Deuil, recorded an account of the French forces' visit to the capital city. Odo offers a great description of the city:

> Constantinople, the glory of the Greeks, rich in renown and richer still in possessions, is laid out in a triangle shaped like a ship's sail. In its inner angle stand Santa Sophia and Constantine's palace, in which there is a chapel that is revered for its exceedingly holy relics. Moreover, Constantinople is girt on two sides by the sea; when approaching the city we had the Arm of St. George on the right and on the left a certain estuary, which after branching from the Arm, flows on for about four miles.[27]

He gives glowing praise of the capital's architecture, describing the splendidness of the palace in detail, writing that the 'exterior is of almost matchless beauty, but its interior surpasses anything that I can say about it. Throughout it is decorated elaborately with gold and a variety of colors [*sic*], and the floor is marble, paved with cunning workmanship.' Despite offering such high praise of the richness of the city, he was equally as critical of the quality of life within the city. He described the city as 'squalid and fetid' and writes, '[the] wealthy overshadow the streets with buildings and leave these dirty, dark places to the poor and to travelers [*sic*]; there murders and robberies and other crimes which love the darkness are committed'. Odo goes as far as to describe the city as lawless, where crime goes without punishment.[28]

Aside from being critical of the city itself, Odo's account offers insight into the relationship between the French and the Byzantines. Even though the French king was treated as a most welcome guest with a banquet and guided visits to Holy sites, the motives of their hosts were questionable. Odo explains that 'many of the king's men feared for him' and even though 'the Greeks furnished us no proof that they were treacherous, I believe that they would not have exhibited such unremitting servitude if they had had good intentions'.[29]

Odo's suspicions of their hosts' intentions demonstrate the rift between the supposed Christian allies and the disingenuous nature of the relationship between the Latin and Greek Orthodox Church. When speaking of Byzantine holdings in Asia Minor, Odo writes, 'The lazy people would have lost all if they had not defended themselves by importing knights from various nations', adding, 'they always lose but since they possess much they cannot lose all at once'.[30]

However, despite the anti-Greek feelings among the French, an agreement was reached where the French would not capture any Byzantian castles or towns and the emperor would provide guides for the Crusaders. The fallout from this relationship ended catastrophically for the Byzantines at the start of the thirteenth century at the hands of French and German Crusaders during the Fourth Crusade.

Emperor Manuel was also uncomfortable with the situation and did not want a foreign army camped outside his capital so, to move the large French army from his lands, he supposedly spread false rumours of a German victory. The thought of missing out on their share of the riches may have motivated the senior French nobles to hurry to cross the sea to Asia Minor.[31]

The French joined forces with Conrad and the remnants of his army and plotted an alternative route south. However, by December, the combined army had reached the Byzantine-controlled town of Ephesus, located in modern-day Turkey. Here, Conrad became ill and was forced to return to Constantinople. His remaining forces merged with the French Crusaders, and now King Louis VII of France led the combined Crusader army to march inland eastwards through the Meander Valley.

The combined Crusader forces faced a tough march through the harsh winter weather, and at first, the army withstood the Turkish attacks until the army needed to cross Mount Cadmus en route to the Byzantine city of Attalea. However, while attempting to traverse Mount Cadmus, the Crusader army lost formation and the baggage train became separated from the rearguard. The path was perilous to trek, and marching beside cliff edges caused the baggage train to slow and stray further from the vanguard. Odo of Deuil describes the scene:

> The mountain was steep and rocky, and we had to climb along a ridge so lofty that its summit seemed to touch heaven and the stream in the hollow valley below descend into hell. Here the throng became congested while ascending, pushed forward, then crowded closely together, stopped, and, taking no thought for the cavalry, clung there instead of going ahead. Sumpter horses slipped from the steep cliffs, hurling those whom they struck into the depths of the chasm.[32]

The baggage train had separated from the rearguard due to confusion about optimal resting places. William of Tyre lays the blame on Geoffrey de Rancogne, who ignored his orders for the vanguard to camp at the summit. William explained that when de Rancogne 'reached the summit, however, the greater part of the day still remained, and Geoffrey decided, notwithstanding his orders, to advance a little farther, for he felt that the march had been too short that day'. The guides suggested that the Crusaders could rest once past the summit. However, the rearguard was unaware of this plan and didn't follow the baggage train.[33]

Whatever the reason, this mistake left the baggage train extremely vulnerable in the hazardous terrain, and it was quickly exploited by the Turkish cavalry. In January, the Seljuk forces attacked the slow-moving middle section, which was utterly helpless without the aid of the rear or vanguard.

When Louis learned of the slaughter, he led a relief force to fend off the Seljuk horseman; however, the French knights struggled to gain the advantage due to the terrain. Odo of Deuil highlighted the desperateness of the situation by detailing that the king escaped death by using a tree root to climb atop a rock so he could fend off the oncoming enemy. Odo paints the picture of King Louis as a warrior, writing, 'To keep from being captured he defended the crag with his bloody sword, cutting off the heads and hands of many opponents in the process.'[34] However, despite writing of his combat prowess, Odo concluded that the king survived not by his martial skill but because the Turkish soldiers did not recognise him and moved on.[35]

Despite the heavy losses, the baggage train survived the perilous climb to the summit. However, a number of senior noblemen were killed in the fighting. William of Tyre names them as 'Count Varennes, man pre-eminent even among great lords, Gauchiers de Montjoy, Evrard de Breteuil, and Itiers de Meingnac and many others'.[36] Such was the disaster that William lamented, 'That day the glorious reputation of the Franks was lost through a misfortune most fatal and disastrous for the Christians; their valour, up to this time formidable to the nations, was crushed to the earth.'[37]

The march across Mount Cadmus was a disaster for the Crusaders. To ensure the army remained intact to reach Outremer, King Louis made a radical decision to turn to the leadership of the Knights Templar. He was so impressed with the example set by the Knights Templar and Master Everard des Barres during the testing march that he wanted the Crusader army to imitate them. Therefore, it was decided that both classes, knight and foot soldier, would take an oath to not flee the battle and would obey every order given to them by the Templar knight assigned to them.

Odo of Deuil recorded some detail of this unprecedented arrangement. He noted that the army 'were given a commander named Gilbert, and he was given associates to each of whom he assigned 50 knights'.[38] Aside from assigning Templar knights, the Templars also insisted on basic rules that the army must follow – significantly, that they must only attack when commanded to ensure they were not baited into charging a false retreat and withdrawing as soon as called back. In addition, the Templars ordered the Crusaders to march in a disciplined order, and the knights who had lost their mounts would march in the rear as archers.[39]

According to historian Jonathan Phillips, the unprecedented decision to give control of the Crusader army to the Knights Templar demonstrates a weakness in Louis VII's leadership and shows just how shaken the Crusaders were by the attack on the baggage train. Also, it is significant to note that very soon after the Templars were formed (1119), they became so highly respected in warfare that the King of France handed over control of the Crusader army to the warrior monks.[40]

Soon the Crusaders were faced with crossing two rivers set a mile apart – a challenge itself for an army to cross because of their muddy banks. Turkish forces strategically held the second river, and it was here that under the Templars' leadership the army of the Second Crusade finally gained victory over the seemingly invincible Turkish cavalry.

The Crusaders repelled several attacks, but food remained scarce despite the new military victories. The Seljuk Turks had enacted a scorched-earth policy that consisted of tactically grazing their cattle, intending to destroy the Crusaders' mounts' food supply. The Seljuks had all their cattle and sheep gathered to graze heavily on the land that the Crusaders needed to traverse.[41] This was a sound strategy as depleting the Crusaders' horses would undoubtedly affect their military powers as well as limiting the transport of equipment and supplies.

Despite the repeated attacks and lack of food supplies, the Crusader army limped towards the Mediterranean coastline and arrived at the Byzantine-controlled port of Adalia towards the end of January. It was here that Louis had planned that he and his army would continue to Outremer via ships. But unfortunately, the Byzantines could not provide enough vessels to carry the Crusader army. Moreover, although the port was a Byzantian territory, the way further east towards friendly Armenian lands meant a long march through hostile Seljuk-controlled land.

The Crusader army could not stay indefinitely at the port while Louis waited for further ships to carry his army. Finally, the French king decided to take the available vessels and sail himself and the leading nobility to Antioch. That meant that the bulk of the army had no choice but to take a perilous march through Seljuk lands with the hope of reaching the safety of the Armenian city of Tarsus.

The Crusaders who were left behind attempted to march to Tarsus but were soon routed by Seljuk attacks. It is after this defeat that Odo records an account of the victorious Turks taking pity on the surviving Crusaders. Odo writes that the Greeks treated the surviving Crusaders terribly, assaulting them and forcing the stronger ones into their service. However, he explains, the Turks showed pity on their vulnerable Crusader enemies by giving them money. He concludes the event by writing that Crusaders should avoid the 'fellow-believers who were so cruel to them'; over 3,000 thousand Crusaders left with the Turks as they had shown them compassion. Most significantly, the Turks did not require the Crusaders to deny their faith.[42] Odo's account is damning of the Greeks' treatment and support of the Latin Christians, but it also tells a story of humanity, with the Turks seeing their defeated enemy as people and offering clemency, which is rarely seen during the cruel and violent Crusade campaigns.

The Second Crusade's plan to copy the First Crusade's march through Asia Minor was a complete disaster. The majority of those who set out from Europe died in the fighting or succumbed to sickness and hunger. The grand armies of Latin Christendom never reached the Holy Land; instead, the Crusaders left a graveyard of Latin dead across Asia Minor. The lords of Outremer were reinforced by a far smaller contingent from Europe. With such a smaller influx of manpower, it seemed unlikely that Outremer would now be able to launch a campaign to take back Edessa. It seemed the Second Crusade had failed before the Crusaders even reached Outremer.

3

THE SIEGE OF DAMASCUS

THE COUNCIL OF ACRE

King Louis of France arrived safely at the Principality of Antioch in March 1148. It was ruled by Prince Raymond of Antioch, who was the uncle of Louis' wife, Queen Eleanor of Aquitaine. Although the remainder of the Crusader army had limped to safety, Louis found himself in a serious amount of debt. Here, Louis VII would start a financial relationship between the French Crown and the Knights Templar.

In a letter to Samson, the Archbishop of Reims, Sugar, the Abbot of St Denis, and Count Ralph of Vermandois, Louis wrote that Everard, the Master of the Temple of France, had travelled from Antioch to Acre to secure Louis a loan to finance the continuation of the Crusade. He also instructed the letter's recipients to ensure they paid the money owed to the Templars as soon as possible.[1] The financial relationship between the French monarchy and the Knights Templar would eventually sour, with dire consequences for the Templars.

The remains of Louis' Crusader army had managed to reach the Crusader territories, but the landscape of the Holy Land had changed significantly since the outset of the Second Crusade. The campaign to retake the city of Edessa from Zengi, the Atabeg of Mosul and Aleppo, had finished in failure before Louis VII reached Antioch. Zengi had been murdered in 1146, and Count Joscelin II of Edessa tried to take advantage of the atabeg's death and recapture the city.

Joscelin's campaign was a catastrophe for the people of Edessa. On 26 October 1146, Armenian guards helped the Franks climb Edessa's walls by ladder and opened the gate for the count and his forces. Joscelin entered the city and the Turks inside fled to the safety of the citadel. However, after six days, and before the Franks could dislodge those taking refuge in the citadel, the city was surrounded by Turkish forces.[2] Joscelin had overestimated the supposed weakness caused by the atabeg's death. As a result, the count was forced to flee the city and abandon the population who had risen up to help restore him.

Michael the Syrian estimated that 30,000 people died during Count Joscelin II's Edessa catastrophes.[3] Such was the slaughter and destruction of the city's inhabitants that the capital city of the first Crusader state seemed unrecoverable. Michael the Syrian described the impact the failed uprising had on the city:

> Desolate Edessa, was like an example of horror. It was clothed in black and intoxicated with blood. It was filled with the stench of the corpses of its sons and daughters who were left to predators. It became the abode of Jackals, and no one entered it except those who searched for its treasures.[4]

With the city of Edessa beyond recovery, Prince Raymond of Antioch suggested that King Louis turn his attention to Aleppo, situated east of Antioch. This would have undoubtedly benefited Raymond's control of the area and expanded into the territory between the principality and the remnants of the County of Edessa, which since the fall of Edessa only consisted of its land west of the River Euphrates. However, Louis had been weakened, losing most of his army in the disastrous march through Asia Minor, and would be unable to support Raymond's ambitions against Aleppo and Nūr ad-Dīn.

Louis left Antioch and marched with his remaining forces south to the Kingdom of Jerusalem, where he would meet up with a recovered Conrad III, who sailed to Acre from Constantinople, arriving in the Holy Land in April. Louis' decision not to strike at Nūr ad-Dīn could be due to several reasons, ranging from lack of manpower and money to a desire to visit Jerusalem's holy sites. However, there were rumours that a disagreement between the French king and Prince Raymond was caused by a great scandal.

Whispers spread of an incestuous affair between Prince Raymond and his niece, the Queen of France. King Louis was humiliated by the scandal of his wife's affair and marched south with his army, having forced Queen Eleanor to leave Antioch with him. John of Salisbury recorded the scandal, writing, 'The attentions paid by the prince to the queen, and his constant, indeed almost continuous, conversation with her, aroused the king's suspicions'. He noted that his suspicion was 'greatly strengthened when the queen wished to remain behind'.[5] This would have undoubtedly ended a friendly relationship between the French Crusaders and the principality.

Although the Crusaders had finally reached Outremer, such were their losses that even combining the forces of France's King Louis VII and King Conrad III of Germany could have little impact on alleviating the threat to Frankish territory. With fewer than expected European troops and after the disastrous attempt to reclaim Edessa by Count Joscelin a few years earlier, a new target for the Second Crusade was needed.

To decide the future of the failing Second Crusade, a Great Council was held in the city of Acre on 24 June 1148. In William of Tyre's work, he recounts many senior nobles in attendance; the names mentioned below address the more significant attendees from the parties of German Crusaders, French Crusaders and lords of Outremer.

The Great Council was attended by Conrad III and his leading men, such as his brother Otto, the Bishop of Freising, the Bishops of Metz and Toul, as well as Theodwin, Bishop of Porto, who was a Papal Legate sent by Pope Eugenius. Other high-ranking nobles included Henry, Duke of Austria, and the young Duke of Swabia, Frederick Barbarossa, who would eventually lead the German Crusaders in the Third Crusade. In keeping with links to future Crusade leaders, William, Marquis of Montferrat was also at the council, and his son Conrad would one day stake a claim for the Kingship of Jerusalem following King Guy's defeat to the Sultan Saladin of Egypt towards the end of the twelfth century.[6]

From the French Crusader camp, King Louis attended with Godfrey, Bishop of Langres, Arnulf, Bishop of Lisieux and Papal Legate, Cardinal Guy of Florence. The French nobility in attendance included the king's brother, Count Robert of Dreux, the king's son-in-law, Count Henry of Champagne, and Count Thierry of Flanders, the brother-in-law of the King of Jerusalem. The young King Baldwin III of Jerusalem attended the council alongside his mother, Melisende, Fulk, the Patriarch of Jerusalem, as well as leading Church leaders such as the Archbishop of Nazareth and the Bishop of Acre, along with the Grand Master of the Knights Templar, Robert of Craon, and the Grand Master of the Hospitallers (the Knights Hospitallers, or Order of Knights of the Hospital of Saint John of Jerusalem), Raymond of Puy.

The lords of Outremer were also in attendance. They included Philip of Nablus (a future Templar grand master), Gerard of Sidon and Balian the Elder, whose son, Balian of Ibelin, would lead the ill-fated defence of Jerusalem against Saladin in 1187.[7]

The significance of naming most of the Christian leaders in attendance at the Great Council is that it demonstrates their collective coalition across Europe and the Holy Land. It also indicates just how influential the Church was on military campaigning in the Holy Land by the attendance by the grand masters of the Templars and the Hospitallers. Such a council of nobles shows just how prominent the monastic military had become so soon after their foundation.

However, despite such a grand meeting of Crusading leadership, historian Mayer describes the direction taken by the council as 'incredibly stupid' and their planned place of attack as 'ridiculous in execution as in conception'.[8] Inevitably, the Great Council of Acre decided to attack Damascus to the east, a city that was relatively friendly to the Kingdom of Jerusalem.

However, Damascus was perceived as the best of the available targets, with the other favoured objectives being the Nūr ad-Dīn-controlled city of Aleppo in the north and a campaign against the Fatimids of Egypt to the south-west port of Ascalon. Following Count Joscelin's failed attempt to retake Edessa and King Louis' disagreement with Prince Raymond, a campaign against Nūr ad-Dīn was not feasible, while the threat posed by the Fatimid-controlled Ascalon was negated by the recent construction of castles at Bethgibelin, Ibelin and Blanchegarde.[9]

Damascus was the largest city close to the borders of the Kingdom of Jerusalem. William of Tyre describes it as 'the largest city of lesser Syria', and 'as the Metropolis of the region', its conquest would undoubtedly be a rich prize for the Franks of Outremer.[10] It was a prize that Queen Melisende's father, Baldwin II, had campaigned against.

Damascus was recently in an alliance with the Kingdom of Jerusalem to counter the aggressive expansion of Zengi, but with Zengi dead and his territories split between his sons, Saif al-Dīn and Nūr ad-Dīn, the threat from the north was significantly lessened. Damascus also allowed the Kingdom of Jerusalem to expand eastwards, as Outremer narrowly hugged the Mediterranean coastline. When looking at the three possible routes of the Second Crusade, Mayer's sharp criticism of the decision to target Damascus seems disproportionate; however, his criticism of these great Christian lords' execution of their campaign against the city is more appropriate.

THE WALLS OF DAMASCUS

The newly reinforced grand army of the Second Crusade marched on Damascus towards the end of July 1148. Ibn al-Qalānisi recorded that the Crusader army, numbering around 50,000 infantry and cavalry, reached the city on 24 July.[11] As the Crusaders approached the city, they had to fight their way through miles of orchards, with the defenders making a desperate attempt to prevent them reaching the river. In the struggle, the elderly lawyer Yusuf al-Findalawi died in battle – he was described by Ibn al-Qalānisi as 'a martyr for the Faith'.[12]

After a hard-fought victory, the Crusader army camped in a well-supplied position among the orchards along the western wall to prepare for a long siege. William of Tyre describes the medieval city, noting that 'it lies in a plain which is arid and sterile except as it is irrigated by ancient canals which bring the water from above for its benefit'. He details the orchard setting of the Crusaders' initial camp:

> On the west, the direction from which our army was approaching, and also on the north, the orchards stretched out five miles or more in the direction of Lebanon and, like a dense, gloomy forest, encircled the city far and wide. To indicate the limits of each orchard and also to prevent trespassers entering at will, these groves are enclosed by walls of mud, for stone is scarce in that region.

William of Tyres' account illustrates the difficulty the Crusaders faced in approaching the city from the orchards as the trees were placed so close together that it made advancing on the walls in great numbers impractical. He explains that despite this, the orchard provided ample food and water for the troops.[13] The well-supplied position also left the army vulnerable, as the defenders could use the dense orchards for cover when attacking the besiegers.

The dense trees that protected the western defences meant that the Crusaders could not utilise their main strength, their heavy cavalry, and it was decided that the army would withdraw from the well-supplied western wall and move to the eastern walls, which had more open ground. However, this meant moving the army to a waterless plain with higher, fortified walls.

William of Tyre wrote that the decision to abandon the camp at the western wall was due to treachery in the Christian army's ranks. He asserts that the lords of Outremer were bribed by the citizens of Damascus to move the Crusader army away from the western wall just as the defences were about to collapse. He wrote that their 'wicked suggestions persuaded the king and the pilgrim princes, who fully relied upon their loyalty and assiduity', informing them that on the east side, there was no orchard and the small wall there could easily be breached.[14]

On 27 July, the Crusaders abandoned their camp in the hard-fought position in the orchard and moved to the barren plain outside the south-east walls of Damascus. However, they soon found their position untenable, having lost access to food or water and now facing the prospect of a prolonged siege as the eastern walls of Damascus were not the small, quick-to-fall defences that had been described. Marching back to the orchards was no longer an option because once the Crusaders had left, the citizens of Damascus had rebuilt and reinforced the fortifications, which would prevent the Christians from returning the way they had come.

Ibn al-Athīr records that the Commander of Damascus, Muin ad-Dīn, had sent a message to his brother, Saif al-Dīn, calling for him to come to his aid.[15] Word soon reached the Crusader camp that the armies of Mosul, led by Saif al-Dīn, and Aleppo, led by Nūr ad-Dīn, were marching to relieve the city of Damascus.

On 28 July, the grand army of the Second Crusade was in full retreat. The resourceless camp and the prospect of fighting both the Damascenes and the sons of Zengi forced the Crusading kings into a humiliating defeat.

Upon discovering that the Crusaders had lifted the siege and taken flight, the Damascene forces pursued them. Ibn al-Qalānisi recorded:

> They showered them with arrows and killed many of their rearguards this way, and horses and pack animals as well. Innumerable corpses of men and their splendid mounts were found in the bivouacs and along the route of their flight, the bodies stinking so powerfully that the birds almost fell out of the sky.[16]

Whether or not there was the treachery in the Crusader ranks that William of Tyre accuses, the Crusader army consisting of two great European kings and all the strength of the nobility of Outremer, failed to take Damascus, which ultimately came down to not having the strength of numbers to defeat the armies of Mosul and Aleppo. Even after his death, the Franks of Outremer shrank in the presence of Zengi's strength.

THE END OF THE SECOND CRUSADE

Conrad III left the Holy Land on 8 September that year, while King Louis VII and Queen Eleanor stayed in the Holy Land until Easter 1149, although this was not for a military campaign but for the royal couple to visit the Christian holy sites. However, before the German King departed the

Holy Land, William of Tyre writes that discussions were held about the Crusaders targeting the city of Ascalon. This seemed a viable alternative to the Franks because it was in close proximity; however, no campaign took place, and Conrad left shortly after to return to Europe.[17]

The Second Crusade ended without any significant gains for Outremer and along with the massive loss of life, it left the Christian territories more unstable and vulnerable than when the kings of Europe had set out. The campaign to retake Edessa never started, and after Count Joscelin's failed attempt to retake the county, it was now truly lost to the Franks. The Council of Acre's decision to send a grand army to take Damascus strengthened the Muslim territories east of Outremer, with Nūr ad-Dīn taking control of Damascus in 1154.

Despite the failings in Outremer, the Second Crusade achieved some success in the Iberian Peninsula. In 1147, Lisbon was captured by English and Flemish Crusaders, who were fighting alongside King Alfonso Henriques of Portugal. In his campaign against the Moors, King Alfonso also fought alongside the Knights Templar and the extent of their support is demonstrated by the gifts granted to them by the Portuguese King. In 1145, the Knights Templar received the castle of Longroiva and a house in Braga, and in 1147, the king granted the Templars all the churches in Santarém. The Knights Templar would have certainly had to have been playing a large part in Alfonso's campaign to justify such gifts.[18]

Although it was a minor victory compared to the early goal of recapturing the original Crusader state, victory at the Siege of Lisbon was a tremendous step forward for the advancement of the Kingdom of Portugal. The fleet of English and Flemish Crusaders who fought at Lisbon would join the forces of Geno, Barcelona and the Templar and Hospitaller orders in the successful 1148 Siege of Tortosa. The success of these sieges compared to the failures in the Holy Land demonstrated that the future of Crusading would involve complete military campaigns rather than the armed pilgrimage of the First Crusade, which was hopelessly copied by Louis VII of France and Conrad III of Germany.

The losses in Outremer shocked Europe and many wondered how a Crusade supported by God and the Church could fail. The defeats were particularly shocking as the Crusade had been led by the great kings of Europe, whereas fifty years earlier, the First Crusade was led by dukes.

Blame for the failings was partially levelled at the Knights Templar, according to John of Salisbury, who recorded the accusations of treachery to the European Christian nobility but also noted that King Conrad firmly exonerated the Templars of any blame.[19] In a letter from King Conrad to

Wibald, the Abbot of Stavelot and Corvey, when recounting the betrayal, the king made no mention of the Knights Templar and simply referred to the traitors as 'they'.[20]

Aside from the mention of blame by John of Salisbury, there is little to suggest that it was the Knights Templar who betrayed the Crusade, but it is significant that when the Christian soldiers failed in their objective in the Holy Land, the finger of blame was pointed at the Knights Templar. This singling out and distrust of the infamous warrior monks shows a hint of the Templars' vulnerability and would eventually be their undoing.

4

A KINGDOM IN CRISIS

THE DEATH OF PRINCE RAYMOND

The Second Crusade, led by two great kings of Europe, set out to the Holy Land to retake the lost Crusader state of Edessa, but upon arriving found that objective unachievable because of the significant losses sustained crossing Asia Minor. After the Great Council of all the powerful Christian nobility, the Second Crusade aimed to strengthen the states of Outremer by capturing the city of Damascus. The hope was to secure more territory for the Crusader states inland. However, the Crusade failed in this second objective, and the once-friendly city would come under the control of the crusader's powerful enemy, Nūr ad-Dīn, in 1154. However, such was the weakness of the Crusader states after the failed Second Crusade that in the summer of 1149, Nūr ad-Dīn invaded the Principality of Antioch. The following catastrophe might have been avoided if the French King Louis VII had supported Prince Raymond of Antioch's desire to attack Nūr ad-Dīn at Antioch's borders.

Keen to strengthen his hold on the north of Syria, Nūr ad-Dīn invaded Antioch and laid siege to the fort of Inab. Prince Raymond mustered a small force and raced to Inab. William of Tyre justifies this rash action, writing, 'for he [Raymond] was a man of undaunted and impetuous courage who allowed himself to be ruled by the advice of no one in matters of this kind'.[1] However, his swiftness may have been exaggerated as conflicting accounts number his force at 4,000 knights and 1,000 infantry, and he allied with a company of Assassins led by Ali ibn Wafa.[2] If Raymond had set out with such a large force, then it brings into doubt the notion of his swiftness to descend on Inab with a handful of troops.

However, the swiftness of Raymond's response was not the main factor in his strategic failings. His arrival caused Nūr ad-Dīn to lift the siege and withdraw, and William of Tyre records that he did so because he was anxious that Raymond would come with a large force, and so he retreated to a safe position until the size of the principality's army was known.

Whether he arrived with a handful of men or a force of 5,000, when Nūr ad-Dīn retreated, Prince Raymond made a huge tactical error. The prince chose not to use the safety of the fort and, believing that the area was now secure, he had his force camp out in the open plain. Unfortunately for Raymond, Nūr ad-Dīn had not retreated and awaited the chance to launch a devastating counter-attack. Raymond's naïve decision to camp his forces in the open provided that ideal opportunity.

The prince's camp awoke to find themselves surrounded by Nūr ad-Dīn's forces and unable to escape. Raymond's army made a desperate last stand but Raymond himself was killed in the fighting. William of Tyre gave him a glowing account, writing that he 'fought valiantly, like the high-spirited and courageous warrior he was'. However, he also recorded that his head and right arm were cut off and his remains were left on the battlefield among the slain. Nūr ad-Dīn had the prince's head and arm sent to the Caliph of Baghdad as proof of the senior Frankish noble's death. Raymond's body was later found and returned to Antioch for burial in the custom of his predecessors at the Church of Saint Peter.[3]

Raymond's swiftness to discount his enemy's threat led to his death and critically weakened the principality's strength. With the prince killed and his forces wiped out, the Crusader state was left at the mercy of Nūr ad-Dīn. Before he began his campaign to take the principality, it is said that he travelled to the Mediterranean coast to bathe in its waters, a gesture to signify that his dominance had spread to the sea.

Aside from the huge blow that was the death of Raymond, another senior Frankish noble was lost, Count Joscelin II of Edessa. Joscelin was responsible for the loss of his capital city in 1144 after marching his troops away to engage with Zengi, who had meanwhile outfoxed Joscelin and attacked the undefended city. Joscelin then caused his people to be massacred after retaking Edessa and abandoning the city and those within in 1146. His incompetence finally caught up with him when he was captured by Nūr ad-Dīn's soldiers in 1150 while en route to defend the Principality of Antioch.

The count had naively left his escort to relieve himself when he was ambushed and taken in chains to Aleppo. He died in captivity. William of Tyre gave a scornful description of the count's life, writing that he 'was a lazy, idle man, given over to low and dissolute pleasures, one who spurned good ways and followed base pursuits' and 'he reaped the result of his dissolute ways and came to a wretched end'.[4]

After the count's capture, to give what remained of the county a chance to withstand Nūr ad-Dīn's expansion, his wife Beatrice sold what lands remained to the Byzantine Empire. However, by 1151, even with Byzantine resources, Nūr ad-Dīn had conquered what remained of the county. The first Crusader state established was the first Crusader state to be lost. The County of Edessa was no more.

To prevent the principality from falling to Nūr ad-Dīn's control, King Baldwin III, the teenage king who co-ruled with his mother Melisende, marched with the Knights Templar to engage with Nūr ad-Dīn's army. Templar knight Andrew de Montbard, the Seneschal of the Temple, wrote to Grand Master Everard des Barres, who had travelled back to Europe after the Second Crusade, to urge him to return to the Holy Land as the situation was so dire. Andrew wrote, 'With his death [Prince Raymond] no more resistance was possible and immediately the Parthians invaded and captured the whole territory of Antioch. They fortified the strongholds which they manned, still man and will continue to man unless divine clemency comes to our aid.' In the letter, Andrew informed Everard that with a loan of 7,000 bezants from Acre and 1,000 from Jerusalem, a force of 120 knights and 1,000 squires marched to Antioch with the King of Jerusalem. However, the situation was so grim that he pleaded for Everard to return to Outremer with knights, sergeants and money.[5]

The arrival of a relief army headed by King Baldwin III and joined by the Knights Templar paused Nūr ad-Dīn's conquest of the region. However, unlike the aftermath of the Field of Blood, the principality's lost territory was not recovered, and the state was significantly weaker. The Franks were forced to sign a treaty with Nūr ad-Dīn that recognised Aleppo's rights to the contested territories of the Summaq Plateau and east of the Belus Hills.[6] It is significant that this treaty was not a great counter-attack by Baldwin and the Knights Templar, which reasserted the Franks' strength. In fact, with Edessa lost and Antioch losing inland territory, it showed the continued decline of the Crusaders' hold over the north of Outremer.

After the victory at Inab, Nūr ad-Dīn styled himself as a champion of Islam, much like his father, Zengi. He set about uniting his territories under the idea of jihad – he sought new mosques and preachers throughout his land to unify the Islamic people in jihad. The head of Prince Raymond was used as a symbol of his victory against the Franks and his status as a champion of Islam.[7] To achieve union among his people, Nūr ad-Dīn also used this religious zeal against the Shi'ites and towards the Sunni people of Damascus, whose alliance with the Franks was deemed unacceptable.[8] After pressure from Nūr ad-Dīn, the people of Damascus opened the gates to the sultan in 1154, which brought added strength to his ever-expanding dominance of the region.

However, Ibn al-Athīr did not share the notion that the sultan was a fanatic. He described Nūr ad-Dīn as having 'a good knowledge of Muslim Law', emphasising that 'he was not a fanatic' but 'held the Holy Law in the deepest respect'. Ibn al-Athīr acknowledged that 'On the battlefield he had no equal', but he also listed the infrastructure the sultan had built, such as walls for cities and fortresses, hospitals and the Great Mosque at Mosul.[9]

The account of Ibn al-Athīr enables us to assess the impact of Nūr ad-Dīn, aside from viewing him as the conquering enemy of the Franks. We can see him as an Islamic leader who advanced the Islamic unity that would come to dominate the dwindling Crusader states of Outremer.

A PRINCESS OF ANTIOCH AND A QUEEN OF OUTREMER

Born in 1130, Baldwin III was the grandson of Baldwin II, who died in 1131. After his father's death, Baldwin III, who was still in his early teens, was crowned as co-ruler with his mother, Queen Melisende, in 1143. Baldwin and his mother were both in attendance at the Second Crusade's Great Council of Acre and the young king even led the march towards the failed siege of Damascus. After the death of Prince Raymond in 1149, Baldwin III found himself ruler of the principality because Raymond's son, Bohemond, was still a child and Raymond's widow rejected Baldwin's plan for her to marry a suitor of his choosing.

Soon after the capture of Count Joscelin, another Crusader state was plunged into crisis as the Count of Tripoli, Raymond II, was murdered by Assassins, a secluded Shia Islamic sect, in 1152. Now the young king found himself temporarily overseeing all three of the remaining Crusader states.

Due to Baldwin III's need to prioritise the management of the Kingdom of Jerusalem, he was unable to engage fully as regent at Antioch. However, his increasing levels of responsibility meant that Raymond's widow, Princess Constance, could rule as regent through her infant son, Prince Bohemond III.

Born in 1128, Constance was the only child of the rebellious Princess Alice of Antioch, who married Raymond when she was only a child. Having never known freedom, Constance was reluctant to give up her new independence so easily. Only a year after the death of her husband, Constance styled herself 'Constance by the grace of God Princess of

Antioch, daughter of Bohemond the younger', which articulated her right to rule as regent legitimately through the Bohemond bloodline.[10]

Constance was the granddaughter of the First Crusade leader, Prince Bohemond, and the heir of that Bohemond bloodline. Constance hoped to succeed where her mother, Alice, had failed, and rule as the rightful princess. However, Constance's newfound independence was immediately threatened as she was pressured to remarry as soon as possible.

Understandably, Constance was reluctant to do so, and the princess rejected a marriage proposed by the Emperor of Constantinople and the three candidates proposed by her cousin, Baldwin III. On Constance's rejection of these proposals, William of Tyre wrote, 'The princess, however, dreaded the yoke of marriage and preferred a free and independent life. She paid little heed to the needs of her people and was far more interested in enjoying the pleasures of life.'[11] Tyre's comments suggest anxiety about Constance ruling Antioch, as the state was a vulnerable border territory. Furthermore, it was argued that her ruling as regent for her young son Bohemond as Queen Melisende had for the young Baldwin was unsuitable because of the need for military experience in the face of the continued threat from Nūr ad-Dīn.

The vulnerability of Antioch and finding an acceptable suitor for Princess Constance was not Baldwin's biggest challenge, as the king was struggling to assert his dominance over the Kingdom of Jerusalem. The fight for control began when Baldwin's strength grew; it worsened his relationship with his mother, Queen Melisende. Once again, the kingdom was split into two factions and civil war seemed inevitable.

To build her support, the queen promoted those loyal to her into the great offices of the kingdom. One such supporter was Manasses of Hierges, a nephew of Baldwin II, who came to Outremer in 1140. Melisende made him the Constable of Jerusalem, and he became a powerful ally for the queen.

William of Tyre gives a scathing account of Manasses, who was not popular with the nobility in Outremer. He records that the newly created constable had 'an insolent attitude of superiority' and 'roused intense hatred toward him on the part of the nobles'. He asserts that those feelings of dislike would have been acted upon if it had not been for the queen's authority.[12]

Aside from the unpopular constable, Melisende also had the support of Elinard, the Prince of Galilee, and through this connection, the support of nobles from the Ibelin family.[13] However, Elinard died in 1148, and to keep control of the region, Melisende made her younger son, Almaric, the Count of Jaffa.

The Crusader states were again in disarray as Baldwin III had built his own support and was strong enough to counter his mother. The king moved to remove Melisende from power. At first, he demanded that his mother agree to divide the kingdom between them, with Baldwin receiving the coastal territories of Acre and Tyre while Queen Melisende held Jerusalem and Nablus. Baldwin stripped Manasses of his role as constable and gave the role and control of the armed forces to Humphrey of Toron.

This new joint-rule agreement through divided territories appeared to have avoided another civil war for control of the kingdom. Unfortunately for the hated Manasses, after the agreement was made, Baldwin amassed a large army and besieged his castle Mirabel and forced him into exile. Then Baldwin took the city of Nablus before laying siege to his mother at the citadel of Jerusalem.

Eventually, a peace deal was reached and Melisende surrendered the city with the agreement that she kept control of Nablus and Baldwin would not move against it in any way. Melisende kept control of Nablus until she died in 1161.[14]

THE SIEGE OF ASCALON

Although Templar Seneschal Andrew de Montbard sent word to Grand Master Everard des Barres warning of the dire state of the Crusader states, the grand master abdicated his role in 1152, becoming the first of the position to retire.

Everard was the Master of the Paris Temple when the French announced plans for what would be the Second Crusade. He rose to prominence during the ill-fated march across Asia Minor to the principality of Antioch, where his leadership and disciplined Templar knights prevented the annihilation of the Second Crusade before it had even reached the Holy Land. However, after going back to Paris after the failed siege of Damascus, he never returned to the region.

His successor was Bernard de Tremelay, who became Templar Grand Master in time to fight alongside Baldwin III as the kingdom attempted to extend its southern border and capture the remainder of the coastline.

Baldwin III built a castle on the ruins of the ancient town of Gaza to strengthen Outremer's southern border with Egypt. Upon its completion, Ascalon would be vulnerable as it blocked the route to Fatimid Egypt. Also, as Ascalon was the lone hostile territory on the coast, it was sandwiched between the new castle and the port of Jaffa. Baldwin gave control of the castle to the Knights Templar – the first castle recorded as being granted to the Templars in the kingdom.[15]

Gaza was an ancient city that lay 10 miles from Ascalon. It was then no more than a ruin, but it is one of the oldest cities in the world and has a long history of conquest and war. The site was originally built by the Ancient Egyptians, taken by the Philistines and then besieged and conquered by Alexander the Great in 332 BCE. After that, the city came under Roman control and was later part of the dwindling Byzantine Empire before it came under Islamic control in the seventh century. William of Tyre writes of the city's former glory and current state of destitution:

> Gaza, a most ancient city, was one of the five cities of the Philistines. It was celebrated for its buildings, and many handsome churches and spacious houses of marble and huge stones, though now in ruins, still gave splendid evidence of its ancient glory. Many reservoirs and wells of living water also still remained. It was built on a slight eminence and enclosed within its walls much widespread territory.[16]

The ruined city was now part of the Kingdom of Jerusalem and would be vital to Baldwin's plan to apply pressure to the isolated Ascalon.

Rebuilding Gaza as a city was too great a project and given Baldwin's aim of securing the southern border of Outremer and capturing the entirety of the coast, a castle was needed to dominate the region. The fortress was built on top of a hill, so its high walls and towers would dominate the area.

Placing Gaza under Templar control proved a shrewd move by Baldwin as they were able to repel several attacks from the Egyptian forces until, after wasting many resources, they deemed taking the castle by force was unachievable. The Egyptians stopped supplying Ascalon by land and now only went by sea, as the caravans were too vulnerable to attack from the Templar knights at Gaza.[17]

With control over the surrounding areas, Baldwin laid siege to Ascalon in January 1153 with all the forces Jerusalem could muster. The king's forces included the Knights Hospitaller and the Knights Templar, who joined the siege with the newly installed Grand Master Bernard de Tremelay.

Ascalon was blockaded by a fleet of ships under the command of Gerard of Sidon, while the Frankish army camped around the city and prevented any allies from reaching Ascalon by land. It had long been desired by the Franks, but it had alluded them for many years as the city was well stocked with supplies and troops from Egypt. According to William of Tyre, 'Ascalon was well defended by walls and barbicans, towers and embankments, and equipped with an incredible amount of arms and provisions. In addition, it had a large population well trained and thoroughly versed in the practice of arms.' He explained that Egypt kept the city so well supplied and defended because it was vital to the security of Egypt's borders as it would be the focal point of Frankish aggression, meaning Egypt was safe while Ascalon still stood.[18]

Despite the blockade by Gerard of Sidon, an Egyptian fleet was able to evade the Christians and successfully reached Ascalon's docks. Before the fleet's arrival, Ascalon had been under siege for several months and the Franks had successfully kept out supplies and reinforcements.

The successful journey of the Egyptian fleet was a major setback for Baldwin's forces because, after months of isolation, the forces of Jerusalem would have been confident of the city's surrender. Instead, the fleet brought with it a plentiful amount of food, supplies and troops, which gave the defenders a huge boost of morale and dashed the Christians' hopes that the city was on the verge of capitulation.

The siege carried on well into the summer as the well-supplied defenders of Ascalon kept the Christian forces at bay. There wasn't a breakthrough for the Franks until the night of 15 August, when the defenders attempted to set fire to the attackers' large wooden siege tower, which the Christians had used to great effect. However, strong winds blew the flames back against the city, causing one of the walls to collapse.

William of Tyre described the event as it unfolded in detail. The sudden collapse of the wall awoke the Franks at the camp, and as one, the troops armed themselves and rushed towards the breach, only to find their way blocked by Templar Grand Master Bernard de Tremelay. According to William of Tyre, the Templars had taken control of the breach and 'he kept the rest back in order that his own people, being the first to enter, might obtain the greater and richer portion of the spoils and plunder'.

This greed later described by William of Tyre would lead to a massacre as forty Templar knights entered the city. Cut off from the rest of the army, they were all slaughtered alongside their grand master, and the collapsed section of the wall was rebuilt. The bodies of the slain Templars were then hung over the walls to taunt the Christian troops.[19]

However, this account of the Templar disaster has been disputed. The Templar deaths and that of the grand master are agreed, but the motive of greed being behind their disastrous assault on the city is unclear. The Templar assault through the breech is not mentioned by Ibn al-Qalānisi. However, in his account of the siege, he describes the incident, recording:

> They pressed upon it with attacks both morning and evening, until at length the way was opened to them to deliver an assault upon it at a certain point in the city wall. Having battered it down, they rushed into the town, and a great host were killed on both sides.

He does not mention the Templars' role, which puts doubt on William of Tyre's accusations of Templar greed and incompetence. In the next line, Ibn al-Qalānisi explains that the citizens of Ascalon sought terms of surrender due to 'necessity and force of arms', which the Franks accepted.[20]

The Templar deaths and their timing close to the fall of the city indicate that their fatal venture was not catastrophic for the Franks' conquest of Ascalon. Templar historian Malcolm Barber argues that as the city fell a week after the assault, on 22 August, the Frankish assault did not suffer the huge setback described by William of Tyre.[21] The significance of the assault aside, the Templar grand master was killed and Ascalon was conquered by Baldwin III, which meant that the Christians now controlled the entire coastline of Outremer, and this would eventually shape the future of the Crusades. The doorway to Egypt was now open.

THE SEEDS OF DISASTER

Baldwin had considerable success in strengthening the Kingdom of Jerusalem's southern border, making gains by building a new strategic castle on the ruins of Gaza and with the capture of Ascalon, the last coastal city on the western shore. However, he also had considerable losses.

The death of Prince Raymond and the imprisonment of Count Joscelin II of Edessa had left the northern states of Outremer vulnerable and weak. While there was an heir in the infant Bohemond III, his mother, Princess Constance, had frustrated Baldwin's attempts to strengthen Antioch's hold on its threatened territories by refusing to marry any of Baldwin's chosen suitors. The princess did eventually choose a husband, however, her choice was not one of Baldwin's suitors. In fact, the man was fighting alongside Baldwin in the Siege of Ascalon when he asked the king for permission to marry the princess.

Constance had chosen to marry Reynald de Châtillon, a French knight. Reynald came from the French nobility, but he was not a man of great influence, nor did he bring great resources. Despite his status, Reynald was a fierce warrior and a despised enemy of the Muslim states. In his account of the Third Crusade, Bahā' al-Dīn refers to him as 'a powerful and violent infidel'. He describes a cruel act carried out by Reynald, whom he refers to as a 'villain'. He recounts 'that during a period of truce [...] a caravan from Egypt was passing by his territory and he broke the truce to attack and capture it, illtreating and torturing the men and imprisoning them in narrow dungeons'.[22]

The newly created Prince of Antioch was also known for being cruel to Christians, and William of Tyre recounts his brutal mistreatment of the Patriarch of Antioch. He records that Reynald had the Patriarch arrested, covered his head in honey, and forced the elderly priest to sit in the Syrian summer sun and suffer the sun's rays and hordes of flies. William explains that the prince's cruelty was because the Patriarch dared to criticise him. However, it showed how brutal and wicked Reynald was in his dealing with those he deemed his enemy.[23]

Reynald's fanaticism for war was a considerable problem for Baldwin III. While the King of Jerusalem was working on an alliance with the Byzantine Empire, Reynald and the Armenian Prince Thoros attacked and ravaged the Byzantine-controlled Island of Cyprus. Baldwin needed Emperor Manuel to agree to allow him to marry the emperor's niece, Theodora, who came with a large dowry that would help the king cope with debts accrued from his costly campaigns.[24] Fortunately, a deal was reached between Baldwin and the emperor, which eased the pressure on Jerusalem's finances and provided support against Nūr ad-Dīn's aggressive western expansion.

Reynald was forced to humble himself in 1158 when a Byzantine army marched towards Antioch. The violent Reynald knew his position was hopeless and threw himself at the feet of the emperor, begging for forgiveness and promising to install a Greek patriarch and give over control of Antioch's citadel.[25]

However, the Prince of Antioch would not be a problem for Baldwin for much longer as he was captured in 1160 and remained a prisoner of Aleppo for sixteen years. There was not a massive political effort to secure the release of such an unpopular figure. But despite his long captivity, Reynald would play a role in Outremer's conflicts with the future Sultan of Egypt, Saladin, and fight in the infamous Battle of Hattin in 1187.

Reynald has a lasting reputation as being one of the villains of the Crusades, a legacy that is depicted in a twenty-first-century film adaptation of the period. Hollywood's depiction of Reynald in *Kingdom of Heaven* will be examined in Chapter 19 of this book.

Despite Baldwin's success in the south with the capture of Ascalon, his greatest failure was his inability to stop Nūr ad-Dīn from taking Damascus. Although his father, Zengi, had longed to bring the rich city under his control, Nūr ad-Dīn had managed to achieve the feat without warfare and bloodshed. Instead, he had taken the powerful Muslim city through diplomatic means and applied pressure when needed. The city was ruled by Mujir ad-Dīn Abaq, whose alliance with Jerusalem was unpopular with the citizens, particularly the tribute paid to the Christians. To cling onto power, Abaq travelled to Aleppo in 1151 to acknowledge Nūr ad-Dīn as his overlord in the hope that this would appease the sultan and prevent a full-scale invasion.[26]

In the winter of 1153–54, Nūr ad-Dīn moved to cut off the shipments of grain from the north, and food soon became scarce in Damascus. In April, he marched on the city, but there was no need for any bloodshed because such was the unhappiness within that the citizens threw open the city gates and Nūr ad-Dīn's banner soon stood tall above the gatehouse. Abaq fled to the citadel, but upon surrendering control of Damascus, he was rewarded with the city of Homs.

With the capture of Damascus, the Crusader states of Outremer were now encircled by hostile states and the Christian territories were reduced. Baldwin III had succeeded in capturing the coast, but under his rule, Outremer had lost a large amount of inland territory.

The aftermath of the Second Crusade was one of continual decline and setbacks. The Second Crusade failed to reclaim Edessa, which resulted in Count Joscelin II's permanent captivity and the eventual loss of the entire county, never to be recovered. The weakness of the Crusaders emboldened Nūr ad-Dīn to invade and capture much of the Principality of Antioch, killing Prince Raymond and thrusting the principality into disarray.

The other failure of the Second Crusade was its inability to capture Damascus. While this was not disastrous in itself, it did have huge political ramifications. The Great Council of Acre's decision to attack Damascus, a city that was a long-time ally of Jerusalem, pushed the city into closer ties with Nūr ad-Dīn. The capture of Damascus meant that not only had his strength and territory grown far beyond that of his father Zengi, but he now threatened the Crusader states of Outremer from the north to the south. Baldwin had gained total control over the coast with the capture of the long-desired city of Ascalon, but this now focused the Christians' attention on Egypt and the wealthy city of Cairo, which would become the setting for power struggles and the target for future Crusades. However, if Nūr ad-Dīn could unite Egypt to his cause, the Crusader states would be entirely encircled and under pressure from a united Muslim power.

5

THE VIZIER OF CAIRO

THE CRUELTY OF BALDWIN III

The city of Banyas was just north of Lake Tiberias (the Sea of Galilee) and south of Damascus and was currently ruled by Humphrey of Toron, the king's constable and loyal supporter. Banyas was a border territory that Humphrey held at great expense. It was vulnerable because it was beside a forest. Unfortunately, the forest of Banyas was the site of one of Baldwin's most ruthless and cruel acts as king.

In February 1157, Baldwin broke a peace treaty for his own gain and slaughtered the Turkoman horsemen camped in the forest. William of Tyre records that this large company of Turkomans had received not just the kings' permission but also a treaty of peace to bring such a large number of horses to the area for the excellent pasturage. With such assurances made, the Turkomans were unprepared for an attack, especially from King Baldwin.[1]

William of Tyre gave some leniency to the king, writing that the plan to attack and plunder the Turkomans for their horses was proposed to him by wicked counsellors and the king's hand was forced by his dire financial situation. The Franks attacked without warning, and the unsuspecting Turkomans were unable to mount a defence. William of Tyre wrote, 'Some, thanks to their swift horses, were able to save their lives by flight; others, spurred on by necessity, escaped by hiding in the woods; but all the rest were either slain by the sword or led into cruel servitude.' He claimed that the number of captives and the amount of loot was so large that it was unequalled in the Crusader states. However, he was scolding in his conclusion of the event, writing:

> This deed brought no glorious or laudable renown to our people, for they had violated a treaty of peace and had maltreated, as they would, an

> unsuspecting people – men who relied upon the good faith of the king and who had, moreover, no means of resisting.[2]

Although the slaughter had brought much-needed resources, the Frankish position would soon come under threat from Nūr ad-Dīn. In May, he defeated a Frankish army, and emboldened by the victory, he mustered his forces and siege weapons and surrounded the city of Banyas.

Nūr ad-Dīn's army contained many siege weapons, and by harnessing his firepower and strength of numbers, he captured the city and forced the survivors to flee to the refuge of the citadel. When King Baldwin learned of Banyas' dire situation, he rushed to relieve the siege and rescue his loyal constable, Humphrey.

In early June, King Baldwin and his forces arrived at the city to the surprise of Nūr ad-Dīn's forces, who chose to retreat and not engage the sizeable Frankish army. The city had been given a temporary respite. However, such was Nūr ad-Dīn's destruction of the city and the ruinous condition of the walls and houses that it is mentioned in both William of Tyre's and Ibn al-Qalānisi's accounts.

The king's forces included senior nobility of the kingdom, such as Odo de St Amand, who was the King's Marshal, and the newly installed Grand Master of the Templars, Bertrand de Blancfort, who accompanied the king's army with a large number of Templar knights. Thinking that the threat from Nūr ad-Dīn had passed, King Baldwin dismissed the infantry units so he could travel back swiftly to Tiberias accompanied by his cavalry.

The king's reduced forces marched south along the River Jordan. Baldwin thought that Nūr ad-Dīn and his army were far from them and lowered his guard, so when the king's forces neared Jacob's Ford, they were totally unaware of the ambush laid for them.

William of Tyre explained that once Nūr ad-Dīn's forces attacked, the Franks 'ceased their trivial chatting, ran to their horses, and took arms'. However, so unprepared were they that it was too late to mount a defence and soon 'their ranks were broken; the foe attacked them furiously at close quarters'.[3]

The Franks were quickly overwhelmed, and the situation was so hopeless that King Baldwin was forced to flee the battle, racing to the safety of the fortress at Safed. Ibn al-Qalānisi's account of the battle mirrors William of Tyre's in describing how quickly the Christian forces were overrun, but he also indicates the level of the devastation inflicted by Nūr ad-Dīn's forces, claiming that 'not more than ten survived'.[4] William of Tyre's account differs where he explains that the number of Christian casualties was low because so many Franks surrendered. This might seem reasonable in the face of certain death; however, William of Tyre was highly critical of the result. He scornfully wrote, 'Warriors renowned for wisdom and experience in war and common soldiers alike, to save their miserable lives surrendered without resistance like the lowest slaves, utterly regardless of the shameful yoke of slavery and the ignominy which would cling to their names forevermore.'[5]

Many senior nobles were captured, including the King's Marshal, the Templar Grand Master Bertrand de Blancfort and eighty-seven Templar knights.[6] The prisoners were taken to Damascus, and the Templar grand master would not be freed until 1159 as part of a peace deal between Nūr ad-Dīn and Byzantine Emperor Manuel. Bertrand de Blancfort was in captivity for two years, but he would not be the last Templar grand master to be taken prisoner.

Following the disaster of Banyas and the king's humiliating flight, Baldwin focused on securing Antioch's future as the principality was once again vulnerable following the capture of Prince Reynald in 1160. He gave control of the principality to Patriarch Aimery, whom Reynald had previously brutalised. Baldwin overlooked Princess Constance's right to rule while her husband was imprisoned, ending the ambitious Constance's control over Antioch.

Despite placing the Latin Patriarch in control, Baldwin was unable to prevent closer ties between the principality and the Byzantine Empire when Princess Constance arranged for her daughter, Maria of Antioch, to marry the recently widowed Emperor Manuel, which drastically strengthened her position in the principality. Stability did not return to the principality until 1163, when Constance's son Bohemond III became Prince of Antioch with the support of the local lords, and Princess Constance was forced from Antioch to Latakia, where she remained until her death.[7] However, Baldwin would not live to see it. He became ill towards the end of 1162 and died in February 1163, only outliving Melisende, his mother and once fierce rival, by two years. Baldwin III was laid to rest in the Church of the Holy Sepulchre.

THE YOUNGER BROTHER

Baldwin was childless and on his deathbed he named his 27-year-old younger brother Amalric as his successor. However, there was some controversy due to Amalric's marriage to Agnes of Courtenay, the daughter of Count Joscelin II of Edessa. The marriage was opposed because Amalric and Agnes were third cousins, so it had to be annulled. Amalric only agreed to this after the legitimacy of their children, Sybilla and Baldwin, was assured. Both would one day rule the Kingdom of Jerusalem, and Agnes married Hugh of Ibelin instead. Amalric was quickly crowned king to avoid opposition to his right of succession gathering momentum.

William of Tyre describes Amalric as 'a man of prudence and discretion, well versed in secular affairs', but notes that he 'had a slight impediment in his speech'. He bore a resemblance to his brother with his aquiline nose and blond hair, however, William of Tyre notes that he was overweight despite not overeating or consuming an excessive amount of alcohol. Most critically, though, he wrote that the king 'abandoned himself without restraint to the sins of the flesh and to have seduced married women' and he overburdened the Church with his financial demands.[8]

The main drive behind Amalric's rule was the acquisition of money, which brought the rich lands of Egypt under his gaze. With the capture of Ascalon by Baldwin III, the rich and resourceful lands of Egypt just over the border tempted the Franks as an opportunity to expand their revenues. The objective of exploiting Egypt's resources started under Baldwin III when he placed an embargo on importing shipbuilding materials such as timber, iron and pitch into Egypt.[9]

With the Templar castle installed on the ruins of Gaza, the Knights Templar had a significant presence at Outremer's border, which brought them into conflict with Egypt. In 1154, they were able to exploit a power struggle in Egypt for their own financial gain.

Although in Cairo the caliph was murdered by Abbās, the Vizier of Egypt, and replaced by Abbās' son, Nāsir al-Dīn, the coup ultimately failed, and Abbās and his son were forced to flee Egypt. However, after successfully escaping the fallout in Cairo, the vizier's party were at the mercy of the Franks.

On 7 June, while travelling to Damascus, Abbās and his party were ambushed by a large force of Franks, mainly consisting of Templar knights, and were quickly subdued. Abbās was killed in the ambush, while Nāsir al-Dīn and their resources were captured. As the Templars had the most knights deployed, they acquired most of the loot and took Nāsir al-Dīn as their prisoner. He was eventually sold to the Egyptians for 60,000 gold, but once back in Cairo, he was executed for his part in the violent coup.[10] This demonstrates the Knights Templars' dominance over the southern region of Outremer and the highly volatile political situation in Egypt, one that Nūr ad-Dīn and King Amalric would try to exploit.

FIGHTING ON TWO FRONTS

When Amalric came to power, the political situation in Egypt was dire. The once rich and powerful country that had built the city of Cairo as the seat of Shi'ite Fatimid power was ruled by the 11-year-old Caliph al-Adid, with Shawar in the role of vizier, who actually wielded power in Egypt. However, Shawar was overthrown by his chamberlain, Dirgham. Given the fractious state of power in the region, losing one's power often resulted in one's death, so Shawar was forced to flee Egypt while Dirgham killed many emirs to secure his control over Egypt.[11]

In 1163, Shawar fled to Damascus, hoping to secure Nūr ad-Dīn's support and troops to overthrow Dirgham. It was an attractive prospect because if Nūr ad-Dīn could stretch his control from Aleppo to Egypt, he would have Outremer surrounded.

Nūr ad-Dīn tasked his Kurdish general, Asad ad-Dīn Shīrkūh, with leading the army into Egypt to overthrow Dirgham and reinstalling Shawar as vizier. William of Tyre describes Shīrkūh as 'an able and energetic warrior, eager for glory and of wide experience in military affairs' and 'beloved by his followers because of this munificence'. Although he noted that Shīrkūh 'was small of stature, very stout and fat and already advanced in years' and 'afflicted with cataract in one eye', he 'had become rich and had risen by merit from his humble estate'.[12]

From William of Tyres' account, it is clear that Shīrkūh was a highly respected and capable general. However, shortly after Shīrkūh's army invaded, Dirgham was killed in the fighting, struck by an arrow from one of his own men. With his rival dead, Shawar was reinstated as vizier and then, to consolidate his position, he had all the allies and relatives of Dirgham executed.[13]

The newfound stability that the Shawar and Nūr ad-Dīn alliance brought was short-lived as the newly restored vizier wanted the Kurdish general gone. To assist with vanquishing Shīrkūh, Shawar turned to Nūr ad-Dīn's enemy, the newly crowned King Amalric of Jerusalem. Amalric, keen to dislodge Nūr ad-Dīn's influence from the country, led his army into Egypt to join Shawar's forces in ousting Shīrkūh.

Shīrkūh was at the city of Bilbais, north of Cairo, and in the summer of 1164, the combined forces of Shawar and the Franks laid siege to the city. However, due to his vast experience as a military leader, Shīrkūh had organised a strong defence, and the besiegers could not gain the advantage. Nevertheless, the siege would drag on for many months.

While King Amalric was distracted by the prolonged siege in Egypt, Nūr ad-Dīn moved to take advantage by campaigning against the Principality of Antioch. However, according to William of Tyre, before this campaign, Nūr ad-Dīn suffered a rare defeat against Christian forces led by the Knights Templar. William of Tyre writes that in 1163, nobles from Aquitaine – including Godfrey Martel and Hugh de Lusignan – had arrived in Antioch on a pilgrimage. It was here that word was received that Nūr ad-Dīn was resting in the County of Tripoli. The combined Christian force of knights included the two nobles from Aquitaine and Robert Mansel and his forces from Galilee.

The combined Frankish army, led by Norman Templar knight Gilbert de Lacy, took the unprepared forces of Nūr ad-Dīn by surprise. Although he escaped, much of his army was captured or killed and the baggage train was abandoned. William of Tyre records that even Nūr ad-Dīn's sword was left behind with the baggage.[14] The Christians had achieved a rare and decisive victory against the Emir of Aleppo and Damascus, returning with riches captured from the battle.

The wheel of fortune, though, continues to turn, and although Nūr ad-Dīn had barely escaped the Christian army in Tripoli, he returned with his forces to continue his campaign against Antioch, laying siege to the castle at Harim in the summer of 1164. Harim was a vital stronghold for the Principality of Antioch, and the young Prince Bohemond III mustered an army that included Count Raymond of Tripoli and Prince Thoros of Armenia. A large number of Templar knights were also part of Bohemond's relief force.

As the Frankish army approached, Nūr ad-Dīn chose not to engage them in battle and ordered his troops to disperse in an organised withdrawal. However, the Prince of Antioch was not satisfied with merely relieving the Christians at Harim; instead, he had his forces pursue their enemy. Unfortunately, in their pursuit, the Franks had spread their forces too wide, which left them extremely vulnerable to a counter-attack from Nūr ad-Dīn's forces, which they did with devastating consequences.

William of Tyre records how 'trapped in a confined and swampy place, the Christians broke ranks at the first charge, and those who shortly before had caused the utmost terror in the ranks of the Turks became the pitiful sport of that same enemy'.[15] Given the dire situation, many of the Frankish nobility surrendered to save their lives, which William of Tyre regarded as shameful.[16]

Among the powerful lords captured were Prince Bohemond III, Count Raymond of Tripoli and Count Joscelin III of Edessa. They were led in chains to the dungeons of Aleppo. Joscelin was the son of Joscelin II, whose poor leadership had lost the County of Edessa and who was imprisoned in the dungeons of Aleppo before dying while still incarcerated in 1159. Prince Thoros of Armenia, though, was one of the few who managed to flee the disaster.

The Knights Templar in the company were decimated, with sixty Templar knights slain and only seven escaping captivity.[17]

King Amalric blamed Prince Bohemond and Count Raymond in a letter to King Louis VII of France dated 12 January 1165. He wrote, 'The count and the prince arrogantly pursued them to a region that nature had made impregnable, and there the leaders were captured.'[18]

Following the victory, Nūr ad-Dīn continued the siege of Harim, and with Prince Bohemond and Count Raymond taken prisoner, his armies soon captured the vital fortress. Once again, the northern regions of Outremer were in disarray, with their leaders in captivity and losing a critical border defence.

Harim wasn't the only loss for the Franks. On 18 October 1164, Banyas, the city that Baldwin III had liberated from Nūr ad-Dīn's besieging army in 1159, was finally captured by Nūr ad-Dīn. William of Tyre wrote that he captured the city within a few days with relative ease as its lord, Humphrey, the Royal Constable, was in Egypt with the king.[19] The dire situation in the north of Outremer was made possible by King Amalric's distraction in Egypt, which showed that the Franks could not cope with fighting on multiple fronts.

Fortunately, after a large ransom was paid, Prince Bohemond was released from captivity by 1165; however, Count Raymond was kept prisoner for around ten years. The count's decade of captivity prompted the control of the County of Tripoli to return to the Kingdom of Jerusalem, with King Amalric acting as regent while Raymond was held captive. Given the dire situation in Outremer's northern states, negotiations for peace took place, and King Amalric and Shīrkūh marched their armies out of Egypt, leaving Shawar in control of Cairo.

The agreement kept the status quo for several years in Cairo, but Shīrkūh had not given up on his goal of seizing power in Egypt. When word reached him that Shawar had agreed to an alliance with the Kingdom of Jerusalem to come to Cairo's aid if Nūr ad-Dīn should invade, it gave him a chance to re-attempt his play for Cairo. Nūr ad-Dīn feared an alliance between Egypt and the Crusader states and supported Shīrkūh's invasion by providing troops. Shīrkūh took with him his nephew, Yusuf ibn Ayyub, who would be known to Islam as Salāh al-Dīn (and Saladin to the West).[20]

THE ALLIANCE OF JERUSALEM AND CAIRO

In January 1167, Shīrkūh marched his army into Egypt, followed soon after by King Amalric and the army of the Kingdom of Jerusalem. King Amalric agreed to an alliance with Shawar in return for a payment of 400,000 gold dinars to drive Shīrkūh from Egypt. However, Hugh of Caesarea, who was negotiating for the king, insisted that the deal be finalised directly by the caliph himself. Desperate to keep Shīrkūh from taking power in Egypt, Shawar agreed, and Hugh, accompanied by the Templar knight Geoffrey Fulcher, was escorted to the palace in Cairo.

After the alliance was agreed upon, Hugh acted in what can only be viewed as a display of arrogance and disrespect by insisting that the caliph shake his hand without a glove.[21] With the alliance between the Kingdom of Jerusalem and Cairo ratified by the caliph, the Franks moved to intercept Shīrkūh's army.

The Franks pursued Shīrkūh's forces for several days before the two armies met in the desert south of Cairo.[22] In his account, William of Tyre describes two very mismatched forces. He numbers the Franks as consisting of 'barely three hundred and seventy-four knights' and an unspecified number of Egyptian forces and Turcopoles. However, he added that the Egyptians and Turcopoles 'were, for the most part, useless'.

Shīrkūh's army, according to William of Tyre, was more than double that of the Franks. He wrote, 'Shirkuh had twelve thousand Turks, of whom nine thousand wore the breastplate and helmet and the other three thousand used only bows and arrows. He had, in addition, ten or eleven thousand Arabs who, according to their custom, fought with lances only'.[23]

Despite the difference in size, the battle was inconclusive, with neither emerging a clear winner. Shīrkūh's nephew, Yusuf ibn Ayyub, distinguished himself in the battle by capturing the disrespectful negotiator Hugh of Caesarea after he was abandoned by his men.[24] After the battle, Amalric regrouped his forces near Cairo, while Shīrkūh marched his remaining forces north to Alexandria.

The ancient city of Alexandria lies west of Cairo and consists of two ports separated by a narrow stretch of land.[25] Upon receiving news of Shīrkūh's forces taking the city, King Amalric marched his forces north, laid siege to the city and blockaded the ports. Although Yusuf ibn Ayyub stoutly led the defences in keeping the Franks out, food was quickly running scarce, and as they were besieged so far from their Syrian lands, the outlook was bleak. However, King Amalric was aware of his kingdom's vulnerability while campaigning in Egypt and could not afford to maintain a lengthy siege. A treaty was agreed upon by Shīrkūh and King Amalric in which Alexandria was to be surrendered, all prisoners were to be released and Shīrkūh's forces would be able to leave Egypt unharmed. Also, it was agreed that King Amalric's standard was to be flown from the top of the Lighthouse of Alexandria as a symbol of the Kingdom of Jerusalem's victory.[26]

The treaty at Alexandria was very much a victory for the Franks, as the Kingdom of Jerusalem agreed to a new alliance with Cairo that meant that the Franks received an annual tribute of 100,000 dinars and installed a Latin prefect and a garrison of troops in Cairo. Egypt had become a client state of Amalric's kingdom, with the display of King Almaric's banner symbolising his victory.[27]

Shīrkūh's ambitions of taking Egypt would have been significantly set back if this new alliance had lasted. However, it did not last long. King Amalric strengthened his ties to the Byzantine Empire by marrying the emperor's niece, Maria Comnena. Now emboldened by the closer ties with the Byzantines, Amalric was not satisfied with the annual tribute and believed that he now had the forces to conquer Egypt.

In October 1168, Amalric decided not to wait for the arrival of the Byzantine fleet and chose to press on with the invasion with the support of the Knights Hospitaller. However, the Knights Templar, one of the major military forces, did not back the invasion and chose not to participate.

The Templars argued that this new expedition was unethical as it broke the treaty with Shawar. However, other factors may have played a part, as the Templars had lost a large number of knights in 1164 at Harim, and the loss of Banyas had happened while the majority of the Templar forces had been on the previous Egyptian campaign with King Amalric.[28] This disagreement between the Knights Templar and King Amalric was not the first and would not be the last.

CONFLICT WITH THE KNIGHTS TEMPLAR

In 1166, King Amalric had already soured his relationship with the Knights Templar after he was highly critical of the their surrender of a fortification to Shīrkūh, which William of Tyre describes as 'an impregnable cave, lying beyond Jordan on the borders of Arabia'.[29] The king was en route with an army to lift the siege when news came that the Templars had surrendered the castle. King Amalric was so furious that the defenders had surrendered so easily that he had twelve Templar knights hanged as punishment.

While Amalric was king and the castle was in his realm, the Knights Templar were outside his jurisdiction and answered only to the Pope. In executing brothers of the Knights Templar, King Amalric acted outside his authority and damaged his relationship with the order.

Another more severe breakdown in the relationship between him and the Knights Templar came in 1173, although this one could have thrown the Crusader states into civil war. In 1173, King Amalric attempted to negotiate an alliance with the Assassins, the secluded Shia Islamic sect based in the Lebanese Mountains. Their leader was known as the Old Man of the Mountain, and although their numbers were few and their territory small, they were feared due to their devotion and belief in tyrannicide to achieve their goals.[30] William of Tyre describes the Assassins's methods:

> If there happens to be a prince who has incurred the hatred or distrust of this people, the chief places a dagger in the hand of one or several of his followers; those thus designated hasten away at once, regardless of the consequences of the deed or the probability of personal escape. Zealously they labor [*sic*] for as long as may be necessary, until at last the favorable [*sic*] chance comes which enables them to carry out the mandate of the chief.[31]

His description demonstrates why both Christians and Muslims feared them, as both had suffered from attacks on their leaders. The Assassins killed Raymond II of Tripoli and even tried to assassinate Saladin.

In 1173, King Amalric was in the midst of forging an alliance between Outremer and the Assassins and had an envoy from the Assassins as his guest during talks. However, the Templars, whose lands bordered the Assassins', had a long-standing agreement that they would pay the Templars an annual tribute of 2,000 gold coins. If an alliance between the Assassins and the Crusader states was formed, King Amalric would wave their annual tribute if they were baptised and converted to Christianity.

While an alliance between the Franks and Assassins would have brought stability to Outremer, the Knights Templar would lose a large sum of annual income. The action taken to prevent this financial loss, described by William of Tyre below, would significantly affect the Templar's legacy because it tore up the notions of piety and poverty and their mission to protect travellers that Hugues de Paynes had founded the order on in 1119.

When Abdallah, the Assassin envoy whom William of Tyre described as 'wise and eloquent, skilled in counsel', was being escorted back to the Assassins' territory, he was set upon by a group of Knights Templar.[32] In a perversion of their founding mission, they killed Abdallah, who was travelling under the kings' protection. When the news of the envoy's murder reached King Amalric, he was furious and sent men to have the murderer apprehended. The man responsible was Walter de Mesnil, a one-eyed Templar knight. However, Grand Master Odo de St Amand refused the king's request, arguing that the man responsible was to be sent to the Pope for punishment. The grand master also 'forbade anyone, on the part of the Pope, to lay violent hands upon the said brother'.[33]

King Amalric was not perturbed by orders from the Templar grand master, or even in the Pope's name, and went to Sidon, where the grand master and Templars were lodged. Once the culprit was identified, King Amalric denounced Walter de Mesnil as a traitor and had the disgraced Templar taken by force, placed in chains and imprisoned at Tyre.

Although the Templars answered only to the Pope, King Amalric felt this was in his jurisdiction as the actions by Walter de Mesnil had destroyed an advantageous alliance between Outremer and the Assassins. Although he managed to convince the Assassins through diplomatic means that he was not to blame, the potential alliance was in tatters.[34] The Assassin's murder was the king's most high-profile conflict with the Knights Templar, but his failure to secure their support for his 1168 campaign to Egypt would have more devastating consequences.

THE RULER OF CAIRO

In October 1168, King Amalric marched his forces into Egypt, and although he had the Knights Hospitaller leading the army, he had failed to secure the support of the Knights Templar. So confident of success were the Frankish leaders that even though King Amalric wouldn't wait for Byzantine support, the spoils of the conquest had already been divided up, with the Knights Hospitaller set to receive a significant financial reward.[35]

Nevertheless, the sudden swiftness of the king's invasion proved effective. The city of Bilbais fell on 4 November and was brutally sacked by the alliance-breaking Franks.

After the savage conquest of Bilbais, the king's invasion stalled. Meanwhile, Shawar used negotiations with the Franks as a stalling tactic while sending messages to Nūr ad-Dīn begging for aid.

Nūr ad-Dīn provided troops and money, and Shīrkūh, alongside his nephew Yusuf ibn Ayyub, marched an army into Egypt again. When word reached King Amalric of the impending arrival of Shīrkūh, the king mustered his forces and marched to intercept the army before they could cross the Nile. However, it soon became apparent that the Franks were too late, and Shīrkūh's forces had already crossed the river into Egypt.

The Frankish army was heavily outnumbered and in the face of such superior numbers, King Amalric chose to march the army back to Outremer without giving battle. Finally, Egypt was within Shīrkūh's reach and he marched his army on Cairo unopposed.

With the Franks gone, Shawar tried to negotiate a truce with Shīrkūh. However, with Shawar in control, Egypt would not be under Nūr ad-Dīn's control because the vizier kept switching sides towards the Christians. Therefore, Shīrkūh planned to capture Shawar the next time he visited to negotiate – and his nephew would do it.

Bahā' al-Dīn describes the capture of Shawar by Yusuf ibn Ayyub:

> When Shawār came riding towards them, Saladin met him on horseback and rode at his side. He caught hold of his collar and ordered his troops to seize his followers. The latter fled and were robbed by the soldiers. Shawār was arrested and placed in a separate tent.[36]

Shawar was then beheaded, and his head was sent to Cairo as proof of his death. William of Tyre's account does not reference Yusuf ibn Ayyub's involvement; instead, he writes that Shawar placed too much trust in Shīrkūh, whom he refers to as 'the minister of murder'. However, in both accounts, Shawar is ambushed by Shīrkūh's forces and is subsequentially beheaded.[37]

Shīrkūh was installed as Vizier of Cairo on 18 January 1169; he had achieved his ambition of taking power in Egypt. However, despite his victory, he wouldn't be able to enjoy his success for long. On 22 March 1169, he died from a serious case of quinsy (an infection behind the tonsil), although Bahā' al-Dīn links this to his excessive overeating.[38]

With Shawar and Shīrkūh now dead, Yusuf ibn Ayyub, his uncle's successor, was installed as Vizier of Cairo. This latest Vizier of Cairo would become the greatest threat to the Christians' hold on the Holy Land.

The installation of Shīrkūh and then Yusuf ibn Ayyub as vizier highlights how catastrophic King Amalric's foreign policy was. The king aimed to expand Outremer's reach and steal the resources of Egypt for the Franks. However, the result was a united power of Aleppo, Damascus and Cairo against them. The Crusader states were now hemmed in against the Mediterranean coast, with only the Byzantines to the north to help them keep hold of their vulnerable northern states. And the Franks soon discovered that the southern lands of the Kingdom of Jerusalem were now as vulnerable as the contested northern frontier of Outremer. Yusuf ibn Ayyub, who would become known as Salāh al-Dīn (or Saladin), would use his position to decimate the Kingdom of Jerusalem and push the Frankish presence to near extinction.

PART 2

THE AYYUBID DYNASTY

6

THE RISE OF SALĀH AL-DĪN

KING AMALRIC'S FINAL INVASION OF EGYPT

Despite Saladin's huge impact on history, there is no surviving account of his physical description.[1] However, Bahā' al-Dīn, a member of the sultan's household, provides a detailed account of his character in his biography.

Saladin was born between 1137–38 at Takrit Castle, where his father, Ayyūb ibn Shādī, was a governor in the service of Atabeg Zengi. In his biography of Saladin, Bahā' al-Dīn describes the sultan as 'one of the great heroes, mighty in spirit, strong in courage and of great firmness, terrified of nothing'.[2] Of Saladin's faith, he writes, 'Whenever he hears the Koran, his heart was touched and his eyes would fill with tears on most occasions.'[3] 'Saladin was just, gentle and merciful, a supporter of the weak against the strong' and 'Each Monday and Thursday he used to sit and dispense justice in public session, attended by the jurisconsults, Qādīs and the doctors of the religion'.[4]

Of Saladin's desire for jihad, Bahā' al-Dīn explains:

> The Jihad, his love and passion for it, had taken a mighty hold on his heart and all his being, so much so that he talked of nothing else, thought of nothing but the means to pursue it was concerned only with its manpower and had a fondness only for those who spoke of it and encouraged it.[5]

His leadership and zeal for reclaiming the lands the Crusaders took would push the Franks into the sea and launch the infamous Third Crusade.

His dominance and conquests aside, Saladin was also known for his generosity, which Bahā' al-Dīn notes 'was too public to need to be recorded and too famous to need to be recounted'.[6] He also details his behaviour, describing him as 'a paragon of chivalry, generous, extremely modest and had a welcoming face for any guests that arrived'.[7]

Bahā' al-Dīn's insight into Saladin was as the iconic leader and champion of Islam. However, long before Saladin would build a dynasty, he had to create a strong foundation as Vizier of Cairo.

His first test as ruler came in October 1169 when King Amalric marched an army into Egypt to unsettle the balance of power, which had been heavily tilted against the Franks. The subjugation of Egypt by one of Nūr ad-Dīn's lieutenants was disastrous for the Crusader states and Outremer was now surrounded to the south and east.

The control of Egypt was vital to King Amalric's foreign policy and had been the focus of much of his kingship. To break up Nūr ad-Dīn's control over Egypt, he launched another invasion in the autumn of 1169, though this time, the king brought with him the Byzantine navy. The target of King Amalric's attack was the port city of Damietta, located on the eastern shore of the River Nile. The Frankish army reached Damietta on 29 October and then made camp to await the arrival of the fleet, which had been delayed by adverse weather.[8]

With the arrival of the Byzantines, the combined Christian forces chose to delay the attack further to make final preparations. It is because of these delays, according to William of Tyre, that the city that had been lacking in armed defenders was now strengthened with reinforcements.[9] Bahā' al-Dīn's account details that when Saladin 'realised the seriousness of the enemy's plan to attack Damietta, he sent to the town and supplied it with sufficient men, champion horsemen, supplies and weapons of war to make him confident of its defence'.[10] In their delay, the combined Christian army had weakened their position.

Now, the only way to capture the city was to construct siege equipment. William of Tyre describes 'a lofty tower of seven stories was built, from the top of which the entire city could be surveyed. Other machines of various kinds were also constructed. Some of these were designed to hurl huge rocks for battering down the walls, others, to protect the sappers', who would undermine the fortified walls to cause them to collapse.[11]

Despite the construction of siege engines, the persistent attacks by the Franks were beaten back, and it soon became clear that the combined Christian force did not have the manpower to dislodge the defenders. Had the Franks used the initiative to launch an attack when Damietta was poorly defended, they may have succeeded, but in their delay, they allowed Saladin to draw from his vast resources to neutralise the Christians' offence.

With the siege doomed to failure, King Amalric negotiated a withdrawal and the combined army retreated from Egypt. The combined force broke up, with the fleet sailing home, and King Amalric marched his forces back to Ascalon, arriving in late December. This was the final act of his attempt to dominate Egypt which, aside from some short-term success, ended in total failure. The invasion of 1169 was a final attempt to break up the powerhouse he had created through his own shortcomings.

While King Amalric's disastrous attempt to capture Damietta would be the last of his invasions, the Frankish assaults on Egypt would continue, with Egypt being the future target of the Fifth Crusade.

CHANGING OF THE GUARD

Saladin had control of Egypt through his role as Vizier, but he was still second in command to the Fatimid Shi'ite Caliph al-Adid and he was also one of Nūr ad-Dīn's lieutenants. However, in September 1171, Saladin's control over Egypt would be complete. The health of the young caliph was failing him, and Saladin could bring the country under Sunni rule.

On Friday, 10 September, Saladin had the Shi'ite caliph's name replaced with the Sunni Abbasid Caliph of Baghdad during Friday prayers at the mosque in Fustat. The following day, Saladin showed his strength by having his vast army march through the streets of Cairo and demonstrating his total control over the country.[12] The young caliph died three days later, on 13 September, bringing an end to the Fatimid dynasty.

Despite the potential threat to his reign, Saladin spared the lives of the caliph's children, allowing them to remain in the palace but forbidding them from having children to ensure the dynasty's end.[13] Although the coup had been bloodless and Saladin had shown respect after al-Adid's passing, he had brought Egypt back under Sunni rule and made himself the Sultan of Egypt. However, Saladin was still subservient to Nūr ad-Dīn, so effectively, Nūr ad-Dīn's lands now stretched from Aleppo, in the north, to Damascus, in the east, and Cairo, in the west. The Crusader states were truly encircled.

With the resources of Egypt at his disposal, Saladin was more akin to an equal engaged in an alliance, than a lieutenant. This new power base could have mobilised an all-out attack on Outremer and pushed the Christians back to the sea. However, no such coordination took place between the two powers. Saladin launched an offensive against the castle of Kerak in 1173 without support from Nūr ad-Dīn, who was campaigning in northern Syria, but the castle held out, and Saladin's forces withdrew without success.

The uneasy alliance between Egypt and Syria would end in 1174 when Nūr ad-Dīn fell ill on 6 May and died on 15 May. His death from quinsy was most advantageous to Saladin as, according to Ibn al-Athīr, 'Nūr ad-Dīn was making preparations to invade Egypt and take it from Saladin'.[14] Nūr ad-Dīn's death effectively avoided a Sunni civil war between Syria and Egypt, which would have only benefitted the Franks.

When writing of Nūr ad-Dīn's death, William of Tyre described him as 'a just prince, valiant and wise' and 'a religious man'.[15] In Ibn al-Athīr's eulogy, he writes that Nūr ad-Dīn 'was known throughout his realms as a wise and just ruler'. He lists his virtues as 'austerity, piety and a knowledge of theology'. He also notes that 'On the battlefield he had no equal; he carried two bows and quivers into the fray with him.'[16]

It is true that the Franks were rarely able to gain the upper hand in their wars against his Syrian forces. He stopped the mightiest princes of Europe from capturing Damascus during the disastrous Second Crusade (1145–49). He defeated and killed Prince Raymond at Inab in 1149 and, in 1150, he captured the disgraced Count Joscelin II of Edessa, whose strategic failures had enabled Nūr ad-Dīn's father, Zengi, to conquer and massacre the inhabitants of Edessa in 1144. More recently, Nūr ad-Dīn had turned certain failure into a victory at Harim in 1164, where he captured the young Prince Bohemond III and Count Raymond of Tripoli. In reviewing some of Nūr ad-Dīn's victories over the Franks, it is clear why King Amalric saw the death of his fiercest enemy as the perfect opportunity to strike at his territories.

King Amalric wasted no time mustering all the forces he could in his kingdom and marching on the city of Banyas. When the Franks besieged the city, Nūr ad-Dīn's widow offered to pay a large sum for the king to abandon the siege and grant a brief period of peace. William of Tyre was particularly scathing of King Amalric in his account, writing that the king 'in the hope of extorting a larger bribe, at first pretended to spurn her plea and continued the siege'.[17]

The Franks continued the siege for over two weeks but could not gain an advantage over the defenders and instead accepted the offer to withdraw. This event may appear innocuous as the Franks made no significant gains or significant losses in this siege, but upon the journey home, King Amalric became ill, suffering from dysentery. He died on 11 July 1174 and was still only in his late thirties.

The Kingdom of Jerusalem was in a dire situation following his death, which left weak leadership, and a kingdom divided, but despite the Crusader states' vulnerability, Saladin chose not to attack the Franks but instead moved to pursue the late Nūr ad-Dīn's territories. The Zengid (or Zangid) empire had been broken up on Nūr ad-Dīn's death with his young son, al-Malik al-Sālih Ismāīl, who had fled to Aleppo, named as a successor, while Nūr ad-Dīn's nephews, Saif al-Dīn and Imād al-Dīn Zengi, held Mosul and Sinjar respectively.

In October, Saladin marched upon Damascus at the head of a large army to take control of the young al-Sālih's guardianship. Nūr ad-Dīn's death had created a power vacuum in Damascus, and Ibn al-Muqaddam, one of Nūr ad-Dīn's commanders, seized power supported by a group of emirs. However, the infighting that followed led him to request Saladin to come to Damascus' aid. In November 1174, Saladin marched to Damascus at the head of a huge army, was welcomed into the city and took control of the citadel.

Bahā' al-Dīn's account states that Saladin came to the city to assume guardianship of the young al-Sālih, entered the city unopposed, visited his father's house, and distributed large sums of money to welcoming citizens.[18] Without bloodshed, Saladin had achieved what the Second Crusaders could not and had now extended his power from Cairo to Damascus, surrounding the vulnerable Kingdom of Jerusalem.

Saladin, now the unopposed Sultan of Egypt, had expanded his power into Syria and his resources and armies with it. The Christians' weakened state without King Amalric provided him with the chance to wage war against the Franks from his new position of strength. The combined might of Cairo and Damascus united under Saladin threatened the very existence of the Crusader states.

However, the Franks could breathe a sigh of relief for now as Saladin turned his attention towards Nūr ad-Dīn's former territories of Homs, Hama and Aleppo. He arrived at the city of Homs on 8 December 1174; it was under the control of an emir, a former lieutenant of Nūr ad-Dīn. The garrison refused to surrender, and the following day, Saladin captured the city, but the garrison hid themselves within the citadel, and Saladin's forces could not dislodge them. With the city of Homs under his control, Saladin marched his forces to the city of Hama, which was also held by a former lieutenant of Nūr ad-Dīn. While the citadel resisted, it was soon surrendered to the Sultan of Egypt.[19]

With Homs and Hama captured, Saladin set his sights on Aleppo, where Nūr ad-Dīn's young son and heir, al-Malik al-Sālih resided. Aleppo would not roll over at Saladin's arrival on 30 December and fiercely resisted the Sultan of Egypt's aggressive expansion. In his account, Ibn al-Athīr describes how Nūr ad-Dīn's young son inspired the hearts of the city's stout defenders:

> A young boy, twelve years old, rode out, gathered the people of Aleppo and said to them, 'You know well my father's kindness to you, his love for you and his good rule over you. I am his orphan. This wicked man, who repudiates my father's goodness to him, has come to take my lands. He respects neither God Almighty nor his creatures.

He describes how al-Malik al-Sālih's words reduced the people of Aleppo to tears and they offered to defend him and his lands.[20] Ibn al-Athīr was a supporter of the Zengid dynasty and gave a seemingly more impartial view of Saladin, which resonates with his mention of al-Malik al-Sālih's remarks about Saladin not respecting God, contrasting with chronicler Bahā' al-Dīn's description of his piety and faith.[21]

Saladin's attempt to conquer Aleppo would eventually end in a stalemate in July 1176, despite his forces winning two battles against the alliance between Mosul and Aleppo. The peace between Saladin and the rulers of Mosul and Aleppo included an agreement that the territory Saladin had taken in Syria was to be acknowledged as part of his growing empire.

During his lengthy campaign against Aleppo, he became the target of the Assassins and narrowly escaped their attempts on his life. The first attempt in 1175 was foiled before reaching Saladin after being recognised by a local ruler. In 1176, a second attempt was made, and Saladin survived due to the protection of his armour, leaving him slightly wounded.[22]

This peace ended two years of campaigning between Egypt and Syria, and Saladin would soon turn his attention back to the Kingdom of Jerusalem.

THE LEPER KING

King Amalric's heir was his 13-year-old son, Baldwin IV. Although his daughter Sibylla was older, the line of succession favoured males, but Sibylla would still one day ascend the throne. Baldwin was crowned king in the Holy Sepulchre just a few days after his father's death. The young king was not yet old enough to rule, so Count Raymond of Tripoli, who had just been released from almost a decade in captivity, was appointed as regent until Baldwin came of age.

Baldwin had a lonely childhood as his mother, Agnes of Courtenay, was sent away, and her marriage to Amalric was annulled, a condition of Amalric becoming king as they were third cousins. His sister was raised in the St Lazarus Convent at Bethany, run by Amalric's sister, Yvetta. In his early years, Baldwin's close companion and a prominent parental figure was his tutor, the Crusade chronicler William of Tyre.

William of Tyre's role as Baldwin's tutor enabled him to give details about the future king's childhood. He described Baldwin:

> [He] was comely of appearance for his age, and far beyond the custom of his forefathers he was an excellent horseman and understood the handling of horses. He had a retentive memory and loved to talk. He was economical but always remembered both favors [*sic*] and injuries. In every respect he resembled his father, not alone in face but in his entire mien; even his walk and the tones of his voice were the same. His intellect was keen, but his speech was somewhat halting.[23]

However, it was William who made a tragic discovery about the prince when he was only 9 years old. He noticed that when Baldwin was playing with his peers, he demonstrated no reaction to being pinched on the arm by the other boys. Upon closer inspection, William discovered that Baldwin's right arm and hand were partially numb, so he could not feel the pinching. Baldwin's condition only worsened as he got older, and it soon became apparent that he was suffering from leprosy. William describes the worsening condition of the young Baldwin IV, 'The extremities and the face were especially attacked, so that his faithful followers were moved with compassion when they looked at him'.[24]

Despite Baldwin's condition, he was still crowned king and has been described by historians as a disaster. The young king was blamed for selfishly refusing to abdicate and overseeing a kingdom split into factions, leaving Outremer vulnerable to the ever-expanding power of Saladin. However, historian Thomas Ashbridge asserts that recent accounts of his reign have focussed on the young king's determination to defend the Crusader states while shouldering the huge burden of his continually declining health.[25]

The young Baldwin IV came of age in the summer of 1176, and so the regency of Count Raymond came to an end. Baldwin's freedom from the regency coincided with the release of Prince Reynald of Antioch, who was captured in 1160 under King Baldwin III's rule. Reynald was imprisoned in Aleppo for fifteen years and was released after a heavy ransom was paid. Reynald de Châtillon was no longer a prince because his wife, Princess Constance, had died and his stepson had ascended the throne as Prince Bohemond III of Antioch shortly after Reynald's capture.

However, this lack of title would not deter the ruthless Reynald for long and he soon married another wealthy heiress, Stephanie of Milly.

The marriage gave Reynald the lordship of Oultrejourdain (also known as Transjordan), which was mostly desert but was the largest lordship in the Crusader states. Oultrejourdain contained the key castles of Kerak and Shobak and, most significantly, the region contained the trade routes of the King's Highway that connected Africa to Mesopotamia and the Hajj Road, used for Muslim pilgrimage.[26] Gifting a man like Reynald control over two vital routes would eventually be catastrophic for the Crusader states, from which the Kingdom of Jerusalem would never recover.

One year after Baldwin IV came of age, Saladin launched his first invasion of Outremer in the autumn of 1177. Most of the Frankish forces were in the north, with Count Raymond of Tripoli and Prince Bohemond laying siege to the fortress of Harim. Saladin's motive may have been to lift the siege or take advantage of the Kingdom of Jerusalem's vulnerability.[27]

Seeing Saladin advance with a force numbering over 20,000 horsemen, King Baldwin took refuge inside Ascalon alongside Reynald de Châtillon, the king's seneschal, Count Joscelin, the Bishop of Bethlehem, who carried the True Cross, and a force of 600 knights and a few thousand infantry.[28] The Franks were vastly outnumbered.

While the Franks took refuge at Ascalon, and confident in his huge advantage of troops, Saladin allowed his forces to spread out and raid local settlements. The sultan did not expect the Franks to risk battle when their numbers were so inferior. However, the smaller force of Franks boldly ventured from Ascalon and linked up with eighty Templar knights stationed at Gaza with the Templar Grand Master Odo de St Amand.

On 25 November, the Christian forces reached Saladin's army while they were traversing a ford at Montgisard. With Saladin's men still scattered wide and distracted with completing the river crossing, Reynald de Châtillon led a desperate charge towards Saladin's forces. In Ibn al-Athīr's account of the battle, he describes how one 'Frank charged Saladin and got close, almost reaching him, but the Frank was killed in front of him'.[29]

Despite their numbers, Saladin was taken by surprise, and his army was routed and pursued by the Franks. Although this was a clear victory for the Franks, as Saladin suffered heavy losses and retreated to Egypt, the Christians also suffered heavy casualties. In a letter from the Hospitaller Raymond, he details, 'Eleven hundred Christians were slaughtered, while seven hundred and fifty were seriously wounded' and needed to be treated in the order's hospital.[30] Regarding Saladin's losses, historian Michael Haag writes that Saladin lost 'nine out of ten of his infantry and cavalry, about twenty-three thousand men in all'.[31]

The Knights Templar were vital to the Franks' victory at Montgisard as they carried out the devastating cavalry charge that decimated Saladin's forces. The Dean of London, Ralph of Diss, recorded an eyewitness account of the battle, which articulates why the Knights Templar were seen as the elite troops within the Frankish armies:

> Odo the Master of the Knighthood of the Temple, like another Judas Maccabaeus, had eighty-four knights of his Order with him in his personal company. He took himself into battle with his men, strengthened by the sign of the cross. Spurring all together, as one man, they made a charge, turning neither to the left nor to the right. Recognising the battalion in which Saladin commanded many knights, they manfully approached it, immediately penetrated it, incessantly knocked down, scattered, struck and crushed. Saladin was smitten with admiration, seeing his men dispersed everywhere, everywhere turned in flight, everywhere given to the mouth of the sword. He took thought for his own safety and fled, throwing off his mailshirt for speed, mounted a racing camel and barely escaped with a few of his men.[32]

Haag praised the tactics used by the Franks but also credits the Knights Templar as playing a vital role in the victory. He asserts that the victory was 'a perfect illustration of Frankish fighting ability and the superiority they could achieve through rapid and offensive warfare, thanks especially to the Templars'. However, he also argues that had the Franks pursued Saladin back to Egypt or attacked Damascus, they could have dealt the sultan a crushing blow and he blames the Christian nobility for failing to take advantage of this victory.[33]

The battle at Montgisard was a humiliating loss for Saladin. As well as the loss of men and his forced flight, his advisor, the lawyer Īsā al-Hakkārī, was captured. However, he was eventually freed after years in captivity when Saladin paid a ransom of 60,000 dinars.[34]

Baldwin IV claimed the victory that day – the young, sickly king defeating the great Saladin, a seasoned military general at the head of a much larger army. The credit for the victory should go to the Christians' implementation of a heavy cavalry charge, which, when timed perfectly, had a devastating effect on its target. The Knights Templar, whose strict military leadership was shown during the long march of the Second Crusade, would have helped carry out such a bold attack. Had the charge not routed Saladin's forces, the situation for the Kingdom of Jerusalem would have been dire.

This time, the bold gamble paid off. In the future, however, a desperate charge with the Knights Templar and Reynald de Châtillon would fail spectacularly and wipe out the Franks' standing army.

THE MASSACRE AT JACOB'S FORD

Following the Franks' stunning victory at Montgisard, King Baldwin hoped to capitalise on the momentum by building strategic fortifications to expand Outremer's borders and gain domination over the frontier areas. One of these areas was the disputed frontier north of the Sea of Galilee (also known as Lake Tiberias) and west of Damascus. The Franks lost control over the area after Nūr ad-Dīn captured the fortress at Banyas in 1164. The Franks had failed to retake Banyas, so King Baldwin, working in cooperation with the Knights Templar, began constructing a new fortress on the west bank of the Upper Jordan at Jacob's Ford. The site, also known as the House of Sorrow, has biblical significance as it was believed to be where Jacob had mourned the alleged death of his son, Joseph.

The construction of the frontier castle began in October 1178, and its completion was so paramount to the king that Baldwin moved his court to the construction site and even minted new coins to pay the workforce.[35] When the tower and a perimeter wall was completed in April 1179, control of the castle was handed over to the Knights Templar.

Saladin could not let the Franks have a castle so close to his territory because it shifted the balance of power back to Outremer. The castle offered the Franks a strong defence and would also enable them to launch attacks against nearby Damascus. Saladin had initially offered the Franks the large sum of 60,000 dinars to demolish the castle without fighting, but King Baldwin refused.[36] With the financial incentive rejected, Saladin had to take the castle by force.

Before Saladin's final assault on the castle, there were skirmishes and battles between the Franks and Saladin's forces. The Christians could not mirror their heroics at Montgisard and were bested by Saladin's forces, which resulted in the loss of senior Christian nobility. The king's constable, Humphrey, was killed, and the Templar Grand Master Odo de St Amand, who had led the Templars in the devastating charge at Montgisard, was captured. William of Tyre is scathing in his record of Grand Master Odo's capture:

> Among the Christians who were captured at that time were Eudes [Odo] de Saint-Amand, the master of the Knights Templars, a wicked man, haughty and arrogant, in whose nostrils dwelt the spirit of fury, one who neither feared God nor revered man. Many people laid at his door the loss and never-dying shame of this disaster. It is said that within the year he died a captive in a squalid prison, mourned by no one.[37]

Although the Franks lost their grand master, they did manage to kill one of Saladin's commanders with an arrow in one of the assaults on the castle at Jacob's Ford, which forced Saladin's forces to retreat.

However, in August 1179, Saladin launched a full-scale attack on the Templar castle, determined to take it at all costs. The building work was still incomplete when Saladin launched his full-scale attack. Although the tower and one surrounding wall were finished, the outer wall was still under construction. Haag describes the castle:

> A vast rectangle constructed of 20,000 enormous blocks of stone each of which was 7 feet long, its walls over 20 feet thick. This was only the first phase; the plan was to enclose the inner structure within an outer rectangle, creating a concentric castle which would have been larger than anything in Europe and the largest in the East.[38]

If such a castle was to be completed, the Franks would dominate the region and pose a significant risk to Damascus. With the first phase of construction finished, and according to the description above, the castle was certainly defendable but was still vulnerable without its planned outer wall.

When Saladin launched his all-out assault on the castle in August, his attack had to be swift and devastating as Baldwin IV was mustering a relief force at Tiberias. Ibn al-Athīr's account details the fierce fighting and the Templars' desperate defence:

> One of the common people in a ragged shirt climbed the barbican of the fort and fought on the wall when he reached the top. Others of his comrades followed him. They were joined by the troops, and the barbican was taken. At that, the Franks retired behind the walls to defend themselves and their fort until reinforcements could reach them.[39]

Saladin could not afford a lengthy siege because the relief force from Tiberias would eventually arrive, so he ordered that the sappers mine under the castle walls. However, when the fires in the mine were lit, the castle walls did not collapse due to their thickness. It seemed that the Templar defenders would be able to cling on for the arrival of Baldwin IV. When it became apparent that the wall would not collapse, the fire was extinguished, and the mine was expanded. The second attempt was successful, and the wall collapsed on 30 August.[40]

With the wall down, Saladin's forces poured through the breach, and although the Templar knights made a final stand, they were soon overrun. The castle was captured before King Baldwin's relief force could arrive.

Saladin demonstrated his ruthlessness in the siege at Jacob's Ford when dealing with the Christian's elite Templar forces. Before the castle fell, he rejected the defenders' terms of surrender, and with King Baldwin's forces still so far from Jacobs Ford, the Templar knights holding out were doomed.[41]

It was said that to evade capture, the Templar commander threw himself into the fire started by the sappers.[42] The Templar dead numbered around 800, and many of them were executed at Saladin's orders upon capture, which foreshadows the fate of the Knights Templar at the Battle of Hattin almost ten years later.

With the Templars defeated, Saladin's forces demolished the castle and took 700 prisoners, which included eighty Templar knights, and the substantial spoils of 1,000 suits of armour back to Damascus.[43]

Although the castle was incomplete, its loss was hugely significant for the Kingdom of Jerusalem and the Knights Templar. For the Franks, it showed that they had failed to capitalise on their success at Montgisard and nullify the threat Damascus posed after its union with Cairo. For the Templars, not only did they lose their grand master, but they also lost hundreds of their forces and their reputation as the elite force of the Franks who had humiliated Saladin at Montgisard was tarnished.

Saladin's forces had defeated the Knights Templar in the field and captured a Frankish castle, crushing its garrison. He had avenged the loss at Montgisard and stabilised the union of Egypt and Syria. However, he needed to bring Aleppo and Mosul into his growing empire before his unification of the Islamic territories could be complete.

7

THE BEGINNING OF THE END

SALADIN'S ZENGID CONQUESTS

Despite his victory in crushing the castle at Jacobs Ford, Saladin agreed to a two-year peace with the Kingdom of Jerusalem, which enabled him to focus on subjugating Aleppo and Mosul. After 1180, the Islamic political landscape in the region changed following the death of the Abbasid Caliph, which was then followed by the death of the Emir of Mosul, Saif al-Dīn, who was succeeded by his younger brother, Izz al-Dīn. This sudden change in leadership was followed towards the end of 1181 by the death of the Emir of Aleppo, al-Salih, the heir of Nūr ad-Dīn, who died when still a teenager. The death of al-Salih greatly boosted the perception of Saladin as the true heir to Nūr ad-Dīn, as the young al-Salih had been seen as the legitimate heir to the Zengid dynasty.

In September 1182, Saladin marched his army across the Euphrates and began to capture vast Zengid-controlled territories, such as the former Crusader state capital of Edessa, before laying siege to the city of Mosul. However, despite a lengthy siege through the winter into 1183, Saladin was unable to capture Mosul and, therefore, decided to switch his focus to Aleppo. Saladin had instead captured its surrounding territories to weaken Mosul.[1]

Aleppo came under the control of Imād al-Dīn Zengi, who was Saif al-Dīn's older brother. Saladin needed to prevent a strong union between Mosul and Aleppo, so he abandoned his siege of Mosul and instead laid siege to Aleppo on 21 May 1183. Aleppo did not have the strength to withstand Saladin's attack and negotiated a surrender deal. The agreement was concluded by 11 June and allowed Imād al-Dīn Zengi to have control over his former lordship at Sinjar, which was taken by Saladin in December 1182. Bahā' al-Dīn's account depicts how magnanimous Saladin was in the subjugation of Aleppo, writing, 'A settlement was reached between them and the Sultan received him [Imād al-Dīn Zengi] in his tent, giving him a splendid gift and some handsome horses. He gave robes of honour to several of his men.'[2]

Saladin justified his war against the Zengid dynasty by claiming that a united Islam was the only way to dislodge the Christians from Jerusalem. Saladin wrote to the caliph to argue that he was right to attack the Zengid territories because he was distracted from defeating the Franks by their continued opposition to a united attack on the Crusader states. Saladin suggested that he should subdue any Muslim who refused to take part in the jihad against the Franks.[3]

If Saladin wanted to wage a decisive war against the Franks, he needed to bring Mosul under his control. In 1185, he once again marched his army and laid siege to the city. However, several months into the siege, although Saladin's forces had captured the surrounding territories, Mosul still resisted.

On 3 December, disaster struck when Saladin developed a fever at the village of Kafr Zammā and then travelled to Harran while ill. Bahā' al-Dīn described Saladin's condition, 'He showed great fortitude and did not ride in a litter. He arrived at Harrān very sick and extremely weak. His life was despaired of and a rumour went around that he had died.'[4]

It was in this weakened state that a peace deal was agreed with Izz al-Dīn, the Emir of Mosul. He was to recognise Saladin as his overlord, and according to Ibn al-Athīr, the deal included that 'the khutbah [sermon] should be in Saladin's name on all the pulpits of his lands and the coinage struck in his name'.[5] Saladin would recover from his illness in 1186, having achieved his goal of uniting Egypt with the lands of the Zengid dynasty.

The Crusader states had been unable to negate the threat posed by Zengi and then his son Nūr ad-Dīn, losing Edessa to Zengi and then struggling to hold back the advance of Nūr ad-Dīn as his forces pushed the northern state back towards the sea. The future of the Crusader states looked bleak against the united power and resources of the Zengid dynasty and Saladin's Egypt.

THE LANDLESS FRENCH KNIGHT WHO WOULD BE KING

While Saladin had united Syria and Egypt, the Kingdom of Jerusalem was once again in disarray. The kingdom was split into two camps: those for Count Raymond of Tripoli and those who supported Guy de Lusignan, the Count of Jaffa and Ascalon.

The health of Baldwin IV grew worse as the leprosy took hold. William of Tyre describes the young king's condition, 'His sight failed and his extremities became completely deadened so that his hands and feet refused to perform their office.'[6] With his health failing him, Baldwin was forced to appoint a regent to rule in his stead but chose not to appoint Count Raymond, who was regent until he came of age, but instead, his sister's husband, Guy de Lusignan.

Guy was a Poitevin knight, who managed to earn political power through marriage after recently arriving in Outremer, in a similar fashion to Reynald de Châtillon. Reynald managed to become a prince, but Guy's marriage to Sibylla put him high in the line of succession for the throne of Jerusalem.

Guy de Lusignan was not Sibylla's first husband, as she had first married William, the Marquis of Montferrat, in 1176. William was deemed a very suitable candidate for Sibylla's hand as the marquis had close ties with the European elite, being cousin to King Louis VII of France (his father was the brother of the king's mother). William was also the cousin of the Holy Roman Emperor Fredrick I, who was the nephew of William's mother.

William of Tyre highly praised the good personal qualities of the Marquis of Montferrat, writing, 'The marquis was a rather tall, good-looking young man with blond hair. He was exceedingly irascible but very generous and of an open disposition and manly courage.' He also praised his knightly prowess, 'He had been trained in arms from his earliest youth and had the reputation of being experienced in the art of war. His worldly position was exalted - in fact, few if any could claim to be his equals.'[7] However, despite his family connections and the high qualities associated with him, the marquis would die early in the marriage after catching malaria. He died at Ascalon in April 1177. Sibylla was pregnant and gave birth to their only child, the future Baldwin V, after the marquis' death.

Despite the tragedy of William's death, King Baldwin needed to find another suitable candidate to wed Sibylla because of his own continually declining health. The next candidate was Baldwin of Ibelin, the brother of Balian, who had recently married Baldwin IV's widowed stepmother, Maria.

Unfortunately, Baldwin of Ibelin was captured in 1179 during a battle before the loss of the castle at Jacob's Ford that also took the life of Templar Grand Master Odo de St Amand. Baldwin of Ibelin's ambition for the throne of Jerusalem was at the mercy of Saladin, who set his ransom at the huge sum of 200,000 bezants. He was unable to raise enough to cover such a sum but paid enough to be released with the expectation that the rest would be paid later.

Before he could be wed to the king's sister, he had to clear the rest of this substantial debt to Saladin. However, while he was in Constantinople, arranging for the emperor to cover his debt, Sibylla was instead married to Sir Guy, an unknown landless knight from France.[8]

If Baldwin of Ibelin had married Sibylla, it would have handed a lot of power to the Ibelin family, who had been growing in influence. Due to his declining health, King Baldwin feared being usurped so marrying his sister to the landless fourth son of a French lord would somewhat keep the balance of power.

William of Tyre explained that the reason for Sibylla's sudden marriage to Guy de Lusignan was because in 1180, Prince Bohemond of Antioch and Count Raymond of Tripoli were en route to Jerusalem, and the king's symptoms of leprosy had progressed so much that he feared the powerful lords would take his crown or marry his sister off to their advantage. So, he hastily married his sister to Guy to prevent the greater lords of Outremer from taking advantage of his poor health.

William of Tyre was not scathing in his comments on Guy de Lusignan's character, but he did not offer the same level of praise afforded to William of Montferrat. He commented that the king 'might have found in the kingdom nobles of far greater importance, wisdom, and even wealth, both foreigners and natives, an alliance with any one of whom would have been of much greater advantage to the kingdom' and referred to Guy as 'a young man of fairly good rank'.[9]

Roger of Howden gives insight into Guy's qualities and also how the relationship came to be. Roger describes that Guy and Sibylla's relationship began as a secret affair, 'The king's sister, seeing therefore that this Guy was handsome, chose him to be her husband. But not daring to make her will known to her brother, she loved him secretly, and he slept with her.' In Roger's account, upon learning of the affair, King Baldwin wanted to execute Guy but spared him on the advice of the Knights Templar and other advisors. Instead, the king allowed his sister to marry the landless French knight since his options were limited, but on the condition that his infant nephew, Baldwin succeed him.[10] In a rapid rise, Guy had become the Count of Jaffa and Ascalon and was the stepfather of the heir to the throne.

Baldwin IV's health continued to decline, and he began to lose his sight and develop paralysis. It was clear he could no longer continue to carry out his duties, so in 1183, Baldwin made Guy regent. However, in the autumn of that year, Baldwin deposed Guy and once again resumed control of the Kingdom of Jerusalem. Mayer states that the reason Guy was deposed was his refusal to allow his forces to march away from a position well supplied with water to avoid a high-risk battle.[11] The significance of this event will be revealed later in the following chapter.

To bring some stability to the kingdom and clarify the succession, King Baldwin's infant nephew was crowned as Baldwin V on 20 November 1183. Guy de Lusignan's sharply rising career began to decline as Baldwin IV stripped him of the County of Jaffa and then placed Count Raymond III as Baldwin V's regent. However, Raymond refused to be Baldwin V's guardian, as he feared he would be implicated in the event of the young king's death, so Baldwin's great uncle, Count Joscelin III, became his guardian.[12] He only accepted the regency if he was financially compensated and with the assurance that he would hold the position for ten years. It was also agreed that in the event of the young Baldwin V's death within those ten years, the regency would pass to the closest heir until a council consisting of the Pope, the Emperor of Germany and the kings of England and France could decide if Sibylla (the daughter of Countess Agnes, King Amaury's first wife) or her half-sister, Isabella (the daughter of Queen Maria, King Amaury's second wife) would succeed Baldwin V.

Count Raymond was given the city of Beirut as compensation for carrying out his duty as regent.[13] However, his second term as regent would quickly come to an end.

Baldwin IV finally succumbed to his illness and died in 1185, and the already-crowned child King Baldwin V succeeded his uncle with Raymond ruling as regent. However, the young Baldwin V died just a year later, in 1186.

Count Raymond's agreement for succession was in ruin, and the supposed Great Council to decide the next ruler would not take place. Instead, with the support of the Templars and Eraclius, the Patriarch of Jerusalem, Sibylla and Guy took the crowns for themselves. Count Raymond was betrayed by Count Joscelin III. Joscelin seized the city of Beirut for himself and sent Raymond back to Tiberias, banning him from the young Baldwin V's funeral.

In 1184, the Templar Grand Master Arnold de Torroja (who succeeded Odo de St Amand), died while on embassy to Italy tasked with informing the European nobility of the threat Saladin posed to Outremer. In 1185, a Flemish knight, Gérard de Ridefort, was elected as his successor. He held a grudge against Count Raymond of Tripoli, dating back to before Gérard joined the Knights Templar. Count Raymond had supposedly promised him an advantageous marriage to Stephany of Botron but instead gave her hand to Plivan, a rich man from Pisa, after receiving a lot of money from him. The betrayal greatly angered Gérard, who joined the Templars after this, since Templar knights are forbidden from marriage.[14]

The *Lyon Eracles* account of the coronation describes the Templar Grand Master Gérard de Ridefort playing a key role in the ceremony, with Gérard, Patriarch Eraclius (or Heraclius) and Reynald of Châtillon securing the crowns of Jerusalem for Sibylla's coronation. However, Gérard played an even greater role when, after Sibylla was crowned queen she called Guy forward to receive his crown and the Templar grand master helped her place it upon Guy's head. Gérard de Ridefort then, according to this account, said, 'This crown is well worth the marriage of Botron.'[15]

Accounts of the coronation differ. For example, Roger of Howden claims that the Crusader state nobility, Templars and Hospitallers agreed that Sibylla would succeed her young son as queen if she divorced the divisive Guy de Lusignan. Sibylla agreed to this on the condition that she could choose whomever she wished for her husband. Supposedly, after she was crowned in the Holy Sepulchre, she chose Guy to be her husband and king, causing outrage among those in attendance. Guy of Bazoches' account says that they demanded she divorce Guy, but Sibylla refused.[16] Regardless of whether Sibylla tricked the barons or refused to leave Guy, the landless French knight whom Baldwin IV had stripped of his regency was now the King of Jerusalem.

The coronation of Sibylla and Guy had a disastrous effect on the unity of the Kingdom of Jerusalem, and the kingdom that was split into two factions was now on the verge of civil war. So aggrieved was Count Raymond of Tripoli by the elevation of Guy that he turned to the Crusader states' greatest enemy, Saladin.

Ibn al-Athīr wrote that Count Raymond became regent 'because at that time the Franks had nobody more influential than him, none braver and none more excellent in council'. And because of Baldwin V, 'he was ambitious to be king'.[17] With the death of the young Baldwin V, the count's ambitions had come to nothing, but following the coronation, Raymond allied himself to Saladin so that he would support him against King Guy. Ibn al-Athīr's account of this agreement details that 'Saladin along with the Muslims rejoiced at this and promised him aid and help to gain all that he wanted. He guaranteed that he would make him an independent ruler for all the Franks. He held several of the count's knights as prisoners and these he released.'[18]

Count Raymond's siding with Saladin would soon have deadly consequences for the knights of Outremer, especially for the Hospitaller and Templar orders. Raymond was such a powerful and influential figure in Outremer that William of Tyre had titled the last and incomplete book of his chronicle *Could Jerusalem be Saved by Raymond of Tripoli?*[19]

The loss of the Count of Tripoli was detrimental to the kingdom's fight for survival, and so vital was his support that despite Raymond refusing to give homage to King Guy, Guy was forced to send a delegation to Raymond to agree a peace deal. This included the Templar grand master, Hospitaller Grand Master Roger de Moulins, Archbishop Joscius of Tyre, Balian of Ibelin and Reynald of Sidon.[20]

However, while the delegation travelled to Tiberius, a terrible massacre occurred that foreshadowed the destruction of the Kingdom of Jerusalem.

THE MASSACRE AT THE SPRINGS OF CRESSON

Saladin had spent the last remaining years of the reign of King Baldwin IV expanding his empire to include the Zengid dynastic territories of Aleppo and Mosul. With his strength and resources greatly enhanced, he could crush the Crusader states, and Frankish Lord Reynald de Châtillon gave Saladin the excuse he needed.

Bahā' al-Dīn describes the 'accursed Reynald' as 'a monstrous infidel and terrible oppressor'.[21] Ibn al-Athīr recorded that 'Reynald, lord of Kerak, was one of the greatest and wickedest of the Franks, the most hostile to Muslims and the most dangerous to them.'[22]

From his castle at Kerak, Reynald dominated the trade route through the Oultrejourdain, and Saladin had agreed on a truce with Reynald to prevent him from pillaging Muslim caravans on the route. However, Reynald broke that truce when he attacked and pillaged a particularly large, rich caravan with an armed escort. Reynald took the goods and animals for himself and made the merchants his prisoners. Bahā' al-Dīn records Reynald's vile crime, stating that he imprisoned and tortured the merchants, and when his victims mentioned the truce with Saladin, he mocked them, saying, 'Tell your Muhammad to release you.'

When news reached Saladin of Reynald's treachery and brutality, he vowed that if God delivered him into his hands, he would personally kill him.[23] Now that Saladin had brought Aleppo and Mosul under his control, he could turn his attention to the Crusader states and reclaim Jerusalem from the Franks, so the actions of Reynald de Châtillon would prove costly.

In April 1187, Saladin marched his forces from Damascus and laid siege to Reynald at Kerak castle. Reynald hid behind the castle walls while Saladin's forces plundered his land. Count Raymond's lands were safe under the secret treaty with Saladin, which included the County of

Tripoli and his wife Eschiva's Principality of Galilee, which was part of the Kingdom of Jerusalem. It was this secret treaty that led to a massacre of Templar knights.

Saladin ordered his son, al-Afdal, to lead a raid into the Crusader states and to do this he would need to march his army past Tiberias. Due to the treaty with Saladin, Count Raymond permitted al-Afdal to march through his land en route to raid Outremer on the condition that he cross the River Jordan at sunrise, return to his own land by sunset and leave the property and inhabitants of his lordship alone.

Raymond sent word to the local populace to stay inside their homes and to let al-Afdal and his forces march through the territory unopposed.[24] However, al-Afdal's incursion into Outremer coincided with Guy's delegation travelling to bring about peace with Count Raymond. Word soon reached delegation members, the grand masters of the Knights Templar and Knights Hospitaller and the Archbishop of Tyre, who were residing at the castle of La Fève.

The grand masters were so greatly alarmed by the news of Muslim forces marching into the Crusader states that they immediately mustered what men they could. The next day, a force of eighty Templar knights and ten Hospitaller knights joined with a force of forty royal knights at Nazareth. The small mounted army rode several miles before finding al-Afdal at the Springs of Cresson with an army of 7,000.[25] A letter from Pope Urban III numbers the armies slightly lower, claiming the Christians had only 110 knights against al-Afdal's 7,000 troops. The letter is also charitable towards Templar Grand Master Gérard de Ridefort in not blaming him for what followed.[26]

The *Lyon Eracles*, however, states that upon seeing that the Christians were totally outnumbered, Gérard de Ridefort ignored the advice of Hospitaller Grand Master Roger de Moulins and Jacques de Mailly, the Templar marshal, who was the military commander of the Knights Templar. Instead, the Templar grand master led a desperate charge against the much greater army.

Perhaps Gérard de Ridefort hoped to emulate the devastating Templar charge from the battle at Montgisard ten years ago.[27] However, the gamble did not pay off, and the small army of Templars, Hospitallers and Frankish knights were massacred. Hospitaller Grand Master Roger de Moulins and Templar Marshal Jacques de Mailly were killed in the slaughter, with Grand Master Gérard de Ridefort and a handful of knights being the only survivors.

A letter sent to the German Emperor Frederick I, dated July 1187, endeavoured to provide some justification for the Templar grand master's folly by suggesting that the knights had no choice but to attack, 'A horde of Turkish barbarians entered the land of Nazareth, pillaging and plundering', without making any reference to Count Raymond's agreement with Saladin. The letter also emphasised the Franks' piety, noting, 'They made the sign of the cross, and with the words, "Christ is our life and death is our reward", they launched an attack.'[28] The *Lyon Eracles* account of the battle makes no mention of a pious sacrifice but highlights that the Templar grand master scoffed at the advice of the Hospitaller grand master and Templar marshal.

Despite the massacre, al-Afdal kept his promise to Count Raymond and crossed the river at sunset without pillaging or harming the local population.[29]

The battle saw the loss of senior members of the knightly orders, over 100 knights, as well as precious equipment and arms. However, the slaughter did bring about the reconciliation of King Guy and Count Raymond. Ibn al-Athīr's account explains that the reconciliation was only brought about due to the backlash Raymond received from the visiting nobles and his own men, with the Patriarch threatening him with excommunication and declaring his marriage invalid. Fearful of the repercussions, Count Raymond ended his treaty with Saladin, travelled to meet King Guy and pledged his loyalty.

The loss of the knights from Nazareth and the Templar and Hospitaller knights weakened the military strength of the Crusader states. Boosted by the recent victory over the infamous Knights Templar, Saladin marched his vast army into Outremer towards Lake Tiberias. He had joined his forces together with al-Afdal, and Ibn al-Athīr details that Saladin 'reviewed his army and estimated that he had 12,000 cavalry with regular fiefs and military stipends, as well as volunteers'.[30] This was an army assembled from Saladin's vast resources of manpower to crush the Franks and reclaim the Holy City of Jerusalem.

8

THE BATTLE OF HATTIN

PREPARING FOR WAR

On 27 June 1187, Saladin crossed the River Jordan with his vast army and attacked the city of Tiberias on 2 July. The defenders were outnumbered and the town quickly fell, with only the citadel holding out against Saladin. Taking refuge inside the citadel was Count Raymond's wife, Princess Eschiva of Galilee.

In response to Saladin's invasion, King Guy ordered the Frankish troops to muster at the Springs of Saffuriya, near Nazareth. Ashbridge estimates that he was able to muster a force of 18,000, which included only 1,200 knights and 4,000 light cavalry. This was one of the largest Frankish armies to march under the True Cross,[1] which also included mercenaries hired with money from King Henry II in penance for the murder of Archbishop Thomas Becket in 1170. The Templar grand master took the 30,000 silver marks that the Templars were entrusted with and used it to hire mercenaries to fight under the banner of King Henry II.[2]

Even with the additional influx of mercenaries, the Christian army was dwarfed by Saladin's army, which had a cavalry of 12,000 and 30,000 volunteers.[3]

Saladin's attack on Tiberias was an attempt to lure the Christian army away from their well-supplied and strong position at Saffuriya. Guy turned to the senior nobles of the kingdom for advice on how to proceed and he was presented with two opposing strategies. Count Raymond implored the king to not march from the security of this camp to engage Saladin as his army was too great.

Count Raymond's words of caution seemed to have been heard, and the consensus among the king and senior nobles was to remain at Saffuriya. However, that night, Gérard de Ridefort warned Guy that Count Raymond was a traitor and had no love for the king or kingdom.

His distrust of Count Raymond can be linked back to the count denying him the hand of Stephany of Botron. The Templar grand master proposed that the army should engage the enemy forces because Saladin would attack the Christian camp and force King Guy into a shameful retreat.[4]

The following day, the Christian army marched from their camp, which was well supplied with water, to Tiberias. The king may have been motivated by the memory of his disgrace and the stripping of his regency after refusing to abandon a well-supplied position to engage the enemy in 1183. Mayer proposes that as the Templars spent King Henry II of England's money without permission on so many mercenaries, they were forced to meet Saladin in battle to justify using these funds.[5]

Imād al-Dīn's account states that when the news reached Saladin that the Franks had taken the bait and were marching towards him, 'he rejoiced to hear that they were on the march'. He was a scholar and secretary to Saladin, and recorded him saying:

> If our objective is gained, our request will have been heard in full and our ambition will have been achieved. Thanks be to God, our good fortune will now be renewed, our swords sharp, our courage valiant, our victory swift. If they are really defeated, killed and captured, Tiberias and all Palestine will have no one left to defend them or to impede our conquest.[6]

The Christians were marching into a trap, which Saladin sprung by moving his forces to block the Christian army from reaching Lake Tiberias. They were in the open with no source of water in the height of summer, making slow progress as they were constantly harassed by Saladin's skirmish troops. The Christian army was forced to make camp on the waterless plain, while Saladin's army had access to a bountiful supply of water. They endured a miserable, sleepless night, unable to quench their thirst, ready for battle.

Despite having access to an abundance of water and superior numbers, giving battle to the Franks was still a gamble because if the fighting did not go their way, they would be trapped in enemy territory. Bahā' al-Dīn explained, 'The Muslims were well aware that behind them was the Jordan and before them enemy territory and that there was nothing to save them but God Almighty.'[7] The following battle was for the highest stakes, death or captivity for the defeated, while the victorious would dominate the Holy Land and surrounding regions.

The morning brought further misery for the Christian army as some of the Muslim forces set fire to the dry grass and the wind carried the smoke and flames towards the Christians. Ibn al-Athīr describes the Christians' dire situation, 'Thirst, hot weather, the heat of the fire, the smoke and heat of the battle all combined against them.'[8]

The *Lyon Eracles* account details the Christian army's early tactics and an event that features in some form in most accounts of the battle. Facing fire and a superior force, King Guy turned to Reynald de Châtillon and the Templar grand master for urgent advice, who advised him to engage Saladin's forces. The king's brother, Aimery de Lusignan, was the Constable of Jerusalem and was ordered to prepare the battle divisions. Count Raymond led the vanguard, which included Bohemond, the eldest son of the Prince of Antioch, and Count Raymond's four stepsons, Hugh, William, Ralph and Oste. Balian of Ibelin and Count Joscelin were in the rearguard.[9] The significance of the names listed in the account is that they include the prominent nobles who escaped the disaster of the Battle of Hattin.

Count Raymond and the vanguard charged at Saladin's forces, which parted to counter the charge and allowed the Christian knights to pass through them. Ibn al-Athīr's account informs that Saladin's nephew, Taqī al-Dīn, was in charge of that division and believed his troops would be unable to withstand the count's charge, so he ordered his men to part to allow Count Raymond's company to flee the battle. The army then closed its ranks to prevent any other Christian escapes.[10]

The *Lyon Eracles*, however, paints a more heroic departure for Count Raymond as it claims Saladin's army opened its rank at the charging Franks but then closed in on them and surrounded the unit. In the fighting, only twelve knights of Count Raymond's company escaped, which included himself, the son of the Prince of Antioch and Count Raymond's four stepsons.[11]

During the battle, the Knights Templar also tried a drastic charge into the enemy forces' ranks. The Templars had previously achieved a great victory at Montgisard in 1177 with this tactic. However, the grand master had recently had his forces slaughtered at the Springs of Cresson only a few months prior.

The fate of the Knights Templar in the battle is recorded in a letter sent to Archumbald, a Hospitaller in Italy, 'At around the third hour the master of the Temple charged with all his brothers. They received no assistance, and God allowed most of them to be lost.'[12] Although it gives no number for Templar losses, a letter sent by Terricus does detail the number of Templar knights slain. Terricus was the senior surviving Templar from the Battle of Hattin, and he recorded that at Hattin, 'Two hundred and thirty of our brothers were beheaded that day.'[13]

To understand how devastating a loss this was to the Knights Templar, it's important to note that when Benjamin of Tudela visited Jerusalem around 1168, he said that the Templars had 300 knights.[14] This would suggest that the Kingdom of Jerusalem lost almost all of its Templar knights at the massacre at the Springs of Cresson and then the Battle of Hattin. Barber estimates that in 1180, there were only 600 Templar knights stationed throughout the whole of Outremer, so the losses sustained in these two events were devastating not just to the Templar order but also to the survival of the Crusader states.[15]

THE HORNS OF HATTIN

Ibn al-Athīr's account gives insight into why the Christians' attacks failed to gain any advantage. He explained that the Christians' repeated charges came close to pushing Saladin's numerically superior forces back. However, despite their ferocity, the Christians sustained heavy losses with each attack. This enabled Saladin's forces to use their superior numbers as, according to Ibn al-Athīr, 'The Muslims surrounded them as a circle encloses its central point.'[16]

The remaining Christians retreated to a nearby hill, one of a pair known as the Horns of Hattin. Here, atop the hill, the Christians attempted to make a final stand. They tried to raise their tents to strengthen their position, but because they were attacked so fiercely, they could only erect the king's tent. Ibn al-Athīr records that the king had only 150 knights remaining in his forces, as the rest had been killed or captured. From that hilltop, the Christians again made desperate charges against Saladin's troops, but they were unable to break through.[17]

In his account of the final moments of the battle, Ibn al-Athīr shares what Saladin's son, al-Afdal, told him. The eyewitness account describes the Christians' desperate struggle and demonstrates how the battle could have gone the Christians' way, had their charges succeeded:

> I was alongside my father during this battle, the first I had witnessed. When the king of the Franks was on the hill with that band, they made a formidable charge against the Muslims facing them, so that they drove them back to my father. I looked towards him and he was overcome by grief and his complexion pale. He took hold of his beard and advanced, crying out 'Give the lie to the Devil'. The Muslims rallied, returned to the fight and climbed the hill. When I saw that the Franks withdrew,

pursued by the Muslims, I shouted for joy. 'We have beaten them!' But the Franks rallied and charged again like the first time and drove the Muslims back to my father. He acted as he had on the first occasion and the Muslims turned upon the Franks and drove them back to the hill. I again shouted, 'We have beaten them!' but my father rounded on me and said, 'Be quiet! We have not beaten them until that tent falls.' As he was speaking to me, the tent fell. The sultan dismounted, prostrated himself in thanks to God almighty and wept for joy.

The battle was over, and the surviving Christians still on top of the hill surrendered. Imād al-Dīn described the aftermath of the battle, 'This field of blood had become a sea of blood; the dust was stained red, rivers of blood ran freely, and the face of the true Faith was revealed free from those shadowy abominations.'[18]

In the letter sent to the Hospitaller Grand Master of Italy, it states that 'no more than 200 of the knights or footsoldiers escaped', noting that 'the Count of Tripoli, the lord Balian [Balian of Ibelin] and Reynald lord of Sidon got away'.[19] This would mean there were only 200 Christian survivors from an army of 18,000.

The lords listed above, along with Count Joscelin, fled from the battle to the port of Tyre. Count Raymond would risk capture had he gone to the citadel of Tiberias and so he abandoned his wife and fled west to Tyre, which would prove vital to the survival of the Crusader states of Outremer.

Aside from the few nobles who escaped, Saladin's forces took the remaining senior figures of the Kingdom of Jerusalem captive. This included King Guy, Reynald de Châtillon, Constable of Jerusalem, Aimery de Lusignan, Plivain, Lord of Botron, and the Templar Grand Master Gérard de Ridefort. In his victory, Saladin also captured the True Cross.

After the battle, Saladin had the King of Jerusalem and the hated Reynald de Châtillon brought before him. What happened during this meeting is addressed in several accounts, although they vary slightly.

Saladin offered the defeated King Guy a cup of iced water to quench his thirst and reassured his royal captive that he need not fear. Guy gratefully drank the iced water and passed the cup to Reynald. However, Saladin informed Reynald that he had not been permitted to drink from the cup. Bahā' al-Dīn explained the significance of this, 'According to the fine custom of the Arabs and their noble ways, if a prisoner took food or drink of water from whoever had captured him, his life was safe.'[20] Since Saladin had not offered the cup to Reynald, his life was not safe. Saladin had vowed to kill Reynald if he ever had the Frank as his prisoner, so he was swiftly executed.

Ibn al-Athīr recorded that Saladin berated Reynald for his crimes and then decapitated him on the spot.[21] Imād al-Dīn and Bahā' al-Dīn's accounts both state that Saladin summoned Reynald a second time, and it was then that Saladin cut off Reynald's arm at the shoulder and he was executed by Saladin's men.[22]

The other noble captives, including the Templar grand master, were taken in chains to Damascus, while the captured Templars and Hospitallers were to be executed. Their execution was not as punishment for great acts of cruelty like Reynald, but as Ibn al-Athīr explains, 'He singled these out for execution because they were the fiercest fighters of all the Franks'. He writes that Saladin had 200 Templars and Hospitallers executed.[23] Saladin gave 50 dinars for each captured Templar or Hospitaller brought to him. Imād al-Dīn paints a vivid picture of the mass execution:

> With him was a whole band of scholars and Sufis and a certain number of devout men and ascetics; each begged to be allowed to kill one of them, and drew his sword and rolled up his sleeve. Saladin, his face joyful, was sitting on his dais; the unbelievers showed black despair, the troops were drawn up in their ranks, the amīrs stood in double file. There were some who slashed and cut cleanly, and were thanked for it; some who refused and failed to act, and were excused; some who made fools of themselves, and others took their place.[24]

Such was the slaughter at the Battle of Hattin that when Ibn al-Athīr visited the site of the battle two years later, he described seeing piles of bones that still remained.[25]

The loss at Hattin proved catastrophic for Outremer and the defeat left the Kingdom of Jerusalem without a standing army that could oppose Saladin's advance across the kingdom. The Franks had suffered heavy defeats before, such as the Field of Blood in 1119 or the death of Prince Raymond in 1149. However, stability had returned with the intervention of the Kingdom of Jerusalem. With the Templars and Hospitallers annihilated, the king captured and his army destroyed, there was no strength left in Outremer to bring stability. The Knights Templar, who had been so vital to the stability of Outremer and a major military force in the Kingdom of Jerusalem, were decimated.

The loss at Hattin was more akin to the catastrophic loss of the city of Edessa in 1144 under the rule of Count Joscelin II, which eventually led to the loss of an entire Crusader state. The loss of Edessa and the tremendous suffering it caused was due to the failings of Count Joscelin II. The loss at Hattin was caused in the short term by a failure in tactics and leadership. However, Saladin's invasion and victory were made easier by the weakened sovereign and disunited nobility, split into two camps about who should succeed to the throne of Jerusalem.

Saladin was free to march his army across the Kingdom of Jerusalem and besiege all cities and castles without fear of the Franks sending a relief force.

9

THE LAUNCH OF THE THIRD CRUSADE

THE SIEGE OF JERUSALEM

After the Christian army was destroyed at the Battle of Hattin and with the kingdom's nobility in chains, Saladin was free to attack the Christian towns and forts. He made use of the momentum brought by his victory and quickly captured Tiberias and then the port city of Acre.

The inhabitants of Acre were offered generous terms and quickly surrendered the city to Saladin. The Franks were given forty days to leave the city with their goods and safe conduct. However, anyone who didn't wish to leave Acre could remain if they paid the customary tax for Christians.[1]

The port of Jaffa, though, was besieged and conquered by Saladin's brother, al-Adil. The men were taken prisoner and the women and children were taken as slaves. In his chronicle, Ibn al-Athīr details the horrific fate of those taken as slaves from Jaffa who he personally encountered and even one who he himself owned.[2]

The castle of Toron tried to hold out against Saladin's forces, but after defending against several assaults, the defenders eventually sought terms of surrender. The defenders were guaranteed their lives, so Toron was surrendered on 26 July and the remaining Franks were allowed to leave unharmed. Then Saladin captured the city of Sidon with no resistance.

The coastal city of Beirut put up a strong defence for several days before eventually asking for terms of surrender, which were granted by Saladin. With their lives spared, the city was surrendered on 6 August.

Saladin then marched his forces to Ascalon and joined with his brother al-Adil's forces to attack the city on 23 August. The defenders put up fierce resistance, and to persuade them to surrender, Saladin had King Guy and the Templar grand master brought to Ascalon to urge the Franks to surrender the city. The city was surrendered on 5 September after agreeing to Saladin's generous terms of safe passage.[3]

Once Ascalon and the surrounding region were brought under control, Saladin turned his attention to the Holy City of Jerusalem. On 20 September, his army arrived at Jerusalem, encircling it. On 25 September, Saladin saw an advantage and moved his troops to the north side of the city to attack the wall beside the Damascus Gate. Once his forces were arranged, they began constructing trebuchets, which the Christians sought to counter by building trebuchets on the north wall.[4]

If the Franks lost their capital city, Jerusalem, it would effectively be the end of the Kingdom of Jerusalem. Who from the nobility was left to lead the defence of Jerusalem? The king and most of the senior nobility were captured at the Battle of Hattin, and from the small list of surviving nobles, the most prominent figure to lead the defence was Balian of Ibelin, alongside the Patriarch of Jerusalem.

The city was filled with those who had been dislodged from the surrounding lands, and Bahā' al-Dīn claims that 'sources estimated the number of soldiers who were there at more than 60,000'.[5] Whether or not that figure is accurate, it indicates that, unlike the previous cities, the people of Jerusalem were prepared to defend themselves.

Ibn al-Athīr's account describes the fierce fighting between the sides. Desperate to keep Saladin's troops from their walls, the Frankish cavalry launched daily attacks on their enemy, and the armies engaged before the walls of Jerusalem, with both suffering losses. However, the Franks were driven back behind the walls, and then the Muslim archers and trebuchets bombarded the defenders on the walls while the sappers began to undermine the wall.[6]

The *Lyon Eracles* details how Saladin used his archers to devastating effect, 'Saladin armed his men and created a shield-wall in front of his archers who shot so quickly that it was like rain. There was not a man so brave in the city who dared show a finger above the walls.' The sappers successfully constructed the mine and set it alight, and to the horror of the defenders, it brought down a section of the wall.[7]

It now seemed impossible for the defenders to prevail, so securing favourable terms of surrender from Saladin seemed the Franks' only hope of survival. Bahā' al-Dīn's account of the siege gives very little detail of the negotiations, but Ibn al-Athīr's account details the negotiations between Saladin and Balian of Ibelin. When the Christians had conquered Jerusalem in 1099 during the First Crusade, they massacred the entire Muslim population. Balian's skills as a negotiator were the only shield to prevent the

Franks from meeting a similar fate. When he first asked Saladin for the inhabitants' lives to be spared, Saladin was unmoved, and Ibn al-Athīr credits Balian with convincing the sultan to change his mind. Ibn al-Athīr recorded that Balian warned Saladin that the Franks only fought because they believed he would offer them favourable terms of surrender. He quotes Balian as saying:

> However, if they see that death is inevitable, by God we will slay our sons and women, burn our property and goods and not leave you to benefit from it by a single dinar or dirham, nor take captive a single man or woman. When we have finished that, we shall destroy the Dome of the Rock, the Aqsa Mosque and other sites and then kill the Muslim prisoners we have, 5000 in number. We shall not leave for you any mount or animal without killing it. Then we shall come forth, all of us, against you and fight you like desperate men fighting for our lives. Not one of us will be killed at that time until he kills many more of you. We shall die nobly or win victory gloriously.[8]

Balian's gamble was the Franks' last roll of the dice, and whether Saladin feared that the Franks could win in a final assault or destroy Jerusalem, the situation could turn glorious victory into a shameful desecration of the Holy City. It was agreed that the Franks would surrender the city and themselves, but each person would be able to buy their freedom and leave the city with their remaining possessions. The price of freedom for each man was to pay 10 dinars, 5 dinars per woman and 2 dinars per child; this was the same price regardless of status. After forty days, those who could not pay the required cost were then doomed to slavery.

The Franks surrendered the city on 2 October, and an attempt was made by the nobles to provide for the poorest, with Balian donating 30,000 dinars to pay for the freedom of as many of the poor as he could.[9] The *Lyon Eracles* states that the Templars and Hospitallers contributed to help liberate the poorest of the citizens, but they did not give as much as they could because Saladin had given assurances that their wealth was safe.[10]

Despite the efforts of the Frankish nobility, a large number of the population were unable to pay. Imād al-Dīn described the desperate measures taken by those who could not pay to escape in his account of the siege. He recorded that some managed to bribe officials, while others resorted to more extreme methods of escape, such as using ropes to scale the walls, hiding within luggage, or even dressing as Muslim soldiers.[11] However, after forty days, those still within the city were taken as slaves, which were believed to be 7,000 men and 8,000 women.[12] Those who managed to escape were escorted to the port of Tyre. Despite holding King Guy prisoner, Saladin allowed Queen Sibylla to leave the city with her wealth and her entourage.

The city's surrender on 2 October coincides with the date when Muhammad made his Night Journey to Jerusalem, where he ascended to Heaven on 2 October. Historian Thomas Ashbridge proposes that the date of Jerusalem's formal surrender was selected to promote the sultan's image as a champion of Islam and that the date would draw parallels between his life and that of the Prophet.[13] Now that the city was under Muslim control, the cross was removed from atop the Dome of the Rock, and Saladin ordered the holy sites to be restored to their former state.

The Aqsa Mosque, which had been adapted to be the headquarters of the Knights Templar, was restored to its original purpose. Of this, Ibn al-Athīr wrote, 'Saladin ordered the mosque and the Dome of the Rock to be cleansed of filth and impurities. All this was duly done.' On the following Friday, the Friday prayers were held in the Dome of the Rock.[14] The Church of the Holy Sepulchre was left intact. However, according to Imād al-Dīn, there was discussion of whether or not to demolish it, but it was decided to leave it untouched as 'when Umar, prince of the believers, conquered Jerusalem in the early days of Islām, he confirmed to the Christians the possession of the place'.[15]

The loss of Jerusalem and the defeat at Hattin sent shockwaves through Europe. Enthusiasm for Crusading was dormant following the failures of the Second Crusade. However, when news of the Franks' defeat at Hattin reached Pope Urban III, he died of shock.[16]

News of Saladin's victory would inspire an armed response from Europe, once again led by kings. A new Crusade was preached, not an armed pilgrimage but a military campaign to recover Jerusalem and the kingdom's lost territories. Saladin would have to defend his conquests against the resurgence of Crusading frenzy.

The Third Crusade was led by one of Europe's most powerful kings, whose lands extended from England across the Channel to Normandy, Anjou and Aquitaine. This English king was Richard I of England, known as Richard the Lionheart. However, before the Crusaders could reach the Holy Land, the Franks had to ensure the survival of Outremer, and with the Kingdom of Jerusalem almost completely captured, they made a stand at the Port of Tyre.

THE SIEGE OF TYRE

The survivors of Jerusalem made their way to the port of Tyre, where many nobles and displaced Christians had gathered. Tyre was an isolated Frankish outpost located north of Acre and south of Sidon, both under the control of Saladin. A letter from Eraclius, Patriarch of Jerusalem, to Pope Urban III reveals the catastrophic list of cities and castles captured by Saladin, 'Gibelet, Beirut, Sidon, Acre, Tiberias, Nazareth, Sebaste, Nablus, Haifa, Caesarea, Arsuf, Jaffa, Ascalon, Lydda, Ibelin, Tron of the Knights, Mirabel, Bethlehem and Hebron'.[17] It was written in September 1187 before the loss of Jerusalem and those sustained from Saladin's 1188 campaign to the north.

Count Raymond of Tripoli was one of the most senior nobles who escaped the battle; however, he died shortly after the catastrophe at Hattin. With no heir, the Prince of Antioch's youngest son, Bohemond, was installed as Count of Tripoli.

Despite the devastating losses, a small glimmer of hope would appear for the Franks in the guise of a new hero, Marquis Conrad of Montferrat. Conrad was the uncle of King Baldwin V, and he would eventually rival King Guy for the kingship of the now-lost Kingdom of Jerusalem. Conrad arrived at Acre shortly after the loss at Hattin. The marquis was almost captured as soon as he arrived when, unknown to him, the city was now under the control of Saladin's forces. Fortunately, Conrad did not sail right into Acre and was able to escape by sailing to Tyre while being pursued by Saladin's navy.[18]

Following his victory at Jerusalem, Saladin set his sights on Tyre, the last significant coastal city in the kingdom still under the Franks' control. Conrad of Montferrat took charge of the city's defences, and when he received word of Saladin's arrival at Acre, he strengthened the city's defensive wall and constructed a large defensive ditch.[19]

Conrad was determined to hold onto the port because its location was vital to receive reinforcements by sea, and his staunch defence of it would elevate his status and make him a rival claimant for the crown. Saladin arrived before Tyre on 12 November, awaiting the rest of his forces and siege engines before moving his camp closer to the city on 25 November.

However, despite Saladin's vast forces, Tyre would not so easily be taken, like other Frankish territories. Ibn al-Athīr describes the city's unusual layout, 'The city was like a hand in the sea with its forearm connected with the mainland and the sea on both sides of it. Fighting was only possible on the forearm.'[20]

After the Crusaders captured Jerusalem in 1099 and began to carve out the Crusader states, the heavily fortified city of Tyre held out against the Franks until 1124, when they finally captured the fort with the assistance of a massive Venetian fleet. Ashbridge describes the challenge facing Saladin, writing that the leader 'found the city to be all but invulnerable. Built upon an island and approachable by land only via a narrow man-made causeway, this compact fortress settlement was protected by double battlements.' He also notes that Tyre was known to have deep-water anchorage, and its inner harbour was protected by a chain.[21]

For weeks, Saladin bombarded the city walls with his catapults while his Egyptian fleet blockaded the city, but despite the attacks from sea and land, the defenders held onto the city. Conrad, with the help of the Knights Templar and Knights Hospitaller, won a naval victory, capturing eleven of Saladin's fleet, which ended his naval blockade. This is detailed in a letter to King Henry II of England dated January 1188 by Terricus, the surviving senior Templar of the Battle of Hattin:

> With the help of the house of the Hospital and the brothers of the Temple, he [Conrad] launched seventeen armed galleys and ten smaller boats in a successful attack against the galleys of Saladin, capturing eleven. He also captured the admiral-in-chief of Alexandria and eight other admirals. Many Saracens were killed. Saladin's remaining galleys escaped from the Christians to rejoin his army. There Saladin had them drawn up on land and burnt, reducing them to ashes.[22]

Conrad's victory against Saladin's fleet was significant as until Tyre, Saladin had seemed unbeatable and whenever his forces arrived at a Frankish settlement, defeat was imminent. However, under Conrad's leadership, the defenders held out through the winter. Seeing that the assault on Tyre was not progressing, Saladin left the siege camp on 1 January 1188 and went to Acre.

Ibn al-Athīr directly blames Saladin for the Franks' frustratingly stout defence of Tyre, 'for he [Saladin] was the person who sent the Frankish troops there and supplied it with manpower and resources from the population of Acre, Ascalon, Jerusalem and elsewhere'.[23]

Tyre was able to use the remaining resources of the Kingdom of Jerusalem, along with the strength of the Hospitallers and Templars, to maintain a coastal foothold in the former Crusader state. In early 1188, the Templars and the Hospitallers still held onto nearby castles at Safed and Belvoir. The Knights Templar held Safed, located just north of Lake

Tiberias, until November 1188, when they were forced to surrender the castle. The Hospitaller-held Belvoir was located east of Tyre, built on the banks of the River Jordan to control entry into the kingdom from the north. However, the Hospitaller defenders were also forced to come to terms with Saladin and surrendered the castle in January 1189.

The surviving Templars and Hospitallers made their way to the island city of Tyre, which added more manpower to the force of Franks holed up there. Ibn al-Athīr was critical of the generous terms of surrender provided by Saladin as it allowed those defeated to regroup at Tyre. He claims that it was these generous terms that escalated the conflict into what would be the Third Crusade:

> Every valiant, devilish champion of the Franks gathered there. Their offensive power became great and their zeal burned brightly. They sent a succession of envoys to Andalusia, Sicily and other islands of the Mediterranean, seeking aid and reinforcements, while support was coming to them little by little. All this was due to Saladin's being remiss in releasing all whom he besieged, so that he ended up biting his thumb in regret and chagrin when that was of no use.[24]

By holding onto Tyre, the Franks were able to maintain a foothold on the lost Kingdom of Jerusalem. They could wait for reinforcements from Europe before launching a coordinated counter-attack. However, while the Third Crusade was being planned, Saladin launched a campaign into Outremer's northern territories, capturing the fortified castles of Krak des Chevaliers, Chastel Blanc, Tortosa and Margat.[25]

Before he could conquer the Principality of Antioch and the County of Tripoli, Saladin's attention was turned towards Acre when the Franks marched on the city in the summer of 1189. The Frankish counter-attack was led by the disgraced and defeated King Guy, whom Saladin had released from captivity in 1188.

THE PREACHING OF THE THIRD CRUSADE

After the failings of the Second Crusade, Europe had little to no appetite for a repeat. During the many crises that befell the Crusader states, the calls for aid went largely unanswered by the European princes. The Kingdoms of England and France were rivals because King Henry II of England controlled most of modern-day France through the Duchy of Normandy, the County of Anjou and, via marriage, the Duchy of Aquitaine, which is known as the Angevin Empire.

Before his ascent to the throne of England in 1154, Henry, who was still a duke at the time, married Eleanor of Aquitaine in 1152, who was several years his senior and had recently had her marriage to King Louis VII of France annulled. As queen, she accompanied Louis to Outremer on the failed Second Crusade and caused a scandal with her close relationship with her uncle, Prince Raymond of Antioch.

The Capetian Dynasty ruled the smaller Kingdom of France, with King Phillip II succeeding his father, Louis VII, in 1180. After the annulment of his marriage, Louis remarried twice, but it was through his third wife, Adela of Champagne, in 1165, that Phillip was born, who was not only the heir to the Capetian Dynasty but a future leader of the Third Crusade.

Archbishop Joscius of Tyre sailed to Sicily following the Franks' destruction at Hattin in the summer of 1187, and despite the decades of apathy towards the Christian cause in the Holy Land, the shocking news had an immediate impact on the west. Pope Urban III was said to have died of shock at the news, but upon hearing from Joscius, William II of Sicily was the first to answer the Franks' desperate call for reinforcements by sending a fleet of ships to Outremer.[26]

Pope Urban III was succeeded by Pope Gregory VII, who died within two months but was still able to issue the papal encyclical *Audita Tremendi* to proclaim the Third Crusade. *Audita Tremendi* described the disaster that befell the Franks in Outremer by likening Saladin to the Devil and addressing the loss of senior Frankish troops, 'The bishops were slaughtered, the king captured, and almost all our men were either put to the sword or taken prisoner. Very few are believed to have escaped.'

Pope Gregory VII specifically mentioned the fate of the Knights Templar, 'also, the Templars and Hospitallers were beheaded in his [Saladin's] presence'. Such was the reputation of the military orders' fighting renown that the news would have shocked European Christendom. To further justify the call to Crusade, Pope Gregory VII described the Franks' enemy as those with 'barbarous ferocity thirsting for the blood of Christians' and their desire was 'adding all their power in this cause to profane the holy and erase the name of God from that land'.[27]

Aside from depicting Saladin as a great evil, the *Audita Tremendi* also offered an explanation for why the Christian army was defeated and the Kingdom of Jerusalem was lost – it was due to the sins of not only the Christians in the Holy Land but of all Christianity.

Gregory VII explained:

> We, therefore, should heed and be concerned about the sins not only of the inhabitants of that land but also of our own and those of the whole Christian people so that what is left of that land may not be lost and their power rage in other regions.

Gregory preached that God had punished the Franks not just because of their sins but those of all European Christians. This notion of collective guilt implored that 'everyone must understand and act accordingly, so that by atoning for our sins, we may be converted to the Lord by penance and works of piety and we may first alter in our lives the evil that we do'.[28] It is with this theme of redemption that *Audita Tremendi* promises 'full remission of their sins and eternal life to those who take up the labor [*sic*] of this journey with a contrite heart and a humble spirit and depart in penitence of their sins and with true faith'.[29] The theme of redemption for one's sin had also been a major theme in Bernard of Clairvaux's preaching for the ill-fated Second Crusade in 1146.

Richard I was the first of the leaders to vow to go on Crusade. He took the cross at Tours in November 1187. His decision to join the Crusade infuriated his father, King Henry II of England, as Richard was a powerful noble, being Duke of Normandy and Count of Poitou.

This decision would have benefited King Phillip II, as Richard was an influential figure in the struggle for dominance between England and France.[30] However, the rival kings met to discuss a settlement on 21 January 1188 at the castle at Gisors in Normandy, which was also attended by Archbishop Joscius of Tyre, who was tasked with preaching the Crusade. At this meeting, the Kings of England and France were moved to join Richard in taking the cross.

The original plan was to march to the Holy Land as for the previous Crusades and to leave around Easter 1189.[31] To fund the Crusade, a tax of 10 per cent on moveable property was required.[32] This was known as the 'Saladin tithe' and was collected by members of the Knights Templar.[33] The fact that the tax had to be collected by the Templars implies that the additional burden was not well received by the people.

The next great leader to take the cross was a veteran of the Second Crusade, the Emperor of Germany. Emperor Barbarossa took the cross in April 1189 at Hagenau and immediately began preparations to march across Europe and then through Seljuk territory, mirroring the doomed marches of the Second Crusade. The German Crusader army started the long march to the Holy Land in May 1189, many months before the Kings of England and France, who had taken the cross months earlier.

The emperor's army included his son, Duke Frederick of Swabia, the Archbishop of Tarentaise, several bishops, three margraves and twenty-nine counts. Other senior nobles, such as Duke Leopold V of Austria, the Archbishop of Breman and Landgrave Ludwig III of Thuringia, travelled to the Holy Land via ship.[34]

However, this would not bring immediate relief to the Franks in what remained of Outremer as the land route to the Holy Land was long and perilous. The German Crusader army did not reach Asia Minor until the spring of 1190.

The English and French part of the Crusade was thrown into disarray when war broke out again between England and France, with Richard turning against his father. However, King Henry II died in July 1189, naming Richard his heir, with King Phillip making nominal gains.

Richard was 32 years old when he ascended to the throne of England. The later Latin account, *Itinerarium Peregrinorum et Gesta Regis Ricardi* (also known *as Itinerarium Regis Ricardi*) describes Richard's physical stature in detail:

> He was tall, of elegant build; the colour of his hair was between red and gold; his limbs were supple and straight. He had quite long arms, which were particularly convenient for drawing a sword and wielding it most effectively. His long legs matched the arrangement of his whole body.[35]

This coincides with Richard's reputation as a warrior; however, it describes Richard's virtues as those of the Ancient Greek heroes, explaining that 'King Richard had the valour of Hector, the heroism of Achilles; he was not inferior to Alexander, nor less valiant than Roland'.[36]

Richard's legacy as the warrior king was due to his success in leading the Third Crusade to undo much of Saladin's conquest of the Kingdom of Jerusalem. He succeeded, where other powerful lords and kings of Europe failed. However, the kings of Europe would not arrive in the Holy Land until 1191, so it was the disgraced King Guy who led the counter-attack against Saladin by laying siege to Acre in 1189.

THE SIEGE OF ACRE

With almost the entirety of the Kingdom of Jerusalem conquered and the Frankish armies crushed, Saladin released King Guy from captivity in 1188. After his release, he mustered a force of 600 knights who had survived the Battle of Hattin. The senior nobles in this small army included Guy's brother, Aimery, the Constable of Jerusalem, his other brother, Geoffrey de Lusignan, who had recently arrived in the Holy Land, and the Templar Grand Master Gérard de Ridefort.

However, the king did not return as a unifier of the Franks; when King Guy and Queen Sibylla arrived before the gates of Tyre, they found them closed. Guy was turned away from the city by the newly arrived Conrad of Montferrat, who had successfully defended Tyre from Saladin's army.[37] Instead, that summer, Guy marched his small army towards the well-fortified city of Acre.

Shut out from the Kingdom of Jerusalem's remaining city, the options left to King Guy were limited. His catastrophic failure at Hattin had lost not only the kingdom but also the will of his remaining people. The *Lyon Eracles* offers insight into Guy's motivations. While marching on Acre may appear to be a desperate or suicidal attack, the *Lyon Eracles* suggests that King Guy was advised that great kings and lords from Europe were on their way and it would be better for his kingship if the arriving Crusaders found him besieging a city instead of waiting for reinforcements.[38]

Guy's army arrived at Acre on 28 August 1189 and established a camp on a hill outside the city. The Frankish army was vastly outnumbered by the defenders. The *Lyon Eracles* describes the disparity, 'There were so many Saracens within the city that there was scarcely one Christian for every ten of them.'[39]

Saladin arrived before Acre and made camp on 30 August, away from the city since the Frankish army was blockading access by land. Bahā' al-Dīn estimated the Frankish army, 'their mounted soldiers numbered 2,000 and their foot 30,000'.[40]

Many skirmishes took place while fresh troops from both sides steadily joined their respective armies. Their numbers were boosted in September 1189 by the arrival of James of Avesnes by sea with 'a fleet of at least 50 cogs', bringing with him a number of Frisians, Germans and Bretons, who aided the camp defences by digging a ditch and constructing palisades and barriers from the ship's wood and also diverting the river that ran through Acre towards their camp.[41] Bahā' al-Dīn writes, 'The armies of Islam came in a steady stream' and 'The first to arrive was the great and noble emir

Muẓaffar al-Dīn ibn Zayn al-Dīn, who was followed by al-Muẓaffar Taqī al-Dīn, the lord of Hamā, with his army'.

Despite the Franks' reinforcements, Saladin reached Acre in September by attacking and routing the Franks positioned to the north and opening up access to the city. However, despite relieving the blockade, Saladin was unable to force the Franks from their camp.[42]

The Frankish army received reinforcements towards the end of September from Conrad of Montferrat, who, despite turning King Guy away from Tyre, arrived by sea with a force of 1,000 knights and 20,000 infantry.[43] The Franks stubbornly dug into their position and continued to repel attacks from Saladin's forces while fresh reinforcements continued to arrive.

With their numbers suitably grown, the Franks dared to venture from their camp on 4 October 1189 with their forces drawn up and launched an attack on Saladin's camp.[44] A letter sent to the Pope by two Italian Crusaders known as Theobald the Perfect and Peter, son of Leo, who fought in the battle, details how the Frankish army was organised for what can be considered the first major battle of the Third Crusade. According to the letter, the Frankish army was split into four squadrons:

> The king, with the Hospitallers and the French, made up one squadron. In the second squadron was the lord marquis and the archbishop of Ravenna, and we were with them. In the third were the landgrave [Ludwig of Thuringia] and the Pisans and Germans. In the fourth were the Templars, the Catalans and certain Germans. The king's brother [Geoffrey de Lusignan] and James of Avesnes remained in the camp.[45]

The letter numbers the combined Frankish Crusader force at 4,000 knights and 100,000 infantry and Saladin's army at 100,000 knights.[46]

At first, it appeared King Guy's forces would be victorious as the centre of Saladin's army collapsed and fled from the Franks' charge. Victory seemed inevitable for the Franks as they raced up the hill, penetrated the camp and reached Saladin's tent, where one of his servants was killed.[47] However, the bulk of the Frankish forces were not behind those in the camp as they were still engaged in fighting the wings of Saladin's army, who resisted the charge. The left wing engaged with those who had attacked the camp, while Saladin rallied what remained of his centre column and attacked the Franks, who had penetrated the camp, from the rear.[48]

Victory had turned to slaughter for the Franks, whose troops were overwhelmed and killed. Bahā' al-Dīn states the Frankish deaths were estimated to be 7,000, while the losses to Saladin's forces were much smaller, at under 200.[49] The letter from the Italian Crusaders contradicts this, noting that Saladin lost 500 knights.[50]

However, all was not lost for King Guy as his brother, Geoffrey de Lusignan, had successfully defended the camp from an assault from Acre. This meant that despite the heavy Frankish losses sustained during the battle, Guy was able to maintain his siege of the city and continue to wait for Crusader reinforcements.

The Franks also suffered the loss of a senior military noble, the Templar Grand Master Gérard de Ridefort. The accounts of his demise differ. The *Lyon Eracles* records that the Templar grand master was killed fighting in the rearguard during the counter-attack by Saladin's forces.[51] Ibn al-Athīr's account of the Battle of Acre provides a differing outcome for the Templar grand master. He states, 'Amongst those taken was the master of the Temple whom Saladin had captured and freed. When he now seized his person, he put him to death.'[52] Whether Gérard de Ridefort was slain in battle or executed, the *Itinerarium Regis Ricardi* describes the grand master with an obituary: 'The Lord conferred such great glory on him, giving him the laurel wreath which he had earned in so many battles and making him a fellow of the college of martyrs.'[53]

Following the Franks' disastrous attack, the attention was shifted to fortifying the camp's defences by expanding the boundaries and digging trenches to enclose the city and expand the land blockade, with the Hospitallers and Conrad of Montferrat laying siege to the remaining parts of the city that were free from the blockade.[54] However, King Guy's forces would have to endure a difficult winter as hopes to starve the population of Acre into submission were dashed by the arrival of the Egyptian fleet in late November. The superior fleet broke the Franks' naval blockade and provided much-needed equipment, supplies and troops to the people of Acre.[55]

As 1189 drew to a close, the Franks managed to hold their fortified camp before the city and maintain their land blockade. However, Saladin controlled the sea and thus was not only able to keep Acre's defenders supplied but also prevent ships friendly to the Christians from arriving. Saladin's mastery of the sea meant supplies were scarce but also the arrival of fresh Crusaders was under threat. For King Guy's siege to succeed, the Franks needed to win control of the sea, as the city would not submit while being well supplied.

The Franks continued to wait for the arrival of the kings of Europe, who would bring the troops and resources they needed. News came that Emperor Frederick Barbarossa was marching his huge army across Europe and he reached Byzantine territory, arriving at Adrianople by the end of November 1189.

The German Crusaders would cross into Asia Minor in March 1190 with an army that would change the balance of power at Acre. While the news was of great concern to Saladin, King Guy and his coalition of Christian forces waited for the arrival of the German Emperor with great anticipation.

10

THE CLASH OF CHAMPIONS

STALEMATE

Throughout 1190, the siege continued with close margins of success and hard fighting with little gain. On 25 March, Conrad of Montferrat sailed a large fleet from Tyre to wrestle control of the sea from Saladin. A naval battle was fought, but neither side would achieve an overwhelming victory as Saladin's navy managed to reach the safety of Acre's harbour. The Franks had to contend with the use of Greek fire, which was particularly hazardous at sea as water does not extinguish its green flames. At close quarters, each side attempted to board each other's vessels.

The account *Itinerarium Regis Ricardi* details how one Frankish ship was hit by Greek fire and then boarded by the enemy, causing the crew to abandon the ship. This left heavily armoured knights trapped on board due to the certainty of drowning should they try to swim. With no option left, the outnumbered knights were forced to fend off the attackers and were able to keep hold of the mostly burnt ship.[1] Although Ibn al-Athīr claims that more Franks were killed in the battle, Conrad of Montferrat could claim victory, because the Franks had retaken control of the sea.[2]

Conrad's success at sea meant that the army on land could receive supplies and reinforcements, and the Franks could also continue their blockade by sea and land. However, attempts to take the city by land stalled. Although the Franks continued to hold their position within their well-fortified camp, they still faced a war on two fronts, with their attention split between Saladin's army in the field and the hostile defenders of Acre.

To gain the advantage, the Crusaders had constructed three siege towers, which Ibn al-Athīr describes as five storeys high with soldiers packed into each level.[3] The towers were protected against fire with cloth and rawhide, and rope netting was used to prevent the wooden structures from being destroyed by the defenders' stone-throwers. The costly engineering of these siege engines and the lives lost were in vain as each was set alight by Greek fire, which left them inoperable.[4]

Despite the stalemate, control over the sea allowed the Franks to receive fresh recruits of English and French Crusaders. The summer saw the arrival of Count Henry of Champagne, who came with a large force of knights and was given command of the army.[5] The arrival of the count was gratefully received as the Frankish numbers had been significantly reduced following a disastrous ambush on Saladin's camp by the foot soldiers on 25 July. The troops attacked against the wishes of the Frankish leaders and were subsequently killed.[6]

However, the most significant setback for the Franks was the news of the death of Emperor Frederick Barbarossa on 10 June. In April Barbarossa had led his huge Crusader army into Seljuq territory and – unlike his predecessor, Second Crusade leader Conrad III back in 1147 – he successfully repelled an ambush on 18 May near Iconium. He had agreed on a treaty with Sultan Kilij Arslan II. However, the sultan's eldest son, Qutb al-Dīn Malik Shah, was Saladin's son-in-law and paid no heed to his father's treaty with the German Crusaders.[7]

Barbarossa's victory mirrored that of the First Crusaders' march through Asia Minor as his army succeeded where both Conrad and King Louis VII of France had failed. Neither was able to march across Asia Minor with their large Crusader armies intact, which was a major factor in the abject failure of the Second Crusade. However, Barbarossa would never reach the Holy Land as he died on 10 June 1190 in a freak accident.

Having reached the safety of the Christian land of Armenia, Barbarossa attempted to swim across the River Saleph but drowned. The accounts of the emperor's death vary, but *Itinerarium Regis Ricardi* explains that he grew impatient as the army slowly crossed the river, so he decided to swim across. Of the emperor's death, Ibn al-Athīr wrote, 'Their emperor entered it [the river] to wash himself and drowned at a spot where the water did not reach a man's waist. God saved us from his evil.'[8] The death of the emperor meant that the massive German Crusader army broke up, while the remaining few were led by Barbarossa's son, Duke Frederick of Swabia.

The news of the emperor's death was a devastating blow to the morale of the Christian army at Acre. *Itinerarium Regis Ricardi* describes the impact of the tragic news, detailing how the defenders mocked the Franks for holding out for the arrival of the emperor and celebrated in the city with dancing, trumpets and drums. According to the *Itinerarium Regis Ricardi*, 'The Christians were shattered by this news. They were afflicted with incredible grief, almost desperate, mortally wounded by this bitter disaster, because it was true that they had expected to achieve their end with the emperor's help.'[9]

It wouldn't be until October 1190 that the emperor's son, Duke Frederick, arrived before the walls of Acre. Even though he brought with him a much smaller force, his arrival was a boost for the Frankish army. Upon arrival, he had several siege engines constructed to assault the walls, but they were soon burned by the defenders.[10]

While the combined Christian army waited for the arrival of the Kings of England and France, many more senior European nobles continued to arrive to provide support for the siege. The Crusaders' ranks were swelled by the arrival of several French counts and Henry II's former Chief Justiciar, Ranulf de Glanville, and prominent Church leaders such as Baldwin, the Archbishop of Canterbury, and Hubert, the Bishop of Salisbury.[11]

The arrival of fresh recruits continued until the winter, which would be terrible for those in the camp as food supplies quickly ran out. So scarce was food that the nobles were forced to eat their warhorses, and it was reported that the people were forced to eat grass and herbs to quell their hunger pains.[12]

With the Christian camp weakened by famine, it was further devastated by disease, which Bahā' al-Dīn claims saw 100–200 dying daily.[13] That miserable winter saw the deaths of many significant Christian nobles, including Barbarossa's son, Duke Frederick, and Baldwin, the Archbishop of Canterbury.

Earlier that year had seen the death of Queen Sibylla and her two young daughters due to illness. This meant the end to Guy de Lusignan's legitimacy to rule, as his right as king was through Sibylla's bloodline. With the death of Guy's wife and daughters, Sibylla's younger sister Isabel became the rightful heir to the throne of Jerusalem (which was in title only).

Sibylla's death caused another crisis of succession, which once again split the Franks into two separate factions – those who supported Guy and those who supported Isabel's claim. A plot by Guy's rival, Conrad of Montferrat, caused further division within the camp when Isabel was taken from her husband Count Humphrey's tent and forced to seek an annulment to her marriage to enable her to marry Conrad. A papal investigation in 1213 recorded several witness statements about the event, and one detailed that it was the barons' view that 'Humphrey will be no use at holding the kingdom'. They heard them say, 'let us take away his wife and give her to the marquis, who will rule the kingdom well and will provide a good market'.[14]

Isabel's marriage to Humphrey was annulled on the grounds that she was 8 when they were wed and were, therefore, too young to marry.[15]

Conrad was popular among the lords as he was the hero who led the defence of Tyre when all other territories fell to Saladin, and his marriage to Isabel gave him a greater claim to the crown than Guy.

The famine continued into 1191 until improved weather enabled ships to bring much-needed supplies. However, the combined Christian forces lacked a unifying leader after the loss of Emperor Barbarossa and with Jerusalem's throne in contention. However, the first of the kingly leaders of the Third Crusade was able to reach the Holy Land alive.

The King of France, Phillip II, arrived at Acre on 20 April 1191, bringing six ships laden with supplies, horses and troops.[16] He did not bring the numbers hoped for, but his arrival did boost the morale of the combined Christian forces.[17] It would be many months before the King of England arrived with a much larger force as he was waylaid at the island of Cyprus.

LIONHEART

On route to Acre, three ships from King Richard's fleet were shipwrecked at Limassol on 24 April. However, when Richard arrived at Cyprus on 6 May, he found that the ship's supplies had been looted and the survivors were imprisoned by Isaac, the ruler of Cyprus. Richard defeated and captured Isaac on 31 May, then preceded to conquer the island's strongholds.

After taking control of Cyprus, a vital location between mainland Europe and the Holy Land, Richard sailed for Acre, arriving at the siege on 8 June.[18] He came with twenty-five galleys laden with soldiers, weapons and supplies.[19] With him was Robert de Sable, the new Templar grand master, who was a vassal of the Angevin Empire and also fought alongside Richard's older brother, Henry the Young King, in an unsuccessful rebellion against Henry II. Robert was also involved with Richard's preparations for the Crusade and was appointed one of the five justiciars commanding the Crusader fleet.[20]

The significance of Richard's close relationship with the new Templar grand master was that the English king agreed to sell the newly conquered island of Cyprus to the Knights Templar for 100,000 bezants. The Templar-acquired island would have given them their own independent state.

Richard arrived at Acre with significantly more troops than his rival, Phillip II, but according to Bahā' al-Dīn, even though Richard had a reputation as an experienced warrior and was more affluent, the French king had higher royal status than the English king.[21] When Richard learned that Phillip was offering three gold coins a month as payment to knights in his service, such was the competition between them, he decided to offer each knight wishing to enter his service four gold coins a month.[22]

The rival kings were also on separate sides of the succession crisis between Guy de Lusignan and Conrad of Montferrat. Phillip supported Conrad's claim, while Richard supported Guy, who had sailed to meet Richard at Cyprus to obtain the English king's support in retaining the crown.[23] Conrad was a relative of the French king, while the Lusignan family were vassals of the English king. Fearing he would be arrested, Conrad fled back to Tyre, and the dispute between Guy and Conrad would not be settled during the siege of Acre.

With the arrival of Richard, the main Crusader forces were finally all mustered before the walls of Acre. However, soon after arriving, Richard fell ill and was confined to his tent, thus delaying the Christian assault on the city. He was suffering from Arnoldia, which causes hair and fingernail loss and can even cause blindness.[24] Bahā' al-Dīn noted that so severe was the king's illness 'that it preoccupied the Franks and discouraged them from making their attacks'.[25]

With Richard unable to fight, Phillip II chose not to wait for the English monarch to recover. He attacked the city with newly constructed siege engines. Still, the defenders withstood the assaults and destroyed the siege towers with Greek fire.[26] However, with the arrival of King Richard and the English Crusaders, the pressure on the Acre garrison was too great, and despite repeated attacks on the besiegers by Saladin, on 12 July 1191, the city surrendered to the Crusaders, just one month after King Richard's arrival.[27]

Bahā' al-Dīn details the terms agreed between the Crusaders and the Acre garrison in that the defenders 'would give up the city and all the engines, equipment and ships it contained and hand over 200,000 dinars, 1,500 prisoners of common, unremarkable background and 100 prisoners to be specified by the Franks'. The terms also included the return of 'the Holy Cross, provided they themselves could leave in safety, taking all their personal wealth and goods and their children and womenfolk'.[28]

With Acre now in the control of the Crusaders, the city and spoils were divided between the Kings of France and England. King Phillip moved into the Templars' former Acre headquarters, while King Richard lodged in the Royal Palace. Phillip and Richard's standards were raised high from the battlements to visually demonstrate its capture by the Crusaders. However, one of the senior leaders of the Crusade, Duke Leopold III of Austria, also had his banner erected atop the battlements alongside the kings' banners, but Richard had the duke's banner torn down. Richard's action would have severe consequences for him in the future.[29]

With the lengthy siege of Acre complete, the King of France decided to depart. Phillip II had only been in the Holy Land for a few months. However, before he left, the dispute between Guy de Lusignan and Conrad of Montferrat needed to be addressed. It was agreed that as Conrad had married Princess Isabel, heir to the Kingdom of Jerusalem, he would become king in the event of Guy of Lusignan's death. In compensation for Conrad's effort in capturing Acre, he received the County of Tyre. It was also agreed that if Guy, Isabel and Conrad perished, King Richard would decide who should receive the monarchy.[30] King Phillip sailed for home, leaving Richard in complete control of the Third Crusade.

The victory at Acre came at a high cost to the Christian forces, and as Mayer informs, the list of the nobility who died during the lengthy siege included 'Queen Sibylla, Patriarch Heraclius [Eraclius], five archbishops, six bishops, four abbots, a prior, a deacon, two dukes, a landgrave, ten counts, three viscounts, and thirty more great nobles', including Templar Grand Master Gérard de Ridefort.[31] Despite the losses of senior figures, the Crusaders' capture of Acre didn't just provide a critical port for receiving reinforcements; the real significance of the capture was that inside Acre's inner harbour was the majority of Saladin's navy with around seventy ships now in the hands of the Crusaders.[32] With these, the Crusader's fleet grew significantly and would prevent Saladin from contesting the Franks for control of the Mediterranean Sea.

Following the surrender of Acre to the Crusaders, there was a delay in the ransom payment and exchange of prisoners. Ibn al-Athīr's account explains that Saladin had intended to meet the Crusaders' demands and had raised 100,000 dinars to pay part of the ransom but hesitated due to fears of betrayal. To ease the anxiety, Saladin's advisors suggested he turn to the Templars to guarantee the safe release of prisoners as 'they were people of religion who hold with keeping faith'. However, when Saladin wrote to them, the Templars replied, 'We shall not swear nor give any guarantee, because we fear our side's treachery.'

Saladin and his advisors feared that the Crusaders would not keep their word and after receiving the ransom money, the Crusaders would keep the more senior prisoners hostage to seek more.[33] Ibn al-Athīr's account demonstrates that despite the enthusiasm for the Templars' mass execution in the aftermath of the Battle of Hattin 1187, the order was seen by their enemies as having more integrity than the lords of Outremer or the Crusader kings.

The *Itinerarium Regis Ricardi* proposes that Saladin was delaying the ransom payment and sent envoys and gifts to King Richard to prolong the situation and achieve more advantageous terms.[34] However, on 20 August 1191, the Crusaders had the Muslim prisoners brought outside the city and brutally executed in sight of Saladin's advance guard.[35] Richard justified his actions in a letter to the Abbot of Clairvaux dated 1 October 1191:

> On Saladin's behalf it had been agreed that the Holy Cross and 1,500 living prisoners would be handed over to us, and he fixed a day for us when all this was to be done. But the time-limit expired, and, as the pact which he had agreed was entirely made void, we quite properly had the Saracens that we had in custody – about 2,600 of them – put to death.[36]

Historian Mayer asserts that Richard had the prisoners executed because Saladin was unable to secure the resources required in the agreed surrender of Acre,[37] while Bahā' al-Dīn suggests that Richard's motive for ordering the mass execution is unclear. He informs that it was believed that Richard 'had killed them in revenge for their men who had been killed or that the king of England had decided to march to Ascalon to take control of it and did not think it wise to leave that number in his rear'.[38] The *Itinerarium Regis Ricardi* asserts that the decision to execute the several thousand prisoners was not Richard's alone, but agreed by 'a council of greater people, which decided not to waste time waiting any longer for anything'.[39]

Richard has been widely criticised for this act, as historian Ashbridge explains: 'No event in Richard's career has elicited more controversy or criticism than this calculated carnage.'[40]

THE BATTLE OF ARSUF

With Acre made secure, Richard continued the campaign to recapture the Christian losses, and his forces left Acre on 22 August 1191 to begin the perilous march south to the port of Jaffa. Richard led the remaining Crusaders alongside the Duke of Burgundy, who led the French in their king's absence. When the Third Crusaders left Acre, it was a few days short of two years since the siege of Acre had begun. The recovery of Jerusalem was the ultimate aim of the Crusade, but first Richard marched along the coast towards Jaffa to establish a coastal base to retake the Holy City.

Historian Jonathan Riley-Smith proposes that this march south and the ensuing battle demonstrated the prowess of Richard's leadership.[41]

King Richard was in the vanguard, while the Duke of Burgundy and the French were in the rearguard. The army marched along the coast and was supported by a fleet that shadowed the army, protected its right flank and provided supplies to the troops. Mayer describes Richard's coastal march as 'a model of Crusade tactics' and maintaining this strict formation while marching was vital to keeping the army intact. Mayer details that at the centre of the column were three squadrons of knights and the left flank was protected by dense infantry formations.[42]

Richard's march south mirrored Louis VII's march across Asia Minor in the Second Crusade. The Templars played the same vital role in being given command of the rearguard. During the lengthy march, the Crusaders were vulnerable to repeated attacks from Saladin's forces. In one such attack, the Templars suffered significant losses, losing many horses that had been defending the foot of the column from Saladin's troops.[43]

Although the Crusader army was repeatedly attacked during the march to Jaffa, Saladin decided to change tactics and go for an all-out assault on Richard's forces. The Crusaders had safely marched through the forest of Arsuf, fearing an ambush from Saladin's forces. However, it was on the open ground south of the forest that the Crusader column was vulnerable to Saladin's superior numbers. On 7 September, on the plains north of the town of Arsuf, Saladin launched a heavy attack. His forces numbered around 30,000, while the Crusader army stood at around half that total.[44] In a letter, Richard describes, 'We set out for Jaffa, but on approaching Arsuf we were met and savagely attacked by Saladin and his Saracens.'[45]

The *Itinerarium Regis Ricardi* details that Richard established his forces into twelve squadrons, which were then divided into five battalions. It provides further details of the battalions:

> That day the Templars commanded the first battalion of the army. After them the Bretons and Angevins marched in order; after them in the third battalion King Guy with the Poitevins; in the fourth battalion the Normans and English who had been assigned to convey the royal Standard; the Hospitallers formed the last battalion. That rearguard was made up of an elite body of knights, divided into separate squadrons [...] The archers and crossbowmen were drawn up in the last rank of all, bringing up the rear of the army.[46]

The rearguard faced the lion's share of the onslaught as Richard had organised his troops to not directly engage the enemy but in a defensive formation that could continue the march under heavy attack. Victory for the Crusaders would have been ensuring the army's survival until Arsuf was reached. The Hospitallers were charged with defending the foot of the column and were so strained by the weight of the violence inflicted on them that they twice pleaded with King Richard to be allowed to fight back against Saladin's forces with a cavalry charge. However, Richard denied these requests, even though the second plea came from the Hospitaller Grand Master Garnier of Nablus.

The Crusaders' archers were able to keep Saladin's forces back with continuous volleys, and drew praise from the *Itinerarium Regis Ricardi*, which described them as 'essential' and 'valiant'.[47] However, the knights in the rearguard could not stand the inaction against the onslaught indefinitely and charged at Saladin's forces against Richard's orders.

The unauthorised charge began with the cry of 'Saint George!' from two knights who could not continue to hold back, recorded as the Hospitaller marshal and Baldwin of Carron. The Hospitallers charged, followed by the Count of Champagne, James of Avesnes, Count Robert of Dreux and their knights. This charge was eventually joined by King Richard and his retinue, who were forced to follow the Hospitallers as the tightly packed defensive formation had been thrown into disarray.

The cavalry charge needed to inflict a devastating blow to the morale of Saladin's forces or the Crusaders would be overrun. Fortunately for the Crusaders, the Hospitallers' charge had caught Saladin's forces unaware.[48] The *Itinerarium Regis Ricardi* described how the 'Turks who had deliberately dismounted from their horses to fire darts and arrows more easily at our people all lost their heads at once in that military engagement; the knights knocked them down and our foot soldiers beheaded them'.[49]

Saladin's forces attempted a counter-attack, but the Crusaders forced them to retreat to Arsuf Forest. Although neither side won a decisive victory, as both armies were still intact, the Crusader army was able to continue its march to Arsuf. Ibn al-Athīr believes that had the Crusaders continued to pursue, 'the rout would have continued, and the Muslims would have been destroyed'.[50] Saladin's losses were estimated at 7,000, including thirty-two emirs, and the Crusaders claimed their losses to be less than a tenth of those.

The Crusaders did lose one of their earliest leaders, James of Avesnes, one of the first to answer the call to Crusade, who arrived with a fleet at Acre in September 1189. His body was found by a search party of Templars and Hospitallers, and he was buried at Arsuf.

The Battle of Arsuf was not a decisive victory for the Crusaders as Saladin's army remained intact, but it was a significant dent in his unbeatable image.

It was the Christians' first major victory in the field against Saladin since the disaster at Hattin in 1187. Mayer explains that the significance of the victory went beyond the Crusader columns' survival because it meant that the 'legend of Saladin's superiority had been destroyed'.[51]

The Crusaders' victory belonged to the Hospitallers, who had held the rearguard against Saladin's heavy attacks and then subsequently put those troops to flight with a devastating charge. The Templars were not involved in the Hospitallers' attack as they were leading the vanguard, and although the Templars had repelled attacks from the rear at great cost earlier in the march, the day belonged to the Hospitallers.

11

THE END OF THE THIRD CRUSADE

THE MARCH TO JERUSALEM

A few days after the victory at Arsuf, the Crusaders captured the port of Jaffa. Saladin changed his tactics following his defeat and adopted a more defensive strategy. Ibn al-Athīr recorded that the Crusaders were now perceived as stronger and better resourced following their capture of Acre. In a meeting between Saladin's emirs, it was decided that Ascalon should be demolished to prevent the Crusaders from capturing it and the garrison suffering the same horrific fate as those in Acre. The demolition of Ascalon began on 11 September, and when word reached Richard, he called a council of Crusader nobles to determine how the Crusade should proceed.[1]

Richard pressed his desire to march on Ascalon, drive off Saladin's forces and prevent the port's destruction. However, this view was not shared by the nobility, who, according to the *Itinerarium Regis Ricardi*, believed the best strategy was to rebuild Jaffa so they could hasten their march to Jerusalem. The majority of those at the council favoured this approach, so Ascalon was destroyed without a struggle. The author of the *Itinerarium Regis Ricardi* is highly critical of this decision:

> O destructive stubbornness of the idle! The more they seemed to be taking wise precautions for themselves and conveniently avoiding labour and expense, the more they would repent later! For if they had driven the Turks out of Ascalon then, the whole land could have been cleared of them.[2]

Here, the Crusader momentum stalled as the forces camped at Jaffa while the port's defences were strengthened. However, this gave Saladin the time to complete the demolition of Ascalon.

Saladin left Ascalon on 23 September and travelled to Ramla to oversee that castle's destruction too.[3] The Crusaders could not solidify their hold on recaptured territory if the fortifications were destroyed.

The outcome of the council at Jaffa was a failure of Richard's kingship. As Crusades historian Ashbridge explains, 'Richard seems not to have recognised it at the time, but he had failed a critical test. The events at Jaffa exposed an ominous deficiency in his leadership skills.' Ashbridge proposes that Richard made the mistake of believing the nobles would favour military strategy, not realising that it was 'underpinned by religious ideology – one that relied upon the overwhelming and imperative devotional allure of a target like Jerusalem to create unity of purpose with the army'.[4] The Crusaders' failure to march on Ascalon led to the port's demolition, and now that the Crusade had stalled at Jaffa, Saladin had been able to dismantle the fortified places between Jerusalem and the coast.

The Crusaders remained at Jaffa for several weeks before attempting the march to Jerusalem. However, the further the Crusaders marched from the coastline, the more vulnerable they were, as their supply line could be intercepted, leaving Richard's forces isolated. Saladin's dismantling of the fortifications along the road to Jerusalem prevented the Crusaders from establishing a position in the region beyond the coastline.

This period saw several skirmishes. One such event on 29 September almost led to King Richard's capture. He was surveying the surrounding region, accompanied by only a small number of his household, when he was ambushed by Saladin's forces. Richard was able to escape when his companion William de Préaux was mistaken for the king and taken prisoner. Although Richard escaped, several of his retinue knights were killed.[5]

The warrior king was not one to sit on the sidelines, and eventually his reckless risk-taking would catch up with him. Winter began to set in before the Crusaders could reach Jerusalem, only reaching Ramla on 22 November. Saladin moved his forces to Jerusalem, where he remained for much of winter.

Despite the onset of winter, the Crusaders continued to march inland, reaching Latrun Castle on 22 December 1191, less than 20 miles from Jerusalem.[6] Now so close to their goal, the decision was made to return the Crusader army to the coast.

According to the *Itinerarium Regis Ricardi*, the Knights Templar highly influenced this decision. The Templars, along with the Hospitallers and lords of Outremer, urged Richard not to press ahead with an attack on Jerusalem as they would be at risk of being attacked by Turkish forces in the mountains and then the army would be forced into a battle with them as well as Saladin's forces garrisoned in Jerusalem. Also, they argued that even if they succeeded against these odds they would struggle to hold the city, because once it was captured the Crusade would be effectively completed. It was proposed that 'the advance should be deliberately postponed in order to retain their military strength and the common people's forces. These would only remain together for as long as the pilgrimage was not complete, for as soon as their vow was discharged the army would break up.'[7]

The concern about troops immediately returning home upon completion of their Crusading vow was well founded as many Crusaders had done this following the First Crusade in 1099. This lack of manpower in the early eleventh century had been a significant factor in the creation of the Knights Templar, as the Kingdom of Jerusalem's forces were stretched so thin they could not police the roads of the kingdom, which led to the deaths and robbery of many pilgrims.

ASSASSINATION OF A KING

Despite the closeness to the Crusades' ultimate goal, the Crusaders marched back towards the coast and Richard spent January 1192 rebuilding Ascalon. While it was still under construction, the leader of the French Crusaders, the Duke of Burgundy, left and took the French with him. King Richard and the duke had had a dispute over funds, as the duke could not pay his men, but Richard refused to loan him the money.[8] The departure of the duke and the French knights was a significant setback for the Crusaders, as they made up a large part of the army. The duke went to Tyre with Marquis Conrad of Montferrat, who was secretly negotiating with Saladin.

The *Itinerarium Regis Ricardi* reveals the details of the peace deal between Conrad and Saladin:

> He [Conrad] would go to Saladin and swear that he would observe peace between them from then on, and in return he would receive half of the city of Jerusalem, which he would hold from Saladin, and the castles of Beirut and Sidon, and half of the country on this side of the River [Jordan].[9]

Bahā' al-Dīn's account also mentions Conrad's negotiations with Saladin, informing that the Lord of Sidon acted as negotiator for the marquis and adding that several senior Frankish lords had given him their support.[10] The *Itinerarium Regis Ricardi* also named Balian of Ibelin as a co-conspirator, the man who survived the Battle of Hattin and led the defence of Jerusalem.[11] This demonstrated that Conrad, as well as being married to the late Queen Sibylla's younger sister Isabel, had the support of the remaining lords of Outremer as the man to inherit the crown.

However, this peace treaty would never be enacted as unforeseen events would prevent it. The first incident was the arrival of the Prior of Hereford as an ambassador from England. The ambassador had a letter from Richard's Chancellor, Bishop William of Ely, informing Richard that England was in dire straits and many of the men Richard had appointed to govern in his absence had been expelled and some killed. The letter blamed Richard's brother John and informed that the royal treasury had been spent.[12]

The news demonstrated that Richard could not remain in Outremer indefinitely and needed to return to England. This meant that if Outremer was to survive beyond the Third Crusade, then the Crusader states required a leader to unite behind. They needed a king.

Although Richard had initially backed Guy's claim to the kingship, Outremer needed a king to unify the Crusader states. Guy had failed to do that during his disastrous reign. In April, Richard held counsel with the army leaders, and after explaining his need to depart, he asked which, Guy or Conrad, they wished to be elected as king. The leaders wanted to make Conrad king as he was a stronger leader than Guy.[13]

Guy was left without a kingdom and was compensated with the island of Cyprus, which the Templars had given back to Richard as they had not invested the resources to secure it. He paid 60,000 bezants and promised to pay a further 40,000. However, he never paid his remaining balance to Richard.[14]

Despite being designated the next King of Jerusalem, Conrad would not live to take the crown. Soon after receiving the news from Richard's messengers that he had been elected, Conrad was murdered.

On 28 April, Conrad was riding homeward in Tyre when two men rushed upon him and preceded to stab the marquis. The man who would be king fell dying from his horse, quickly succumbed to his wounds and was buried at the Hospital of St John in Tyre.

The assassins were quickly captured and killed. They had been the marquis' servants and had been lying in wait to carry out the murder.

Initially, there were several suspects for who had ordered Conrad's murder. The *Lyon Eracles* states that the assassins had served the Old Man of the Mountain (Rashīd al-Dīn Sinān), and he had ordered Conrad's murder because the marquis had captured a merchant ship that belonged to him and then had refused to release his ship or his men.[15] Bahā' al-Dīn places the blame on Richard, claiming that the assassins confessed, 'The King of England put us up to it'.[16] Ibn al-Athīr claims that it was Saladin who ordered the assassination of the marquis, explaining that the men disguised themselves as monks and became associated with the Lord of Sidon and Balian's son, the Lord of Ramla. Then, over six months, they gained the trust of the marquis before carrying out his murder.[17]

It is not known for sure who ordered the murder, but Richard did not have much to gain from Conrad's death as he wanted stability to return to the Crusader states to enable him to depart for England. Likewise, Saladin had been negotiating with Conrad to reach an agreement on returning territories of the Kingdom of Jerusalem and ending the Third Crusade. It is possible that the Old Man of the Mountain had him killed because he was deemed too troublesome.

With the death of Conrad, Count Henry of Champagne was the next candidate for the crown. Henry and Isabel were married on 5 May, a few days after Conrad's murder. The kingdom's stability was at stake, so the royal marriage was a priority to secure the future of the royal line. To complicate matters, the queen was pregnant with Conrad's daughter, Maria.[18] Maria was born in 1192 and would eventually rule as Queen of Jerusalem.

With the ascension of Henry of Champagne, Richard had united the lords behind a king and brought some stability to the Crusader states. However, Richard was needed back in England, and it was deemed that although the Crusaders could have recaptured Jerusalem, they would not have been able to hold the city after he had departed for home. Richard needed to bring the Third Crusade to a satisfactory conclusion by negotiating a peace deal with Saladin.

Richard and Saladin had been negotiating since Richard's capture of Jaffa; however, no agreement had been reached as Richard demanded the return of all the Kingdom of Jerusalem's land and a substantial tribute from Egypt. Despite the exchange of gifts between Richard and Saladin, no agreement was reached, and the war continued.[19]

Richard turned his attention towards the border with Egypt, and after a short siege, the Crusaders captured the fortress of Darum on 22 May 1192. In June, the Crusaders once again planned to march upon Jerusalem, a move favoured by the French lords yet still opposed by Richard. He urged against this action as he believed that the Crusaders did not have the forces to capture or hold the city.

To counter the growing frustration and division within the Crusader army, Richard proposed that the direction of the Crusade should be decided by lords of Outremer who sought their lost territories as well as the Templars and Hospitallers. It was agreed that twenty men would determine the best route for the continuation of the Crusade: five Templars, five Hospitallers, five Outremer lords and five French lords. The appointed delegates agreed that the best strategy was to not besiege Jerusalem but to launch a campaign into Egypt. However, this was not well received by the French Crusaders, who demanded they besiege Jerusalem.[20]

With the Christian factions in disagreement, the army began to break up, disheartened that Jerusalem was no longer a viable target, and Richard returned to negotiations with Saladin. However, after lengthy talks throughout July, the two could not reach a peace deal. Richard had given up his demands for the return of Jerusalem, now only asking for monks and priests in the Holy Sepulchre, but the sticking point was the refortification of Ascalon. The sultan demanded that the walls of the city be demolished, but Richard refused.[21]

Following the failed peace negotiations, on 28 July Saladin laid siege to Jaffa, which was vulnerable as Richard had left for Acre. He attacked the fortified port with trebuchets and sappers. The defenders held out until 31 July, when a large section of the curtain wall collapsed after heavy bombardment from trebuchets and was undermined by the sappers. The remaining defenders fled inside the citadel as Saladin's forces captured the town. However, Saladin soon received word that Richard was en route to Jaffa with a relief force for what would be the final battle of the Third Crusade.[22]

THE BATTLE OF JAFFA

When news reached Acre that Saladin had attacked Jaffa, a force of Templars and Hospitallers set out to relive the city by land.[23] Richard, though, made for Jaffa with a sizeable force by sea.

Richard's fleet of ships arrived off the coast of Jaffa on 1 August and motivated Saladin to hastily negotiate the citadel's surrender. Some of those held up in the citadel surrendered, fearing the relief force was too small to liberate them. However, the number of ships off the coast increased to thirty-five, giving those still in the citadel hope that Jaffa would be retaken and their lives saved.

Inspired by the large Crusader fleet, the defenders launched a sortie from the citadel, but it was short-lived as they were soon forced back.[24] The number of Crusader ships had reached fifty-five; their lack of action inspired the desperate actions of a priest mentioned in both the accounts of Bahā' al-Dīn and the *Itinerarium Regis Ricardi*.

The Crusader fleet delayed attempting to land as they believed that Jaffa had been captured and there were no longer any defenders to liberate. However, Richard spotted a priest racing into the sea from Jaffa and swimming towards the Crusader fleet.[25] Bahā' al-Dīn witnessed the same man leap from the citadel and land unhurt in the sand before running into the sea and desperately swimming towards the Crusader ships.[26]

Now knowing that the citadel was still under the control of the defenders, Richard ordered the fleet to head for the shore before launching a reckless attack by jumping into the sea to lead the attack on Saladin's forces at the shore. The *Itinerarium Regis Ricardi* describes that the 'outstanding king shot them down indiscriminately with a crossbow he was carrying in his hand, and his elite companions pursued the Turks as they fled across the beach'.[27]

Richard's actions were witnessed by Bahā' al-Dīn, who described him, 'The first galley to deliver its men on land was his [Richard]. He was red-haired, his tunic was red and his banner was red.'[28] Richard's gamble paid off, and he captured the shore before driving Saladin's forces from Jaffa.

This was the site of the last battle of the Third Crusade, which, although a victory for the Crusaders, demonstrated the vulnerability of any Christian territorial gains further away from the coastline. After the fighting at Jaffa, Richard and Saladin continued their negotiations through envoys, and eventually a compromise was reached between the two leaders.

The negotiations continued throughout August, with Ascalon still proving to be the sticking point. Saladin would recognise Frankish control of Jaffa, but they must surrender Ascalon. Richard could not agree as he had recently rebuilt the port at great expense. Though Richard was suffering from ill health, he was desperate for the war to end so he could return to England to re-establish control over his realm. However, at the end of the month, he agreed to surrender control of Ascalon with the help of Saladin's brother, al-Adil (known as Saphadin to the Crusaders), and a peace agreement was reached and approved by Richard on 2 September 1192. The *Itinerarium Regis Ricardi* provides a detailed summary of the agreement:

> Ascalon, which had always been a threat to Saladin's authority while it remained intact, was to be destroyed. It should not be repaired by anyone within a period of three years beginning from next Easter. But after three years Ascalon would be ceded to whoever was occupying it, irrespective of who had the greatest power. Saladin also conceded that Joppa [Jaffa] should be restored to the Christians. They could inhabit it freely and peacefully, along with all the region around, the coast and the

> mountains. He sanctioned an inviolable peace between the Christians and Saracens. Both should have safe and free passage everywhere, and access to the Lord's Holy Sepulchre without any exactions, and free passage through the whole country for those carrying any sort of goods for sale. Commerce was to be exercised freely.[29]

On 3 September, Saladin ratified the deal and extended the terms of peace to the Principality of Antioch and County of Tripoli, but only as long as Prince Bohemond III and his son Bohemond, the Count of Tripoli, swore an oath to uphold the peace agreement.[30]

The deal meant that Saladin recognised the Frankish territory from Tyre to Jaffa; Jerusalem was to remain under Islamic control, but Christian pilgrims were permitted to enter the city. The Crusaders had by no means secured back the Kingdom of Jerusalem's lost territory, with the Crusader state now reduced to a fraction of coastal land. With Jerusalem not under Christian control, Acre was to become the kingdom's new capital and was known as the Kingdom of Acre. The Knights Templar would move their headquarters to Acre as their infamous first headquarters at the al-Aqsa Mosque, built atop the ruins of the Temple of Solomon, was now truly lost to them.

With the three-year peace deal agreed upon and implemented, Richard departed the Holy Land on 9 October 1192, leaving without ever setting foot in Jerusalem, although he was permitted to by the terms of the agreement. He would never return to the Holy Land. However, before he left, he was able to secure the release of William de Préaux, who was captured when Saladin's forces had believed he was Richard.[31]

Misfortune followed Richard on his journey as bad weather forced the royal fleet to land on the island of Corfu. Unfortunately for Richard, this was within the realm of the Byzantine Emperor Isaac II, whom Richard had greatly angered by capturing the Byzantine-controlled Cyprus, which King Guy now ruled. To remain undetected, he continued with only four attendants but was discovered by Duke Leopold of Austria and captured in Vienna on 20 December.

Although he had made peace with Saladin to attend to the crisis brewing in England, Richard remained a prisoner of the duke for several years until a kingly ransom was paid.[32] He was handed over to Emperor Henry IV, who released him in 1194 after 150,000 marks of silver were paid.[33] Despite his many victories against the great Islamic Sultan Saladin, Richard the Lionheart's Crusade ultimately ended in humiliation when he was held prisoner by the man whose banner he had cast down from the ramparts of Acre.

Fortune continued to turn against Richard, and in 1199 the reckless warrior king ran out of luck and was struck by a crossbow bolt while besieging a castle at Châlus-Chabrol during a war with Phillip II of France, his former Crusading brother in arms, over the Duchy of Normandy. Richard soon died of his injury, and his younger brother John became King of England.

The aftermath of the Third Crusade was disastrous for Saladin and his supporters, as the sultan fell ill with a fever on 20 February 1193, then his condition worsened and he died on 3 March. Of his death, Bahā' al-Dīn wrote, 'This was a day such as had not befallen the Muslims and Islam since the loss of the rightly guided Caliphs. The citadel, the city, the world was overwhelmed by such a sense of loss as God alone could comprehend.'[34]

Following Saladin's death, his empire was split among his sons. His eldest, al-Afdal, became the ruler of Damascus, Jerusalem and all the districts south to Darum. Al-Aziz took control of Egypt, and az-Zahir Ghazi took control of Aleppo. Saladin had united the Muslim territories under a single purpose. But now that he was gone, his empire was split between three brothers. Still, the new status quo would not last, as Saladin's brother, al-Adil, the man who had been instrumental to Richard and Saladin's peace deal, had eyes on reuniting his brother's empire.

The significance of the Third Crusade and events leading up to it mark the end of not just Outremer's supremacy of the Holy Land but also the dominance of the Knights Templar. Before the disaster at Hattin, the Templars had acquired significant lands through Outremer and strengthened their position with the construction of castles. The Templar castle at Gaza gave them control over the Kingdom of Jerusalem's border with Egypt.

Their role as a premier fighting force saw them closely aligned with the military strategies of the Kings of Jerusalem, such as the successful campaign against Egypt by King Amalric in 1167 and the leper king's victory over Saladin at Montgisard in 1177. But however entangled the Knights Templar were with the successes of the Crusader states, they were also highly influential in their defeats. The Templars failed to hold the strategically vital newly constructed fortress at Jacobs Ford in 1179. Their most significant failure was their part in convincing King Guy to move away from the well-watered campsite at the Springs of Cresson, which led to the massacre at Hattin in 1187 and the eventual destruction of the Kingdom of Jerusalem.

Since the early twelfth century, the infamous Knights Templar had grown rich and expanded their territories across Outremer and Europe, but their success was intrinsically linked to the success of the Crusader states. Despite playing a significant role in the Third Crusade, they were unable to take the city of Acre or drive Saladin's army from the field, and their Grand Master Gérard de Ridefort was killed in the Battle of Acre in 1189. It was the rival religious order, the Knights Hospitaller, who helped Richard win the Battle of Arsuf in 1191.

Despite the successes of the Third Crusade, Outremer would never be as powerful as it had been prior to the disaster at Hattin, and neither would the Knights Templar reach the same heights again. Outremer continued as a sliver of coastal land, and the Templars continued to fight for its survival, but if Outremer should fall and the Franks be pushed back into the sea, the Knights Templar would have no purpose.

The eventual decline of the Crusader states over the next 100 years would run parallel to the fortunes of the Order of the Knights Templar.

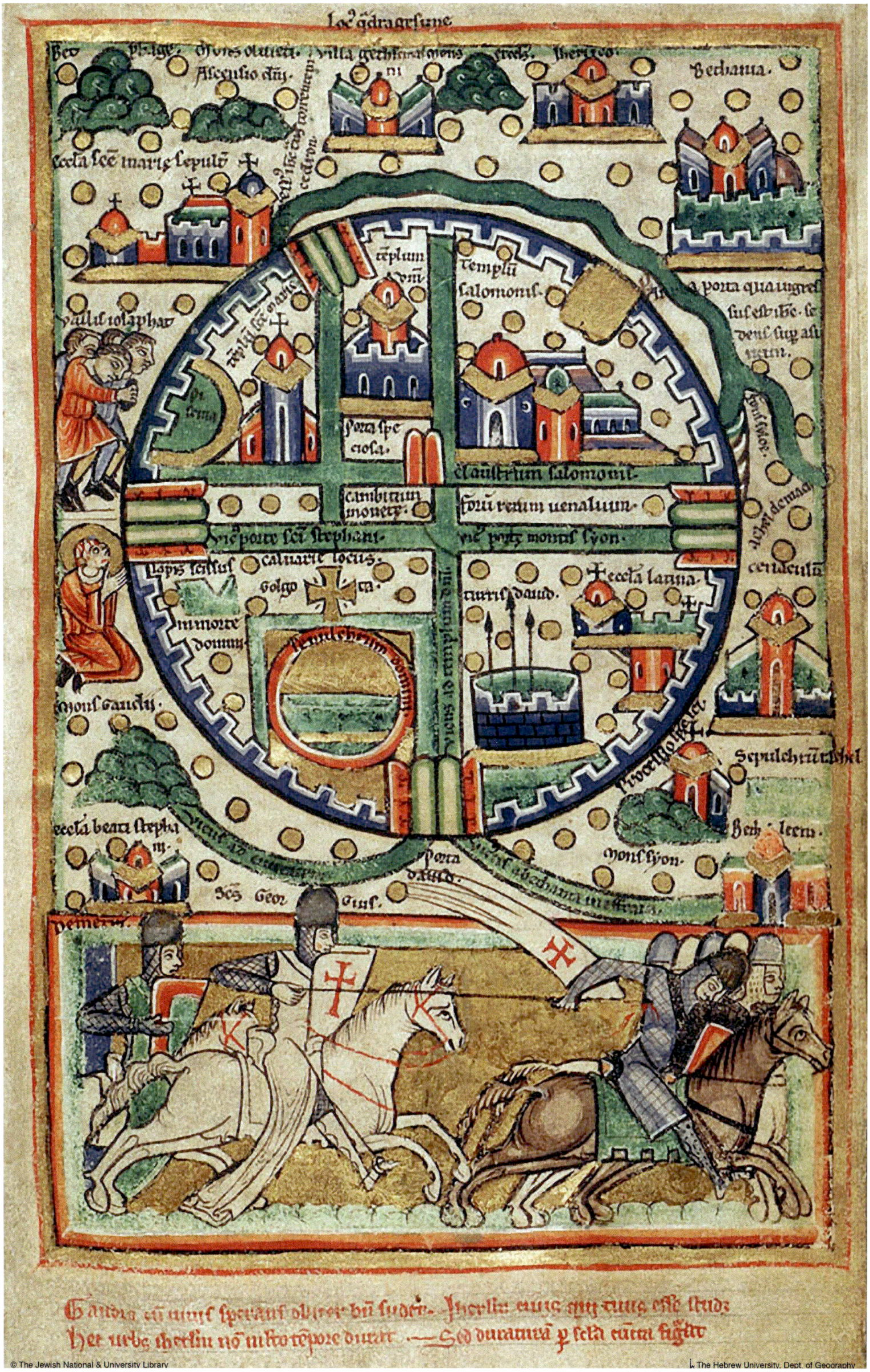

A twelfth-century map of Jerusalem. (Zev Radovan/Alamy Stock Photo)

Ruins of a Crusader castle at Sidon. (Shutterstock)

Templar tunnels under Acre that connected the Templar fortress to Acre's port. (Shutterstock)

Rosslyn Chapel, Scotland – a site associated with the Templar myths of the Holy Grail and Freemasonry. (Shutterstock)

The Battle of Mansurah from a fourteenth-century manuscript. (incamerastock/Alamy Stock Photo)

Robert Eddison as the Grail Knight in the 1989 film *Indiana Jones and the Last Crusade*. (Landmark Media/Alamy Stock Photo)

Joakim Nätterqvist as Templar knight Arn Magnusson in the 2007 film *Arn: The Knight Templar* (*ARN: TEMPELRIDDAREN*). (Moviestore Collection Ltd/Alamy Stock Photo)

Joakim Nätterqvist as Templar knight Arn Magnusson in the 2007 film *Arn: The Knight Templar* (*ARN: TEMPELRIDDAREN*). (Moviestore Collection Ltd/Alamy Stock Photo)

James Purefoy as Templar knight Thomas Marshal in the 2011 film *Ironclad*. (AJ Pics/Alamy Stock Photo)

PART 3

THE FALL OF THE KNIGHTS TEMPLAR

12

THE FIFTH CRUSADE AND THE CAPTURE OF DAMIETTA

THE AFTERMATH OF THE THIRD CRUSADE

After the death of Saladin in 1193, the territories of his vast empire were split among his sons. However, they would soon lose control of their lands to Saladin's brother, al-Adil, known as Saphadin in the west (derived from his honorific title, Saif al-Dīn, which means Sword of the Faith).

Al-Adil was able to take control of Damascus from Saladin's eldest son, al-Afdal, in June 1196. He did not have his father's leadership skills and lost the support of the emirs, with his most trusted supporter, Izz al-Dīn, switching his allegiance over to al-Adil. With his uncle now in control of Damascus, Saladin's eldest son was forced to flee into exile.[1]

Al-Adil's ambition did not stop with Damascus, and he soon took control of Egypt. One of Saladin's other sons, al-Aziz, ruled Egypt following his father's death and had allied with his uncle to wrestle Damascus from his older brother. However, on 22 November 1198 his horse stumbled, causing him to fall, and he died soon after in Cairo. After his death, his brother, al-Afdal was invited to rule Egypt as regent, as al-Aziz's son was too young to rule alone.[2]

As the ruler of Egypt, al-Afdal now had the strength to take revenge on his uncle and remove him from Damascus. With the support of another brother, az-Zahir Ghazi, the Emir of Aleppo, he laid siege to Damascus in June 1199. Al-Afdal was unable to take control of the city and was forced to abandon the siege in December after the arrival of al-Adil's son, al-Kāmil, with significant reinforcements, and returned home due to the harsh winter conditions.[3]

Al-Adil moved to take control of Egypt for himself and invaded, defeating al-Afdal in battle on 25 January 1200. After fleeing to Cairo, al-Afdal surrendered control of Egypt to his uncle and was given minor lands as compensation.[4] Soon, al-Zahir made peace with al-Adil, but he was able to keep control of Aleppo, unlike his brother, al-Afdal, who had lost control first of Damascus and now Egypt to their uncle.

In a relatively short amount of time, al-Adil had reunited his brother's empire, and once again the diminished Frankish Crusader states were surrounded by a united Islamic Empire from Aleppo to Cairo. The timely reforging of Saladin's empire by his brother had extinguished any hope the Franks had of taking advantage of the disunity between al-Adil and Saladin's heirs.

Count Henry of Champagne was the leader of the Crusader states, and he was now the ruler of the newly created state, the Kingdom of Acre (as the Third Crusade ended with Jerusalem still being part of Saladin's empire). However, despite his marriage to the rightful heir, Princess Isabella, Henry chose not to use the title king but went by 'lord of the kingdom of Jerusalem'.[5]

Guy de Lusignan's reign as King of Cyprus ended abruptly with his death in 1194, after which he was succeeded by his brother, Aimery. In his short reign, he restructured the island's society to Western feudalism by redistributing territory to create hundreds of new vassals from the nobles who had been disinherited by Saladin's conquest of the Kingdom of Jerusalem.[6]

The end of the twelfth century brought some territorial gains for the Franks as Sidon and Beirut were captured by German Crusaders in 1197. The recaptured territories once again connected the County of Tripoli to the Kingdom of Acre. However, in the same year, the port of Jaffa, from which the Crusaders had successfully repelled an attack from Saladin's forces in 1192, was captured again by al-Adil. When the relief force from Acre arrived at Jaffa, they discovered the port was already lost.

Jaffa might have been relieved had the army not been delayed by the unexpected death of Count Henry of Champagne. The Lord of the Kingdom of Jerusalem had fallen to his death from a window – it is recorded as a sudden accident in both the accounts of Ibn al-Athīr and the *Lyon Eracles*, with the latter detailing that he fell through the window because the railing failed when he leant on it.[7]

Aimery de Lusignan was chosen as the man to take the crown of Jerusalem, which meant that he was to become Queen Isabella's fourth husband. The monarchy's future was directly from Isabella and not from her later husbands. She had no children with her first husband, Humphry of Toron, but with Conrad of Montferrat she had Maria, who would be

Queen of Jerusalem from 1205. With Henry of Champagne she had three daughters, Margaret, Alice and Phillipa, and three children with Aimery de Lusignan, but they would not rule as it was Conrad's daughter who inherited her mother's title.

Aimery died on 1 April 1205 from eating an excessive amount of fish, and Queen Isabella died soon after.[8] Princess Maria succeeded her mother as queen, with John of Ibelin, who was chosen as regent and ruled during her minority. John was the eldest son of Balian of Ibelin, the defender of Jerusalem, who had died in 1193. John of Ibelin was regent until Maria married John of Brienne in 1210. Maria died in 1212, and King John of Jerusalem ruled as regent for his and the late Queen Maria's daughter, Isabella. The direct line of succession would become convoluted through various regencies and marriages.

Pope Celestine III died on 8 January 1198, and his successor, Innocent III, began calling for a new Crusade to recapture Jerusalem. Innocent believed that the Fourth Crusade should be led by the Pope himself as the supreme Christian leader, not by kings.[9] Innocent's desire to remove control would bring about avoidable setbacks that would change the course of the Crusade and have devastating consequences for one of the eastern powers.

The Fourth Crusade would not be led by kings but by three counts: Theobald of Champagne, Louis of Blois and Baldwin of Flanders and Hainault. Count Theobald died in 1201 before the Crusaders set sail. Before his death, he and the other counts had sent envoys to negotiate passage across the sea with the Venetians. It was agreed that for 85,000 marks, the Venetians would provide transport for 4,500 knights and 20,000 infantry and the target of the Crusade was Cairo, not Jerusalem. The army was to muster by 1202, with Cairo the target of future Crusades because in order for Jerusalem to be retaken and retained, the Ayyubid power would first need to be broken in Egypt.[10]

The Marquis Boniface of Montferrat was elected as the new leader of the Fourth Crusade. However, not all Crusaders mustered at the same point, and a far smaller force assembled at Venice in 1202; the Venetians had prepared for an army of around 30,000, but only 13,000 troops arrived.[11] Despite the diminished forces, the Venetians demanded the Crusaders pay the agreed amount, but the leaders could not raise it.

Kings have deeper pockets than counts, so if Innocent III had not excluded the kings of Europe from planning the Crusade, the following events may not have come to pass. To fulfil their debt, the Venetians required the Crusader army to attack the Christian city of Zara (now known as Zadar and located on the east coast of modern-day Croatia), which had recently rebelled against the Venetians. The Crusaders had little choice but to attack the city, even though it was under the protection of the Pope and the King of Hungary, who had also taken the cross.

Although this caused much disagreement among the senior Crusaders, the army set sail in October, and Zara was captured on 24 November 1202. The scandalous decision of a Crusader army to attack and sack a Christian city set a precedent that would be disastrous for the Byzantine Empire.

The Crusader army stayed at Zara for the winter, and here they received envoys from the German King Phillip of Swabia and Alexius Angelus, whose father, Isaac II, had been the Byzantine Emperor before being deposed and blinded by his brother, Alexius III in 1195. Alexius Angelus had escaped captivity and sought the assistance of Phillip of Swabia, who was married to Alexius' sister, Irene. Despite being the King of Germany, Phillip could not provide the forces needed to remove Alexius III from power; however, the standing Crusader army at Zara could provide the required manpower.

The envoys brought an overly generous proposal from Alexius Angelus for the Crusaders to restore his father, Isaac II, to power. In return, the Byzantine pretender promised to unify the Orthodox Church with Rome, solve the Crusaders' financial troubles and provide troops for a campaign in Outremer. According to Geoffrey of Villehardouin, the envoys of King Phillip of Swabia stated:

> He knows that you have spent your property and that you are poor; he will give you 200,000 marks of silver and provisions for all the members of the army, humble and noble. He will himself go with you to the land of Babylon or will send thither with you (if you think it better) 10,000 men at his expense. This service he will perform for you during one year. And so long as he lives, he will maintain at his own expense 500 knights in the land of Outremer, to guard the land.[12]

The offer was far too good for the Crusader leaders to turn down. However, Alexius' position was so weak that his only currency to wield was promises of generosity, whether they were feasible or not. Trusting in the promises of the deposed emperor's son, the Crusader army attacked Constantinople on 17 July. Alexius III soon fled the city, and Isaac II was restored as emperor, with his son, now Alexius IV, ruling as co-emperor.

Once restored to power, Alexius IV found it challenging to fulfil the promises made to the Crusaders, who remained outside the city. The deal struck with the Crusaders was very unpopular with the clergy and citizens of Constantinople, who resented that a foreign army was camped outside.

Alexius IV and Isaac II were overthrown and killed in January 1204, and Alexius V, from the rival Doukas family became emperor.[13] The new emperor was openly anti-Latin, so the Crusaders planned to break up the Byzantine Empire and create a new state. They attacked Constantinople on 12 April 1204 and captured the city within a day. It was then ransacked for several days. In his account, Nicetas describes the violent acts of the Crusaders, writing:

> Nobles wandered about ignominiously, those of venerable age in tears, the rich in poverty. Thus it was in the streets, on the corners, in the temple, in the dens, for no place remained unassailed or defended the suppliants. All places everywhere were filled full of all kinds of crime. Oh, immortal God, how great the afflictions of the men, how great the distress![14]

The city was stripped of its wealth and relics such as the blood of Christ, a piece of the True Cross, part of St John, an arm of St James, a foot of St Cosmas and a tooth of St Laurence, as well as relics of another twenty-eight male saints and eight female saints and fragments from sixteen holy sites.[15] The Crusaders' ill-gotten gains were estimated to be valued at 900,000 silver marks, 500,000 of which were given to the Venetians to settle the Crusaders' outstanding debts.[16]

Now that the Crusaders' debts were settled, the army was free to travel to Outremer, but this never happened. After the conquest of Constantinople, senior Fourth Crusader Baldwin of Flanders was elected as the first emperor of the newly created Romania, the Latin Empire of Constantinople. The newly conquered territory was then divided among the French and Venetians, and several new Latin states were created, such as the Principality of Achaea, which consisted of southern Greece and the Duchy of Athens. The chosen Crusade leader, Marquis Boniface of Montferrat, who had failed to be elected as the new emperor, echoing the actions of the First Crusaders hundreds of years before, carved out a kingdom for himself – the Kingdom of Thessalonica, stretching from the coastal city of Thessalonica, south towards Athens. The Venetians acquired many of the islands, including Crete and Rhodes.

The Fourth Crusade destroyed the power of the Byzantine Empire, ending the Crusading role of the Byzantine Emperor, who had been so influential in Crusading since Alexius I appealed to the Latin West for aid in 1095, which led to the First Crusade. While the Fourth Crusade was successful for its leaders, who had won themselves new land and destroyed the seat of the Latin Church rival, it had spectacularly failed in its original aim to help the cause in Outremer.

Pope Innocent III had called for a new Crusade to retake Jerusalem; however, that target was changed to Cairo to try to break Ayyubid power. The Fourth Crusade never left Europe and instead subjected fellow Christians to horrific violence and created new Latin Crusader states in the conquered Byzantine territories. These would not last long. The Kingdom of Thessalonica was retaken by a former Byzantine state, the Despotate of Epirus, and by 1261 Constantinople was recaptured by the Empire of Nicaea, founded after the Fourth Crusade and seen as the Byzantine successor state.

A NEW CRUSADE

Despite the Fourth Crusaders attacking and sacking a Christian city, Pope Innocent III called for another Crusade to the Holy Land. The Fourth Crusade had weakened the states of Outremer when many Frankish knights left for the newly created Latin states in Greece as these new lands were far from the Ayyubid Empire, which stretched from Cairo to Aleppo.

In November 1215, Innocent III held the Fourth Council of the Lateran, which debated issues such as Transubstantiation, the limits of translating the Bible into vernacular language and another Crusade to the Holy Land. Innocent III would not live to see the results of his planning as he died in July 1216, before the Crusader armies could muster in 1217 in the southern Italian ports.[17]

Innocent was succeeded by Honorius III, who attempted to convince Frederick to uphold his crusading vow but was forced to negotiate the German king's involvement as Frederick wanted the Church to bestow on him the title of Holy Roman Emperor. The negotiations continued as other great Christian lords began to arrive in Italy with their armies.[18]

The Kings of England and France, despite playing a prominent role in the previous Crusade, were too preoccupied because King John of England and King Phillip III of France had been at war over the English lands on the Continent. King John, significantly weakened by the losses of these lands, became engaged in a civil war with his barons, who turned to Phillip III's eldest son, Prince Louis, to depose the English monarch.

The King of Germany and Sicily, Frederick II, took the cross in 1215, but he postponed his involvement. While Frederick stalled in August 1217, King Andrew II of Hungary and Duke Leopold VI of Austria and their armies assembled in Spalato (Split, in modern-day Croatia) and soon sailed for Outremer.

In Acre, King Andrew and Duke Leopold joined with King John of Jerusalem, Prince Bohemond IV of Antioch, King Hugh I of Cyprus, the senior Frankish lords and masters of the military orders, Knights Hospitaller Grand Master Herman of Salza and Knights Templar Grand Master William de Chartres. Unlike the Fourth Crusade, the Knights Templar were involved with the early planning of the Fifth Crusade. The treasurer of the Paris Templars processed the funds raised to finance the new Crusade, and an early plan had King John and Duke Leopold join with the Templar and Hospitaller grand masters in Cyprus, although that proposal was changed.[19]

Despite the armies of the Fifth Crusade mustering in 1217, the momentum stalled as the Crusaders achieved little, which caused King Andrew of Hungary, Prince Bohemond of Antioch and King Hugh of Cyprus (who died on the return journey) to abandon the Crusade in January 1218.[20] In the spring, the Templars, with the assistance of Walter of Avesnes, began constructing Pilgrim Castle, also known as Atlit. This was an impregnable fortress that overlooked the coast south of Hafia and north of Caesarea. Pilgrim Castle replaced the original fort known as Destroit. Oliver of Paderborn described the impressive fort in his chronicle of the Fifth Crusade:

> Two towers were built at the front of the fort of hewn and fitted stones of such greatness that one stone is with difficulty drawn in a cart by two oxen. Both towers are one hundred feet in length and seventy-four in width. Their thickness encloses two sheds to protect soldiers. Their height rising up much exceeds the height of the promontory. Between the two towers a new and high wall was completed with ramparts; and by a wonderful artifice, armed horsemen can go up and down within. Likewise another wall slightly distant from the towers extends from one side of the sea to the other, having a spring of living water enclosed.[21]

Oliver of Paderborn's description indicates how the imposing Castle Pilgrim dominated the region and enabled the Templars to hold the region until 1265, when the castle was surrendered to Mamluk Sultan Baybars. It quickly showed its significance as it became the Crusader fleet's muster point for the next part of the Crusade.

The Crusaders arrived at Castle Pilgrim in May and the Egyptian port of Damietta was chosen as the first target for the Crusaders' invasion of Egypt. Paderborn described Damietta as 'the key to all Egypt', due to its location and fortifications, which provided the ideal base from which to march to Cairo.[22]

The campaign in Egypt hoped to emulate the success of King Amalric against Saladin's uncle, Shirkūh, in 1167 (see Chapter 5), which resulted in Egypt becoming a client state of the Kingdom of Jerusalem, albeit temporarily.

In May 1218, the Crusaders set up camp on an island in the Nile across from Damietta. Al-Adil's son, al-Kāmil, was now the Emir of Egypt and had marched his army from Cairo and assembled his forces before Damietta.[23] The Crusaders began their attack on the chain tower, which stood in the Nile, and connected a huge chain across the river to Damietta to prevent ships from sailing further into Egypt. After months of assault on the tower using siege engines, the Crusaders captured it on 24 August.[24]

The Bishop of Acre, James of Vitry, explains the ingenuity behind the Crusaders' capture of the tower, describing that some Frisians constructed a floatable bridge by tying two boats together and constructing on top 'a rotatable bridge on which they put a ladder and a fortification to protect the whole machine'.[25] After months of failed assaults, the bridge allowed the Crusaders to surround the towers, and the attackers built a huge fire that forced the defenders to surrender.[26]

Soon after the Crusaders captured the chain tower, Saladin's brother, al-Adil, who had reunited Saladin's empire at the expense of Saladin's sons, suddenly died. If the Crusaders hoped that the death of such a senior figure would weaken the Muslim territories and diminish the strength of his son, al-Kāmil, they were disappointed. The Crusaders failed to establish a foothold on the east bank of the Nile from which to attack the city of Damietta.

Soon after the capture of the tower, Cardinal-Bishop Pelagius arrived at the Crusader camp with reinforcements. He was Pope Honorius III's Papal Legate, and was there to ensure that the Crusade aligned with Honorius' vision for the Crusade.

Throughout the winter and into 1219, the Crusaders remained unable to take advantage of the death of al-Adil and the two armies were locked in a stalemate. The conditions for both sides were dire, with Oliver of Paderborn describing the state of the camp, 'Many of the army were struck down by a certain plague against which physicians could find no remedy in all their skill. A sudden pain attacked the feet and legs, and at the same time, corrupt flesh covered the gums and teeth.'[27]

Despite the deadlock and unbearable conditions, the Crusaders were able to cross the Nile to the east bank on 7 February 1219 because al-Kāmil had deserted the camp. He had received word of a plan to overthrow him and was forced to leave with his army. The Crusaders found the camp defenceless and were able to plunder all that remained.

With the arrival of his brother, al-Mu'azzam, al-Kāmil prevented the coup and banished its architect, Emir Ibn al-Mustūb, from Egypt.[28] Although al-Kāmil had prevented the coup, the Crusaders had surrounded Damietta. The situation in the city was dire, and its defenders and citizens were suffering so greatly that he proposed a treaty that would finally achieve the aims of the Third Crusade. Paderborn recorded:

> Therefore the Sultan fearing dearth and famine, and also because of his desire to keep Damietta, offered the Christians a peace with Coradin his brother on these terms: that he would give back the Holy Cross which had formerly been captured in the victory of Saladin, along with the Holy City and all the captives who could be found alive throughout the kingdom of Babylon and Damascus, and also funds to repair the walls of Jerusalem; in addition he would restore the kingdom of Jerusalem entirely, except Krak [*sic*] and Montréal, for the possession of which he would offer tribute for as long as the truce would last.[29]

The generous treaty would have finally completed the mission of the Third Crusaders, who first laid siege to Acre in 1189 with the goal of recapturing Jerusalem. Even though the Crusaders had not yet captured a significant territory, losing Damietta would leave Egypt vulnerable as it would give the Franks the ideal stronghold for an invasion.

The King of Jerusalem and senior French Crusaders welcomed the treaty as they believed that the return of Jerusalem to Christian rule would benefit all of Christendom. However, Pelagius, the Templars, the Hospitallers and senior Church figures believed that capturing Damietta was the most essential action for the future of Outremer and vehemently opposed the treaty.[30] So, despite it returning Jerusalem to Christian control, the Crusaders rejected the treaty and continued with the siege of Damietta.

In the immediate short term, rejecting the treaty seemed the correct strategy as the city surrendered to the Crusaders on 5 November 1219. According to Paderborn, upon entering the city, the Crusaders learned of the horrific fate of its inhabitants as they 'found its streets strewn with the bodies of the dead, wasting away from pestilence and famine; very much gold and silver, silk stuffs of the merchants in abundance, various household goods in superabundance'.[31]

Even though the situation inside the city was grim, the Crusaders had captured a vital base that they could use to extend Outremer's southern frontier and prepare for the next phase in their conquest of Egypt. Following the capture of Damietta, the Templars raided the coastal town of Burlus to find desperately needed resources. They returned with many spoils, such as 100 camels, horses, mules, oxen and goats, as well as captives, clothing and household items.[32]

ABJECT FAILURE

With the death of al-Adil and the capture of Damietta, the Crusaders had all the momentum, but instead of pressing on with the invasion, they stalled. At Damietta, the Templar Grand Master William de Chartres died, having been ill since 1217 before heading to Egypt.[33] He had been grand master since 1210, and his death caused a crisis of leadership, forcing the order to quickly elect Peter de Montaigu to provide much-needed authority for the Crusade.

In the spring, King John of Jerusalem left Damietta to pursue a claim to the throne of Armenia and to defend Outremer from attack by al-Mu'azzam, the Emir of Damascus and brother of al-Kāmil. Duke Leopold VI had returned to Austria in May of 1219, so in King John's absence, Pelagius became the leader of the remaining coalition of Crusaders, and in Damietta he waited for the arrival of Frederick II.

August saw a fleet of fourteen ships laden with supplies and pilgrims sent by the Doge of Venice intercepted by an Egyptian fleet, who captured the ships, took those aboard captive and seized the Crusaders' much-needed resources.[34] With their forces depleted and supplies captured, the army could only wait for reinforcements to swing momentum back to the Crusaders.

The spring of 1221 saw the Crusaders' prospects improve as reinforcements began to arrive from Germany. In October 1220, Frederick II was crowned emperor in Rome by Pope Honorius, and to demonstrate his commitment to the Crusade, which he had delayed while negotiating with Rome, he sent Duke Louis I of Bavaria. The duke arrived in 1221 with other nobles, including the Bishop of Passau, the Marquis of Baden, and Count Guy of Breinne, which gave the Crusaders reinforcements.[35] Their ranks were further swelled by the return of King John of Jerusalem in the summer of 1221.

After much criticism of their inaction from within the camp, the Crusade leaders held a council to decide on the next course of action. The council included Duke Louis, the grand masters of the Templars and Hospitallers, the Teutonic Grand Master Hermann of Salaza and other senior nobility, who were all unanimous in their support for the Crusader army to march further into Egypt.[36] Reinforced by new arrivals, the Crusaders finally made ready to continue their invasion of Egypt nearly two years after the capture of Damietta.

The Crusaders marched out of Damietta with an army of around 1,200 knights, 400 archers and a vast number of infantry, who were escorted along the Nile bank by the large Crusader navy.[37] They marched south to Mansourah, where al-Kāmil had stationed his army, which he had reinforced following the Crusaders' lengthy indecisiveness at Damietta. At that time, al-Kāmil was joined by his brother, al-Ashraf, while al-Mu'azzam was heading to Damietta.

The Egyptian navy attacked the Crusader vessels, taking control of the Nile. Al-Kāmil had several of his ships sunk in the Nile to prevent the Crusader fleet from passing and cutting the army off from Damietta.[38] Despite gaining this advantage, he once again offered the Crusaders generous terms for the return of Damietta. Ibn al-Athīr details that the Crusaders were offered the return of 'Jerusalem, Ascalon, Tiberias, Sidon, Jabala, Lattakia and all that Saladin had conquered from the Franks on the coast'. The Crusaders still did not agree, demanding the return of the castle at Kerak and 300,000 dinars to rebuild Jerusalem.[39] Again, had the Crusaders accepted this treaty, the aims of the Third Crusade would have been achieved.

In August, the Nile River continued to rise and the Crusaders were cut off from Damietta. With the river blocked, they could only wait within their camp for reinforcements as the ground flooded. By 26 August, the Crusaders' position became untenable and the army was forced to march back to Damietta. The Knights Templar took the rearguard to maintain order during the hasty retreat.

Maintaining a disciplined march to prevent catastrophe during deadly situations was a role that the Knights Templar had carried out successfully during both the Second and Third Crusades. Oliver of Paderborn described the hazardous conditions the Crusader army had to traverse through:

> When the banks had been burst to a great extent, the superabundance of water, following the declivity of the reservoirs through conduits, softened the earth, made dry by long drought, into sticky mud which held tight the horses' hoofs; it made the open space of the fields quite impassable and greatly hindered horses and riders.[40]

Despite the extremely difficult conditions, the army held together at first, but even the highly disciplined knights of the temple could not prevent the catastrophe that al-Kāmil unleashed on the Crusader army. He had the sluice gates that were used to control the Nile flooding opened, flooding all the surrounding fields, which left the land impassable for the Crusaders. In a letter, Peter de Montaigu described the horrific situation, writing that the army 'lost its packhorses, equipment, saddlebags, carts, and virtually all its essential supplies in the swamps, so that, bereft of food, it could not advance, retreat or try to find refuge anywhere'.[41]

Despite these conditions, the Crusaders fought on while surrounded on all sides by the waters and al-Kāmil's forces. Oliver of Paderborn describes how the Knights Templar lived up to their reputation as fierce warriors and fought to maintain the Crusaders' vulnerable position: 'The Marshal of the Temple with his battle line which he was leading, raised his banner, turned upon those who were pursuing, and forced them to halt and retreat.'[42]

Although the Templars' military prowess is mentioned in Paderborn's account, this was not a repeat of their role in the victory at Montgisard in 1177, nor was it the total disaster of the Battle of Hattin in 1187. Although the Crusader army was trapped, unable to advance or retreat, echoing the situation of the Franks at Hattin, which also featured water in the crisis, the Crusaders were able to negotiate a semi-favourable surrender. Most of them left with their lives.

Thirteenth-century historian Ibn Wāsil informed that there was a lot of pressure from al-Kāmil's nobles to not grant the Crusaders any concessions and capture them while they were so vulnerable and then move to retake Damietta and attack Outremer. Had al-Kāmil chosen to destroy the Crusader army, the soldiers of the Fifth Crusade and Outremer could have suffered a similar fate to the Frankish army defeated at Hattin. However, Ibn Wāsil explains that al-Kāmil was concerned that if they annihilated the Crusader army, it might inspire another Crusade on a much larger scale.[43]

On 30 August, a treaty was agreed between al-Kāmil and the Crusaders, and the Crusader army surrendered. Essentially, the agreement allowed the Crusaders to leave Egypt with their lives, but they had to surrender Damietta. They had previously been offered Jerusalem, but this treaty did not include the holy city.

The failure to win back Jerusalem and the surrender of Damietta appeared as if the Fifth Crusade achieved nothing, yet the Crusader leaders were able to get some minor concessions. According to Oliver of Paderborn's account, the treaty also included the release of Christian prisoners in Egypt, the release of Muslim prisoners in the Kingdom of Jerusalem and the return of the True Cross. The Crusaders were free to leave Egypt with their belongings and an eight-year truce.

Prisoners were exchanged to ensure the terms were kept, and Damietta surrendered to al-Kāmil. The Crusader hostages included many senior nobles such as the Papal Legate, the Duke of Bavaria, the grand masters of the Templars, Hospitallers and Teutonic Knights, and King John of Jerusalem, while the hostages given to the Crusaders included al-Kāmil's heir and the sons of other prominent nobles.[44]

The terms of the treaty were kept, and Damietta was reluctantly surrendered on 8 September. The Templar Grand Master Peter de Montaigu was one of the senior leaders sent to Damietta to explain the treaty's terms and the requirement to surrender the city. Count Henry of Malta, who had recently arrived with a large fleet, and the Bishop of Acre were displeased with the treaty's terms and wished to defend the city.

Count Henry of Malta and Emperor Frederick had sent the fleet to help with the invasion of Egypt, but they had arrived too late. Despite their protestations, it was obvious that their position in Egypt was untenable; the terms of the treaty were upheld and the city was surrendered. Al-Kāmil also upheld his part of the agreement and fed the retreating Crusader army with bread and maize flour for fifteen days.[45]

The Fifth Crusade ended in abject failure; the Crusaders failed in their attempt to conquer Egypt and weaken Ayyubid power. They also twice rejected the chance to return control of Jerusalem to the Franks and fulfil Richard the Lionheart's Crusading ambition. Instead, after years of struggle and death, the Crusaders left Egypt with their own lives as consolation.

The eight-year truce agreement enabled the Frankish forces to regroup while they waited for the arrival of Emperor Fredrick. Had he joined the Fifth Crusade at its onset, he may have swung the balance in the Crusaders' favour. However, the prospect of his hoped-for arrival caused the hard-won momentum to stall while they waited for the emperor who did not come.

13

NEGOTIATION AND TEMPORARY SUCCESS

RETURN OF A KING

Emperor Frederick II's failure to arrive in Egypt doomed the Fifth Crusade, but despite this, senior Outremer lords and military orders were still planning for Frederick's Crusade. As soon as March 1223, King John met with the prominent Frankish lords, the Hospitaller and Teutonic grand masters and William Cadel, the Commander of the Temple. The council of senior Outremer lords concluded that the next Crusade should be postponed for two years, and Frederick II should be wed to Queen Isabel II of Jerusalem (born in 1212), the daughter of King John, who acted as regent during her minority.[1] Her mother, Queen Maria, died shortly after giving birth to Isabel, who effectively became queen while still a baby.

Frederick and Isabel were married in November 1225 in southern Italy. The wedding was attended by King John and other senior nobles of Outremer. However, once he and Isabel were wed, Frederick immediately assumed the royal title of King of Jerusalem, ending John's reign as regent and self-styled King of Jerusalem.

Although John was no longer king, Frederick's marriage to Isabel was seen as a gain for the next Crusade as, for the first time, a European monarch would be a Crusader and monarch of Outremer.[2] In the previous July, Frederick was named the leader of the next Crusade, and the terms were agreed upon in the Treaty of San Germano. However, this stipulated that if Frederick failed to go on the Crusade by August 1227, he would be excommunicated by the Church.

The next Crusade was known as both the Sixth Crusade and the Crusade of Frederick II. This book will refer to it as the Sixth Crusade because a significant time passed between the surrender of Damietta and

Frederick's voyage to Acre. Also, the political landscape had changed in Outremer with Frederick now the ruler of the Kingdom of Acre by his marriage to Queen Isabel. It is important to make this distinction as the later Crusade, also known as the Crusade of King Louis IX, will be called the Seventh.

Although Frederick was now brought into the Crusader states' royal family, he failed to sail to Acre by the agreed time. However, his failure to keep to his Crusading vow was due to misfortune.

Along with Teutonic Grand Master Hermann of Salza and Landgrave Ludwig IV of Thuringia, he had assembled his army at Brindisi to depart for Acre when there was an epidemic outbreak. Despite this, the Crusader force set sail, but three days into the journey, Frederick became seriously ill and Ludwig died, forcing them to return.[3] This misfortune caused Emperor Frederick, the King of Sicily and now Jerusalem, to be excommunicated by the Church.

Pope Gregory IX, who had succeeded Honorius III after his death in March of that year, officially excommunicated Frederick on 29 September 1227. Gregory IX forbade Frederick from going on Crusade until he had received absolution. However, the Pope's terms of papal control of Sicily were unacceptable to Frederick, and while still an excommunicate, he sailed to join up with his Crusader army in Acre on 28 June 1228. Crusades historian Mayer proposes that Frederick needed to succeed in Outremer as it was the only way to improve his standing in Europe, and he went to Acre at great risk to his lands, as the Pope could have considered Sicily an escheated papal fief.[4]

Shortly before Frederick sailed for Acre, Queen Isabel II tragically died after giving birth to Conrad. Following the death of his wife, Frederick now only had claim to the Kingdom of Jerusalem through his infant son.

Although he was excommunicated, Frederick received a hero's reception at Acre, with the chronicle of Roger of Wendover describing how the Templars and Hospitallers 'went on their knees and worshipped him, kissing his knees; and the whole of the Christian army which was present there gave praise to God for his arrival, being now in hopes that by his means there would be salvation in Israel'. Wendover also reported that Frederick was received with great honour worthy of his position of emperor, but when news reached them that he had been excommunicated, the clergy refused him the kiss of peace, would not dine with him and implored him to make amends with the Pope and the Church.[5] This withdrawal of support for Frederick from the senior leaders of Outremer would lead to a feud between the emperor and the Knights Templar.

The emperor's campaign began in November 1228, marching south with his army towards Jaffa. At first, the Knights Templar and Hospitallers followed a day behind Frederick's army, not wanting to be commanded by an excommunicate. This contrasts with the tightly formatted march of the Third Crusade, where the Templars and Hospitallers were vital for keeping discipline while being attacked on all sides by Saladin's forces. However, once at Arsuf, the military orders returned to the main army after agreeing to a marching order that gave the impression they were not under Frederick's command.[6]

While Frederick marched towards Jaffa, al-Kāmil had marched his army out of Egypt and was camped at Gaza in preparation for an attack on his nephew, al-Nāsir Dā'ūd, who had succeeded his father, al-Mu'azzam, who died on 12 November 1227. Al-Nāsir Dā'ūd appealed to his other uncle, al-Ashraf, for aid and he joined his nephew in Damascus.[7] Frederick arrived in Outremer at an advantageous time as there was an ongoing power struggle between Cairo and Damascus.

Given the hostility between the two centres, al-Kāmil was keen to avoid another conflict with European Crusaders – the Fifth Crusade had lasted several years with significant loss of life and property. Frederick also wanted to avoid a lengthy Crusade as his standing in Europe was not secure after his excommunication. Frederick and al-Kāmil engaged in negotiations through their envoys, with Frederick demanding the deal the sultan had offered to the leaders of the Fifth Crusade – the return of Jerusalem.

After much deliberation, on 27 February Frederick was able to secure terms that would bring a further ten years of peace and return the control of Jerusalem to the Franks. The relinquishing of Jerusalem came with the condition that the al-Aqsa Mosque and Dome of the Rock remained under Islamic control and Muslim pilgrims were permitted access to the city to visit these holy sites.[8]

However, Jerusalem was no longer a fortified city as its walls had previously been demolished on the orders of al-Mu'azzam in 1219 to discourage the Franks from attempting to capture and hold it.[9] But although the Franks could not defend Jerusalem as they had done during Saladin's invasion in 1187, the treaty enabled them to control some of the region around the city when lands to the west were returned to the Kingdom of Jerusalem. A letter from Emperor Frederick to Henry III of England details the territory gained through this treaty:

> The city of Bethlehem is restored to us, and all the country between Jerusalem and that city; as also the city of Nazareth, and all the country

> between Acre and that city; the whole of the district of Turon, which is very extensive, and very advantageous to the Christians; the city of Sidon, too.[10]

The return of these lands enabled the Franks to extend their territory and provided a land corridor from Jaffa to Jerusalem. The Templars, however, would never return to their original headquarters because the al-Aqsa Mosque remained under Muslim control. The treaty fulfilled the aim of the Third Crusade, returned control of Jerusalem to the Christians and provided some security for the city by gaining some of the surrounding region. While Frederick boasted of returning Jerusalem to Christian hands, Ibn al-Athīr writes of the loss of Jerusalem, 'Muslims were outraged and thought it monstrous.'[11]

Emperor Frederick had done what Richard the Lionheart could not and returned Jerusalem to Outremer, yet despite this he did not receive the adoration of the Church leaders because he was an excommunicate. So unpopular was the emperor with them that, instead of the grand coronation, on 18 March 1229, Frederick was crowned King of Jerusalem by himself in the Holy Sepulchre.

Although Frederick's claim was through his marriage to his late wife, Queen Isabel II, he only ruled as guardian to his infant son, Conrad. He did not stay long in Jerusalem, and returned to Acre within a week of his coronation. Gerold, the Patriarch of Jerusalem, chastised the emperor in a letter emphasising that Frederick had made empty promises to rebuild the city's fortifications, and the Hospitallers and Templars had agreed to assist the emperor with the vital project. According to Gerold:

> The emperor, who did not care to set affairs right, and who saw that there was no certainty in what had been done, and that the city in the state in which it had been surrendered to him could be neither defended nor fortified, was content with the name of surrender, and on the same day hastened with his family to Joppa.[12]

Frederick did not stay in the Holy Land long as he had urgent matters to attend to in Italy. Despite the short stay, he was accused of wanting to capture the Lord of Beirut and his children and plotting to kill the Templar grand master at a council he had summoned him to. Frederick went as far as laying siege to the Templars' headquarters at Acre, but to no avail.[13] However, thirteenth-century preacher Sibt Ibn al-Jauzī wrote that it was the Templars who wanted to assassinate Frederick, and that was the reason he only stayed in Jerusalem for just two nights.[14]

Aside from the violent feud with the Knights Templar, because of his broken relationship with the Church, Frederick remained unpopular with the local population. Upon venturing to Acre's harbour to depart the Holy Land, he was chased and pelted with tripe and bits of meat by butchers.[15] He had achieved what Richard the Lionheart could not, but the Frankish nobles did not widely celebrate the return of Jerusalem as the deal did not meet their needs by providing the security needed to defend the city. The military orders were also displeased because the treaty prevented them from improving the Hospitaller castles of Krak des Chevaliers and al-Marqab and the Templar castles of Chastel-Blanc and Tortosa.[16]

A crisis in Italy forced Frederick to depart the Holy Land just over a month after crowning himself King of Jerusalem. He left Acre on 1 May 1229 to counter an invasion of southern Italy by Pope Gregory, who was hoping to take advantage of Frederick's absence in the Holy Land.

Frederick successfully defeated the papal army, and in May 1230 a peace deal was secured, with the emperor received back into the Church and his achievements in Outremer officially recognised by it. Gregory IX would again use excommunication for political purposes against Frederick in 1239, citing failure to return Templar property as one of the reasons. Fredrick II's conflict with Pope Gregory continued until his death in 1250; by then, the Pope had called two Crusades against the emperor.[17]

Though the emperor was an enemy of the Catholic Church, Ibn Wāsil says he was 'a sincere and affectionate friend' of al-Kāmil right up to the sultan's death in 1238.[18] However, Sibt Ibn al-Jauzī describes the emperor as 'materialist and that his Christianity was simply a game to him'.[19]

Though Frederick II was a controversial figure in Europe, he used diplomacy to return control of Jerusalem to the Crusader states. Richard the Lionheart had relied on negotiation to bring the long war with Saladin to a close, but he was unable to restore Jerusalem to the kingdom. However, the peace deal and return of Jerusalem to the Crusader states was only a short-term achievement, as the end of the ten-year peace would bring more war and devastation to the Holy Land.

THE MASSACRE AT JERUSALEM

Following the death of al-Kāmil, senior nobles from Europe carried out two small-scale Crusades in 1239 and 1241, known as the Barons' Crusade. Theobald IV of Champagne led a Crusader force southward and retook Ascalon in 1239. However, the Crusaders suffered a crushing defeat at

Gaza when Count Henry of Barr led a force of 600 further south on a foraging raid. Several senior nobles tried to dissuade Count Henry, including Templar Grand Master Armand de Périgord, who succeeded Peter de Montaigu in 1232. The nobles urged caution and insisted Henry should wait for the whole army to move south. However, he and his company were said to have 'replied forcefully that they would do nothing of the kind, they had come there to fight unbelievers and did not mean to keep putting off any encounter'.[20]

In November, Count Henry and the foraging force were attacked and annihilated, with the survivors captured and taken back to Cairo. Count Theobald and the rest of the Crusader army arrived at the site of the battle only to witness the aftermath of the slaughter. Upon learning the fate of Henry and the several hundred foragers, Theobald debated whether to launch an offensive into Gaza to aid their captive comrades but was dissuaded by the Outremer nobles, Templars and Hospitallers, who thought that the prisoners would most likely be killed upon their approach, and thus decided to return to Ascalon.

This decision to leave the captured Christian knights to perpetual captivity caused a great upset as the loss would significantly weaken the already diminished military power of Outremer.[21] The Templars and Hospitallers were singled out as being to blame for not aiding Count Henry of Barr and are mentioned directly in a song, supposedly written by Phillip de Nanteuil, who was captured at the Battle of Gaza and imprisoned:

> If the Hospitallers,
> Templars and brother knights
> had shown our men the way,
> had ridden as they should,
> then all our chivalry
> would not in prison lie.[22]

In 1240, Count Theobald negotiated the return of territories to the north and east of Galilee despite Count Henry's defeat at Gaza.[23]

Theobald's gain did not come due to a position of Crusader strength but because of Ayyubid weakness. After the death of Saladin's nephew, al-Kāmil, his vast territories were fought over by his sons, al-Adil II and as-Salih. Al-Kāmil had designated al-Adil II as the heir, and he succeeded his father as Sultan of Egypt, but he was soon deposed by as-Salih. However, as-Salih's uncle, al-Salih Ismail, had taken control of Damascus in 1239, fracturing the Ayyubid dynasty's strength.[24]

Count Theobald left Outremer in 1240, having extended the Kingdom of Jerusalem's border, although this was due to as-Salih focusing his attention on retaking his lands in Syria rather than significant Crusader strength. However, before he left, Theobald was able to secure the release of the prisoners taken at Gaza, including Phillip de Nanteuil, although the fate of Count Henry of Barr is unknown.[25]

A few months after Count Theobald left Outremer, a second Crusader army led by Richard, Earl of Cornwall, arrived in the Holy Land. Richard was the younger brother of King Henry III of England and arrived at Acre in October 1240. Upon arrival, he led his forces to Ascalon, where the defences were being rebuilt under the supervision of Duke Hugh IV of Burgundy (Hugh was originally part of Theobald's Crusade). Richard put his men to work assisting with the reconstruction of Ascalon's defences.[26] He also ratified Theobald's treaty with Sultan as-Salih, which, Richard explains in a letter, was initially agreed with al-Nasir, the Emir of Kerak, and he also claims was not finalised before Theobald returned to Europe.[27]

With the treaty implemented and Ascalon rebuilt, Richard of Cornwall returned to England in May 1241, leaving the Kingdom of Jerusalem with its largest share of territory since Saladin's conquest in 1187. However, it had been rebuilt through diplomacy and not the sword. The kingdom's re-emergence would not last because these negotiations were not from a position of strength and would soon once more be lost by the sword.

The revived Crusader states had the same problem as back in the early twelfth century – a lack of manpower. The recent Crusaders had returned home, and the newly returned territory was defended by limited forces. This was evident in the massacre at Jerusalem by Khwarizmian forces in 1244.

Following their defeat at the hands of the Mongols, the Khwarizmians allied with as-Salih, who was at war with Ismail, the Emir of Damascus. They were a Turkic people who, in 1219, lost their home in western Turkestan to the army of Chingiz (also Genghis) Khan.[28] With their homeland lost, the Khwarizmian people travelled west and met with as-Salih, who proposed an alliance and instructed them to attack the Kingdom of Jerusalem and settle there.

The Khwarizmians invaded the Kingdom of Jerusalem in the land surrounding Safed and Tiberias before heading south to attack Jerusalem itself. The attack was so sudden, and their forces so great, that the Franks were unable to mount an effective defence, and the Khwarizmians soon captured all the Christian territory south of Toron to Gaza and made frequent attacks on the weakly defended Holy City of Jerusalem.

So afraid were the Christian inhabitants that 6,000 assembled and left the city to flee to the remaining Crusader states territory along the coast. The thousands left with family members and possessions as the Christians believed that the truce agreed with Damascus and Kerak would allow them to travel unharmed through the mountainous region. However, this wasn't the case, and most of those fleeing Jerusalem were killed or captured and sold into slavery. Those who could flee raced onto the plains, but here they were annihilated by the Khwarizmians. Only 300 of the thousands that set out reached the safety of Frankish-controlled territory.[29] Jerusalem was left virtually uninhabited, and the Khwarizmian forces, which numbered 12,000, were free to sack the city.[30]

However, it was not completely abandoned, and a small number of Christians remained in the Holy Sepulchre. On 23 August 1244, Khwarizmians killed every Christian they found seeking refuge in the most holy place. Robert, the Patriarch of Jerusalem, detailed the horrific fate of those remaining Christians in a letter written in November of that year. Helpless Christians were disembowelled and priests decapitated at the altar, the marble that encased the Tomb of Jesus Christ was destroyed and the tombs of the Kings of Jerusalem were desecrated. The letter acknowledges that the previous Muslim inhabitants 'had always shown the utmost reverence for our sites during their numerous occupations of the land of the Christians'.[31]

The violence bestowed by the Khwarizmians does not reflect the city's conquest by Saladin in 1187, who made a deal with Balian of Ibelin to allow the citizens to purchase their freedom and then left the Holy Sepulchre untouched. Instead, it echoes the slaughter of Muslims inflicted by the First Crusaders in 1099.

The Kingdom of Jerusalem did not have the strength alone to defeat the Khwarizmians and appealed to al-Salih Ismail, the Emir of Damascus, and al-Mansur Ibrahim, the Emir of Homs, for an alliance. With the alliance secured, the Khwarizmian forces withdrew to Gaza before the combined Christian and Muslim army.

The Franks were able to muster around 2,000 knights and 10,000 infantrymen, the largest Christian army raised since the Third Crusade, and showed the full strength of the Kingdom of Jerusalem. In Gaza, the Sultan of Egypt provided 5,000 soldiers to join the Khwarizmians, and the two sides met on 17 October at La Forbie, near Gaza. The combined armies of the Franks, Damascus and Homs hardly outnumbered the enemy.[32]

The Battle of La Forbie was a devastating defeat. The armies of Damascus and Homs were routed and fled the battlefield, while the combined might of Egypt and the Khwarizmians annihilated the Franks. In the battle, 300 Templar knights were either killed or captured, including the Templar Grand Master Armand de Périgord, who was taken prisoner and never released.[33]

The military orders suffered huge losses, with only thirty-three Templar knights, twenty-six Hospitallers and three Teutonic knights escaping the battle. Most of the Frankish nobility were killed or captured, while the infantry was slaughtered. The Hospitaller and Teutonic grand masters were also taken prisoner.

The survivors fled for the refuge of Ascalon, before returning to Acre, and with the Franks now unable to field an army, the Khwarizmians were free to roam the surrounding territory, even pitching their tents on the plains outside Acre.[34] All the gains of Emperor Frederick and the Barons' Crusade had been lost, never to be recovered.

The disaster at La Forbie was akin to the Franks' defeat at Hattin in 1187. The kingdom was left undefended and the survivors hid behind walls. At the end of the twelfth century, the Franks of Outremer appealed to Europe for desperate reinforcements and once again began the calls for a new Crusade.

14

THE FINAL CRUSADE TO EGYPT

SAINT LOUIS

At the end of the twelfth century, the disaster at Hattin and the loss of Jerusalem sent shock waves through Europe, and three of the mightiest Christian kings took the cross. However, in the mid-thirteenth century, the massacre at Jerusalem and the defeat at La Forbie did not provoke the same response from the nobility. In 1245, Pope Innocent IV held a council at Lyon where he preached another Crusade but did not rouse a great reaction.[1] In fact, at the council, Innocent excommunicated Emperor Frederick, who still styled himself as the King of Jerusalem, and called for a Crusade against Frederick, who was engaged in a civil war with Heinrich Raspe, Landgrave of Thuringia, followed by Count William of Holland in 1247, who were rivals for the throne of Germany. Although Frederick claimed the title of King of Jerusalem as he ruled as regent through his son Conrad, he was no longer seen as such, because a rival faction in Outremer named Conrad's great aunt, Queen Alice of Cyprus, as regent and expelled Frederick's supporters from the Crusader states.[2]

While the leader of the Sixth Crusade was engaged in civil war, King Henry III of England, whose brother had recently been a leader in the Barons' Crusade, was preoccupied with dealing with his defiant barons who had brought the country to civil war in the reign of his father, King John. However, Henry's rival across the Channel, King Louis IX, had already taken the cross prior to the Council of Lyon in 1245.

Louis was born in 1214 and was only 12 when he was crowned King of France in 1226. In 1244, he was severely ill when he took the cross, possibly motivated by the news of the terrible fate of Jerusalem or perhaps in hopes of a divine cure. It was feared the king would not recover, and according to *The Rothelin Continuation*, the king 'made his will, put his affairs in order, and earnestly begged his brothers to take care of his wife and his children, who were very young and helpless'.

Louis' condition was so poor that those around him feared that he had died, and so his recovery was seen as miraculous.[3] In taking the cross outside of the official call to Crusade, Louis IX was following in the footsteps of his great-grandfather, Louis VII before the disastrous Second Crusade.[4] Unfortunately, like his great-grandfather, his Crusade was doomed to failure.

To raise funds for his Crusade, Louis convinced the French Church to pay a tithe for five years, which raised 190,000 *livres tournois* annually, and 274,000 was raised from taxing the towns.[5] The majority of the lords joined the king's Crusade (Count Theobald of Champagne declined, having recently returned from the Barons' Crusade), including his brothers, Robert, Count of Artois, Alphonse, Count of Toulouse, and Charles, Count of Anjou. Queen Margaret of France accompanied Louis while her young sons and heirs, the Princes Louis and Phillip, remained in France.

King Louis sailed for Cyprus on 25 August 1248 and met his brothers. Here, they waited until May 1249 for the rest of the Crusader forces to muster. The army included 1,900 French knights, and a further 700 knights joined from Cyprus, Outremer, the Templars and Hospitallers.[6] Alongside the knights, the king brought a large infantry that included 5,000 crossbowmen.[7] This Crusader army was larger than the 1,200 knights and 400 archers who had marched out from Damietta during the failed Egyptian campaign of the Fifth Crusade nearly thirty years ago.

King Louis IX arrived at Limassol on 17 September 1248 and met William de Sonnac, who had been elected as Grand Master of the Knights Templar in 1247 following the loss of Armand de Périgord in the Battle of La Forbie in 1244. The relationship between the new grand master and Louis did not begin well.

Soon after the king's arrival, William de Sonnac received messages from the sultan with talk of reaching a peace deal. When William brought this news to Louis, he was forbidden to receive any further messengers without the king's permission.[8]

Despite displeasing the French king, the Templars remained vital to the Crusaders' invasion of Egypt. The fleet arrived off the coast of Damietta and was met by a large force of defenders. On 5 June, the Crusaders used their smaller vessels to attack the well-defended beach. As the boats reached shallower waters, the knights leapt into the water and fought onto dry land to carve a beachhead for the Crusade. King Louis joined his comrades in wading through the water, which evoked Richard the Lionheart's recapture of Jaffa at the climax of the Third Crusade.[9]

The Christian accounts of the battle point to very low casualties for the Crusaders and heavy losses for the Egyptian defenders. Gui, a household knight in service to the Viscount of Melun, claims, 'Nobody on our side fell by the sword except one; but two or three died by drowning.' For the enemy forces, Gui states, 'Many had been killed and a great number mortally wounded or mutilated withdrew into their city in cowardly flight.'[10] In a letter, Robert de Sandford, the Preceptor of the Temple in England, expresses a similar perception of the battle, 'Louis with his troops occupied the land along the coast, killing a great number of the heathen but with the loss of only one of our Christians.'[11]

The Templar Preceptor and Gui's accounts suggest the Crusaders won a significant victory over the Egyptian force, who then fled south to Ashmūn Tannāh, leaving Damietta's citizens at the mercy of the Crusaders. After seeing the army flee, the residents soon abandoned the city, fearful of the fate suffered by their predecessors during the previous Crusader siege of 1218–19.[12]

On 6 June, the Crusader army moved into the unoccupied city and found Damietta loaded with supplies of food and weapons. As the city had been hastily abandoned, the fortifications remained intact, including ramparts, ditches and imposing towers, making Damietta ideal for the Crusaders to use as a base for their invasion of Egypt.[13] Their prospects looked bright after the ease with which they captured Damietta, and the king camped his army beside the city while waiting for the flood season to pass before continuing further into Egypt.

On 20 November 1248, King Louis began the march towards Cairo along the Nile, which enabled a large fleet with supplies to accompany the Crusader army. King Louis' Crusade seemed to have undertaken the invasion at the most advantageous time. On 22 November, the Sultan of Egypt, as-Salih, died after a long illness and this could potentially throw the region into chaos. However, Egyptian Emir Fakhr al-Dīn and the sultan's widow, Shajar al-Durr, attempted to conceal the sultan's death to keep up morale in the face of King Louis' invasion until the successor was installed. In the meantime, Fakhr al-Dīn assumed control of the armies while as-Salih's son, al-Malik al-Mu'azzam Turanshah, was sent for to succeed as sultan.[14]

After leaving the city, the Crusaders made camp at the fork between the Nile and the River Tanis, where the Egyptian forces had camped just across the river to impede the Crusaders' advance. They looked to break the stalemate by launching a surprise night-time attack on the Egyptian camp.

On 8 February 1250, the king led an attack force with his brothers, Robert of Artois, Alphonse of Toulouse and Charles of Anjou, along with a large number of Templars, Hospitallers and Crusader knights across the river via a ford. The location of the ford was revealed to the Crusaders by local Muslims, and this enabled them to launch a surprise attack on the enemy camp.[15] The king ordered that once they were across, the companies of knights must wait for the remainder, but Robert of Artois and the Knights Templar, who were part of the vanguard, disobeyed the king's orders and launched an immediate attack on the Egyptian camp.

So sudden and unexpected was the raid that many of the Muslim forces were still asleep. The Crusaders killed Emir Fakhr al-Dīn, the commander of the Egyptian forces, and any who could not flee were slaughtered.[16] It appeared that Robert of Artois and the Knights Templar had achieved a great victory – but Count Robert's desire to pursue the enemy would turn it into a terrible defeat.

DISASTER AT MANSURAH

Although separated from the main army, Robert of Artois and the Knights Templar pursued the fleeing Egyptians inside the town of Mansurah. The blame for this decision is laid on Count Robert who, according to *The Rothelin Continuation*, believed the enemy to be defeated and questioned the courage of the Templars when they urged the count to reconvene with the remainder of the Crusader army.[17]

Inside the narrow streets, the Crusaders were surrounded and attacked by the Mamluk troops, who were the Egyptian sultan's elite slave soldiers. Ibn Wāsil refers to the mamluks as 'Islām's Templars', demonstrating the strength of the Templars' reputation.[18] The vast majority of the Christian knights were killed, with very few escaping with their lives. Many senior nobles perished, including Robert of Artois and William Longsword, the Earl of Salisbury. The losses for the Templars were devastating, with 300 knights lost and only a handful of the pursuing company escaping the slaughter.[19] Had Robert of Artois not led the foolhardy pursuit into Mansurah, he would have achieved a significant victory. Instead, the Knights Templar and Crusader forces had needlessly lost close to 600 knights.[20]

The Battle of Mansurah was not over, and the Egyptian forces, with their morale boosted by their victory over the king's brother and the Knights Templar, attacked King Louis' troops on the bank of the River Tanis. The Crusaders were able to push them back and establish a camp, but the battle was not a great victory because although they had managed to cross the River Tanis, they had sustained heavy losses and were trapped with Mansurah in front of them and the river behind them.

The Templar forces were a vital part of the Crusader heavy cavalry and were decimated at Mansurah. More misfortune for the Templars quickly followed as Templar Grand Master William de Sonnac was killed when the Egyptians attacked Louis' camp on 11 February.[21] Despite establishing a beachhead across the river, the army could move no further and was plagued by famine and disease, which gave the king a challenging dilemma – for his army to survive, he would have to surrender his hard-won gain and withdraw to Damietta.[22]

On 4 April 1250, Louis decided to abandon his position and retreat to Damietta. The king was urged to travel back to Damietta aboard an armed galley, but Louis refused to abandon his army. In the night, leaving all their tents in place to mislead the enemy, they retreated across the River Tanis and the sick and wounded Crusaders were loaded onto boats while the rest of the army hoped to march back through Egypt on foot.

However, the Egyptian forces became aware of the Crusaders' movements and gave pursuit, turning a tactical withdrawal into a disastrous rout.[23] The retreating Crusaders were chased down and killed or captured, and according to an anonymous Christian account, the royal French standard, 'the Oriflamme was torn to shreds' and the Templars' black and white standard, the Bauséant, was 'trampled underfoot'.[24]

Despite the chaos, Robert, the Patriarch of Jerusalem was able to reach the safety of Damietta on 7 April. In a letter to the cardinals dated 15 May 1250, he explains that he had been informed that the king and remnants of the Crusader army were surrounded at the village of Sarensa. After waiting a day for the king to reach Damietta, Queen Margaret ordered that ten galleys be sent to the king's aid. However, the men couldn't find the king or the Crusader army but eventually came across a mass of bodies in a field near the village. Robert wrote, 'They did find, in a field near that village, a great mass of men who had been put to the sword, naked and decapitated, and countless horses that had been killed.'[25]

King Louis was not among the dead as he had been captured along with his two surviving brothers, the Counts of Poitiers and Anjou, as well as the Count of Flanders, the Count of Brittany and the Count of Soissons. The king was not with the main force as he was seriously ill with dysentery and taking refuge in a village.[26] The troops returning by land were lost, either captured or slain, while the boats returning the sick and injured were also lost when they were attacked and burnt on the rivers.[27]

In captivity, King Louis had little choice but to surrender Damietta and pay 800,000 bezants to ransom himself and the captive Christians. The French king laid out the agreement's details in an August 1250 letter to his subjects, where he articulated that the ransom would release all Christian prisoners captured since al-Kāmil's treaty with Emperor Frederick. The letter states that the agreement included a ten-year truce, and Louis had already arranged for the sum of 400,000 bezants to be paid towards the enormous ransom.[28] This large amount was raised from the king's war chest, and the rest came from the Knights Templar. With a huge part of the ransom paid, Louis, his brothers and senior nobles left Egypt and sailed for Outremer on 8 May. The vast majority of those captured remained in captivity.[29]

The Seventh Crusade was a colossal failure that echoed that of the Fifth Crusade; however, the Seventh showed that even a well-funded and organised operation led by an eminent king of Europe was doomed to failure. Had the Knights Templar not followed Count Robert of Artois into Mansurah, the Crusader armies would not have lost the manpower needed to press on from the beachhead, which they had won at great cost.

The Knights Templar forces had been destroyed, the knights wiped out, their grand master killed and their standard trampled underfoot. They had been crucial to the success of previous Crusades, such as ensuring the survival of the Second Crusade and helping win the battles of the Third. However, in the Egyptian campaigns, the order failed spectacularly.

The Templars' defeat at Mansurah left the Crusader army lacking enough elite troops to continue the invasion of Egypt and, therefore, can be considered a serious factor in the Crusade's failure. However, perhaps if King Louis had realised the hopelessness of the situation sooner, the army could have withdrawn and regrouped, but then the deaths in crossing the River Tanis would have been for nothing.

Louis' adventure in the Holy Land did not end in 1250, as the king stayed in Outremer and oversaw the Crusader states. Louis liberated the remaining captives in 1152 and improved the defences of the remaining Frankish territories of Acre, Jaffa, Caesarea and Sidon. He also established a French garrison of 100 knights in Acre funded by the French monarchy before leaving for France in April 1254.

The Seventh Crusade was the last major campaign to the Holy Land, although King Louis attempted another, known as the Eighth Crusade, to Tunis, sailing in July 1170. However, the king died shortly after, on 25 August, when the army was plagued by disease. With the king dead, most of the Crusader army returned home.

King Louis IX of France was canonised as a saint in 1297. Prince Edward (the future King Edward I of England) arrived in Acre in 1271, but after surviving an assassination attempt, he sailed for home in 1172.[30]

The great Crusade campaigns had ended in failure. Although the Third Crusade won back the coastal territories and the negotiations of the Sixth Crusade temporarily returned Jerusalem, most of them failed. The age of Crusading was over, but a new power had risen in Egypt that would overthrow Saladin's dynasty and utterly defeat the Knights Templar.

15

OUTREMER DESTROYED

NEW POWER RISING

Al-Malik al-Mu'azzam Turanshah arrived in Egypt in February 1250 to succeed his father, as-Salih, as Sultan of Egypt. The new sultan saw the collapse of the Seventh Crusade, successfully captured King Louis and retook Damietta, but there was a plot to murder the new sultan. Al-Malik al-Mu'azzam had lost the support of his father's emirs by promoting those who they deemed unworthy above them and a group of Mamluks moved to kill him in May 1250. The Mamluk warrior Rukn al-Dīn Baybars struck the first blow inside the privacy of the sultan's tent. Al-Malik al-Mu'azzam managed to flee to the riverbank before he was caught and murdered. None of his emirs came to his aid.[1]

It was agreed that as-Salih's wife, Shajar al-Durr, should become sultan as a figurehead, and Izz al-Dīn Aybak al-Turkmāi al-Sālihī would be atabeg and commander of the army.[2] However, Aybak soon married Shajar al-Durr and deposed her to become the first Mamluk sultan, bringing an end to the Ayyubid control of Egypt. The Emir of Aleppo, an-Nasir Yusuf, was the great-grandson of Saladin, and so the Ayyubid dynasty would live on as he controlled Aleppo and Damascus, but Saladin's empire was now split in two, with the elite Mamluk warriors controlling the Sultanate of Egypt.

The aftermath of the Seventh Crusade saw a period of relative peace between Outremer and its Muslim neighbours. King Louis was able to secure the release of the remaining prisoners, and hostilities between the Crusader states and Cairo, Damascus and Aleppo were limited so as not to provoke another mass invasion from Europe.[3] However, despite the relative peace with the Franks, the control of Egypt descended into a violent power struggle. Shajar al-Durr had her husband Aybak murdered in 1257, and then the first female ruler of Egypt since Cleopatra was herself killed by Aybak's supporters.[4] This enabled the Mamluk Qutuz to seize control of Egypt, ruling through Aybak's son, al-Mansur Ali, before assuming the title of sultan for himself. Baybars and the Bahriyaa regiment had been forced to flee Egypt when Qutuz murdered their commander, Aqtay; however, a new enemy from the east prompted Baybars to return to Egypt – the Mongols.[5]

In the early thirteenth century, the Mongol leader Temujin united the nomadic Mongol tribes and was declared the Great Khan of the Mongols with the title Genghis Khan. Under his leadership, the Mongols wreaked havoc in their conquest of Asia, demanding immediate surrender from towns; otherwise, they were massacred. Genghis Khan died in 1227, and by then his armies had conquered Azerbaijan and south Russia. After his death, his sons continued the brutal conquest under the leadership of Great Khan Ogodei, who, over the next ten years, destroyed the Khwarizmian empire (sending the survivors to seek a new home at the expense of the Franks), Iran and Korea. Ogodei died in 1241, which saved Europe from being overrun as the Mongols had swept across Ukraine and Poland in 1240.

Mongke Khan succeeded Ogodei and conquered south China, with the entire country under Mongol control by 1280. In 1258, the Mongols captured Baghdad and murdered the Abbasid Caliph al-Mustasim. In 1259, they took Aleppo, followed by Damascus in 1260.[6] Saladin's Islamic empire had been fractured between the Mamluks of Egypt and Ayyubid descendants of Syria and now faced being lost entirely to the seemingly unstoppable Mongol invasion.

To deal with this crisis, Sultan Qutuz mustered a large army of cavalry and infantry, including Baybars in the vanguard, and marched to meet the Mongol army head-on. The Franks allowed the Egyptian army to march through the Kingdom of Acre because the Mongols had attacked and devastated Frankish-held Sidon.[7] At Ain Jalut, in Galilee, in September 1160, the Mamluk army met the Mongols' invincible army, and Baybars won a decisive victory. The Mamluks recaptured Damascus and Aleppo, which reunited the territory of Saladin's empire.

The Mongols' defeat at Ain Jalut prevented their advancement into North Africa, which historian Mayer proposes was one of the decisive moments of history. Not only was a seemingly invincible force defeated but with the invasion of Africa prevented, 'the continued existence of Islam was assured'.[8]

With the Mongols defeated, the Mamluks cemented themselves as the dominant power in the region. However, Qutuz was murdered by Baybars, who had the support of the other prominent emirs and assumed the title of sultan for himself.[9] The new Mamluk regime would bring an end to friendly relations between the Franks and the Mamluk empire and lead to the destruction of Outremer.

BAYBARS' CAMPAIGN AGAINST THE FRANKS

Now that Baybars had assumed control of the Mamluk empire, which stretched from Cairo to Aleppo, the sultan had no interest in continuing a policy of neutrality with the Franks because even in a weakened state, the Christians had a beachhead to launch an offensive from Europe.[10] It had been Saladin's failure to capture the port of Tyre after the Battle of Hattin in 1187 that enabled the Crusaders to safely bring troops to the Holy Land and ultimately win back part of their kingdom.

Baybars would begin an offensive that would crush the Knights Templar and drive the Franks into the sea. In February 1165, the Mamluks laid siege to Caesarea, capturing the coastal town by 5 March and then capturing Hospitaller-controlled Arsuf on 1 April. So weak were the Franks that they were unable to field an army to stop the Mamluks' advance, though they were reinforced by the arrival of Hugh, the Regent of Cyprus, at Acre with a fleet of galleys and a force of 130 knights and sergeants.[11]

Baybars continued his invasion of Outremer, laying siege to the Templar castle of Safad in June 1266. He attempted to storm the castle; however, each time his assaults failed, sustaining heavy casualties. Safad had recently been reconstructed and was seen to be an impregnable fortification. The fourteenth-century Egyptian chronicler Ibn al-Furāt described the castle at Safad as 'an obstruction in the throat of Syria and a blockage in the chest of Islam'.[12]

In light of the heavy losses and Safad's effective defences, Baybars implemented less-direct methods and attempted to sow dissent among the defenders by declaring that all the Syrian sergeants and archers be allowed safe conduct to leave, hoping to drive a wedge between them and the Franks.[13] The number of defenders stationed at Safad during peacetime was 1,700 men, rising to 2,200 during times of war. However, of that number, only fifty were Templar knights and about thirty Templar sergeants.[14] Discord among the defenders and the loss of Syrian troops would seriously damage the fortress's defences and force the Templars to seek terms of surrender.

Templar Sergeant Leon Cazelier was sent to negotiate with the sultan as he was fluent in Arabic. The sultan agreed that the defenders would be allowed safe passage to Acre upon surrendering. However, once the defenders left the castle, Baybars sent his troops to apprehend them and had the men beheaded and the rest sold into slavery.[15] The chronicle of *The Templar of Tyre* accuses Leon of aiding the sultan with his insidious plan through fear of execution. The chronicler also adds that after the castle's surrender, Leon apostatised and became a Saracen.[16]

The execution of the Templar knights echoes the mass execution of the Templars following the Battle of Hattin in 1187. However, it also contrasts with the mercy shown by Saladin, who allowed the surrendering Franks at Jerusalem in the same year to leave and build a resistance at Tyre. The survival of the port of Tyre provided a beachhead for the arrival of the Third Crusade – Baybars would not show such mercy to the Franks.

The fall of Safad gave Baybars control of Galilee, and in 1268 Jaffa, which the Third Crusaders had fought to recapture and defend, fell to the sultan's forces after a one-day siege.[17] Baybars' troops moved against the Principality of Antioch, laying siege to the capital and capturing the city after a short siege on 18 May.

At the end of the eleventh century, Antioch had taken the First Crusaders a year to capture and became the seat of the second Crusader state. The County of Edessa was the first established Crusader state in 1098 and was then the first state lost, with the Principality of Antioch established shortly after in the same year, which coincidentally was the second Crusader state to fall.

The population of Antioch suffered the same fate as those at the hands of the First Crusaders 170 years prior. The chronicler of *The Templar of Tyre* numbers the deaths at 17,000, with 100,000 occupants taken into captivity.[18] Baybars' forces plundered and destroyed the once-mighty city of Antioch, leaving it in such a ravaged state that it would not recover for centuries.

The Templar outposts in the principality were soon abandoned, and the realm of Bohemond VI, the last Prince of Antioch, was reduced to a sliver of land at the port of Latakia. Bohemond, who was now Prince of Antioch in title only, was not at the siege of Antioch, but was at Tripoli, where he had wrongly expected Baybars to strike.[19] Tripoli would not be spared either.

The speed and ferocity of Baybars' invasion of Outremer and the loss of one of the Crusader states' great cities shocked Christendom, and once again the calls for another Crusade to prevent the collapse of Outremer reverberated throughout Europe. The call was answered by the previous Crusade leader, King Louis IX of France, who led the failed Eighth Crusade to Tunisia in 1270. However, another senior European leader, Prince Edward of England, answered the call to Crusade and arrived in Tunisia with a small group of English Crusaders after Louis' death.

Although the Eighth Crusade had dissolved, and even though Edward had received word that his father, King Henry III, was gravely ill, he stuck to his Crusading vow and sailed for Acre from Sicily in May 1271. Prince Edward and the Templars and Hospitallers led unsuccessful attacks in Mamluk territory.[20] Although they were ineffective, they paused the attack on Tripoli and forced Baybars to manoeuvre his armies to counter these threats.

Prince Edward did not have the resources to challenge Baybars directly in the same way his great uncle Richard the Lionheart had challenged Saladin, but a ten-year peace agreement was reached, which would prolong the survival of Tripoli and the remaining Frankish territory.[21] However, Edward was the only significant figure whose signature was missing from the peace deal, which showed his desire for the war to continue and was seen as troublesome.[22]

Prince Edward was almost murdered at the hands of an Assassin, a Muslim soldier who came to Acre seeking to be baptised and eventually served Edward as a spy, gained the Englishman's trust and was given access to the prince, day or night. After a long deception, the Assassin attacked Edward, who was himself unarmed and dressed for bed, at his bedchamber door. Despite being wounded in the hip with a dagger, Prince Edward incapacitated him with a single punch to the head and then killed him with the Assassin's own blade. Edward was treated with an antidote as it was feared the blade would be poisoned, but the warrior prince made a full recovery.[23] Historian Thomas Ashbridge lays the blame for the attack at Baybars, explaining the sultan hired the Assassin because Edward posed too much of a threat to his ambitions to destroy the Crusader states.[24]

After recovering from the assassination attempt, and with peace now agreed between the Kingdom of Jerusalem and Baybars Prince Edward sailed to England in September 1272. Although the Eighth Crusade, which he had initially sailed for, had failed with the death of King Louis IX, Edward left the Holy Land with a ten-year peace deal agreed with Baybars. He would be King Edward of England later that year after his father's death.

The ten-year peace deal would see the end to Baybars' accelerated conquest of the Crusader states when the sultan fell ill with dysentery while travelling to Damascus following victory against the Mongols and died on 28 July 1277. *The Templar of Tyre* chronicle states that it was believed that the sultan had been poisoned, coinciding with the violent way Baybars seized the crown. In his life, Baybars and the Mamluks had crushed the Knights Templar, and as a warrior Baybars slaughtered the Templar knights at the Battle of Mansurah in 1250, which deprived King Louis of heavy cavalry and effectively defeated the Seventh Crusade. As a sultan, his invasion of Outremer had captured Templar fortifications, most notably at Safed, when he betrayed the Templars by executing the warrior monks upon their negotiated surrender. Although he had not entirely driven the Franks from the Holy Land, his campaign had captured a vast amount of Frankish territory, including the great city of Antioch. His campaign reduced Outremer to a sliver of land clinging to Tripoli and Acre for survival. Unlike Saladin's conquest of the Kingdom of Jerusalem, there would be no mass Crusade in response from Europe, as the Seventh and Eighth Crusades were expensive failures.

THE LAST KING AND THE LOSS OF TRIPOLI

Baybars had intended for his son, Baraka, to succeed him; however, he was soon forced to abdicate and died in exile in 1280. Meanwhile Baybars' former emir, Qalawun, installed Baybars' second son, the 7-year-old Salamish, as sultan to be a figurehead. It wasn't until 1279 that Qalawun himself was proclaimed sultan, and Salamish was sent to Kerak and eventually exiled to Constantinople.[25]

The succession of the crown of Jerusalem was also contested. Since the loss of Jerusalem, the title King of Jerusalem became an honorary one held by the King of Cyprus. When Emperor Frederick's grandson, Conrad III, was executed by Charles of Anjou following his failed reconquest of Sicily on 29 October 1268, the crown passed to King Hugh III of Cyprus. However, the succession was challenged by Maria of Antioch as she was the closest relation to King Conrad III and to his grandmother, Queen Isabella. Although Maria was unable to successfully pursue her claim, she sold her right to the title to Charles of Anjou in 1277.

King Hugh (Hugh I of Jerusalem) did not have the strength to enact his will upon the state and was unpopular with the Templars after trying to reverse the acquisition of the Frankish lordships of Sidon and Arsuf by the military orders. Although Charles of Anjou purchased his claim to the kingship, the Knights Templar opted to support his claim, and King Hugh returned to Cyprus. Charles sent soldiers, led by Roger of Severino as his representative.[26] Roger arrived in September 1277 with letters from Charles, Maria and the Pope declaring that Charles was the true King of Jerusalem and lodged at the Templars' headquarters in Acre. In 1279, Hugh attempted to retake Acre but was prevented by the Knights Templar, who were strong supporters of Charles, and Hugh was forced to flee back to Cyprus. In response to the Templars' betrayal, Hugh destroyed several Templar properties in Cyprus, such as the castle Gastria and the houses at Limassol and Paphos. Hugh attempted to regain his control over the Frankish lands in 1283 at Beirut without success, and died in 1284 without restoring his rule over Outremer.[27]

At that time, Frenchman Guillaume de Beaujeu was the Templar grand master, having been elected in 1273, and under him the Knights Templar had engaged in civil war not just against King Hugh but also Count Bohemond VII of Tripoli, who succeeded his father Bohemond VI as count and titular Prince of Antioch. Guillaume de Beaujeu turned the Templars from their original mission of protecting the vulnerable on the road and a standing army for the Crusades into a political force involved in the rivalries of the local barons.

Guy of Jubail had joined the Knights Templar as a *confrères* (a secular knight associated with the Templars) following a dispute with the Count of Tripoli after Bohemond went back on a marriage agreement with Guy's brother, John. Guillaume de Beaujeu supported Guy of Jubail in his feud with Bohemond, and the Knights Templar engaged in armed conflict with the County of Tripoli.[28]

In 1279, the Templar grand master sent several armed galleys to attack Tripoli. Bohemond responded by attacking the Templars at Sidon, taking prisoners and returning to Tripoli with loot.[29]

The Templars' Tripoli conflict continued until 1282, when Guy and his men were captured and put to death. Then Charles of Anjou died in January 1285, ending the Templars' involvement in internal Frankish political conflicts.

King Hugh I died in March 1284, so his son was crowned King John I of Cyprus and Jerusalem in May. However, within a year, John died, and his brother Henry was crowned King Henry II of Cyprus in 1285 at Tyre.

In 1286, Henry was to be crowned as the last King of Jerusalem. Henry was only able to return to Acre as king due to the support of the Knights Templar against the supporters of Charles of Anjou.[30] His coronation was widely celebrated with a fifteen-day festival at Acre that included jousting and re-enactments of King Arthur and the Knights of the Round Table. *The Templar of Tyre* records it as 'the loveliest festival anyone had seen for a hundred years'.[31] However, the joy and optimism brought by the Crusader states being reunited under King Henry did not last when Sultan Qalawun turned his attention to the weakened County of Tripoli.

Templar Grand Master Guillaume de Beaujeu received intelligence of the sultan's desire to move against Tripoli from Emir al-Fakhri, who was in charge of weapons and part of the sultan's guard. He immediately sent a message to Tripoli to warn them of an attack, but despite the information coming from a source close to the sultan, the warning was ignored, as they were suspicious of the motives of the Templar grand master. As the sultan's armies approached, Guillaume de Beaujeu sent the Spanish Templar

Brother Reddecoeur, the Commander of Tripoli, to urge the city to prepare for a siege. Reinforcements were sent, but many arrived too late after the sultan's armies laid siege to Tripoli on 17 March 1289.[32]

Qalawun had the walls bombarded by mangonels and undermined, capturing Tripoli on 27 April 1289.[33] Although the city was well fortified, as the walls began to fall, the Venetian merchants took to their ships and fled, followed by the Genoese, who feared the Venetians taking all the galleys and leaving them trapped. With the loss of the Genoese, the defenders did not have enough soldiers to keep out the sultans' army.

Despite the efforts of both the Templars and Hospitallers, the city was lost. In the struggle, Brother Reddecoeur was captured, and the Templar Commander Peter of Moncada was killed.[34] Qalawun destroyed the city of Tripoli and built a new one near the ruins.[35]

The County of Tripoli, founded in 1102, was the last Crusader state of Outremer to be formed, with the city itself not brought under Frankish rule until 1109. With Tripoli lost, all that remained of the territory captured during and after the First Crusade was Acre and the remaining sliver of Frankish land.

The loss of Tripoli would bring to pass the loss of Acre. Unlike the loss of Jerusalem, which drew Crusader armies to reclaim some of the Kingdom of Jerusalem, the Crusaders who arrived after the fall of Tripoli brought Acre's destruction.

In August 1290, twenty galleys filled with Italian Crusaders sailed to Acre. Instead of helping to deter further hostilities, this provoked the sultan into action.[36] In Acre, the newly arrived Crusaders murdered Muslim traders from the surrounding villages who had come to the city to sell goods such as wheat. They also murdered many native Christians who were targeted because of their beards.[37]

The barbaric violence was brought to the attention of Qalawun, who was not interested in the Franks protesting their innocence and blaming the newly arrived Crusaders for the murders. The sultan believed they had broken the peace treaty.[38] He demanded that the murderers be brought to justice. However, the lords of Acre chose not to punish the newly arrived Crusaders from Europe and the Templar grand master proposed a radical alternative, suggesting that they send the prisoners who were already awaiting execution and claim they were the guilty ones to appease the sultan.

But this idea was rejected. Instead, according to *The Templar of Tyre*, the Frankish nobles wrote to the sultan that 'these crusaders who had done the deed were foreigners from overseas, and not subject to their justice, and they were unable to lay a finger on them'. Qalawun was very displeased with this response and began preparations to attack Acre.[39]

Despite the looming threat, there was little interest from Europe. The Mongol Khan Arghun sent his envoys to Europe to form an alliance against the Mamluks, though the princes of Europe were more focused on domestic affairs and only gave polite excuses.[40] Had the European nobility responded with more interest, the fate of Acre might not have been sealed. However, virtually isolated apart from the Kingdom of Cyprus, the total end of the Crusader states was almost inevitable.

On 10 November 1290, however, it appeared to the Franks that fortune favoured them, because while preparing to attack, Sultan Qalawun fell ill and died.[41] He was succeeded by his eldest son, al-Malik al-Ashraf, but any Franks who hoped that a change of sultan would stall the attack were mistaken, as he intended to finish what his father had started. With his position as Sultan solidified and having his would-be assassin and rival, the Emir Ḥusām al-Dīn Ṭurunṭāy, brutally put to death, al-Malik al-Ashraf turned his attention to Acre.[42]

THE LAST STAND

Al-Malik al-Ashraf's army vastly outnumbered the Franks holed up at Acre. *The Templar of Tyre* numbers the sultan's forces as 70,000 horsemen and 150,000 infantry. While the Franks had around 700 to 800 mounted units and 13,000 infantry, including non-combatants, those at Acre numbered 30,000 to 40,000.[43] Once it was understood that the sultan was going to Acre, the Franks sent messengers with gifts, but al-Malik al-Ashraf would not be swayed and had the messengers, which included the Templar Bartholomew Pisen, imprisoned, where they perished in captivity.[44]

As the sultan's forces approached, the Franks had a relativity short time to muster the limited fighting forces left in Outremer. The Templars and other military orders summoned knights from Europe, and the defenders were joined by Otto de Grandson, who led a company of English soldiers sent by King Edward I of England.[45] With King Henry absent, six prominent men were placed in command of Acre's defence: Jean de Grailly, Otto de Grandson, the Hospitaller Grand Master Jean de Villiers, the Templar Grand Master Guillaume de Beaujeu and the Masters of the Orders of Saint Thomas and Saint Lazarus.[46]

The Siege of Acre began on 5 April, with the sultan unleashing his vast arsenal of catapults and mangonels upon the fortified city. The Mamluk forces also attacked by undermining Acre's towers and did so much damage to the Tower of the King that the defenders were forced to destroy it so it couldn't be used against them.

In response to such offensive pressure, Templar Grand Master Guillaume de Beaujeu, Otto de Grandson and Jean de Grailly led a surprise night-time sortie to destroy the Mamluks' siege engines. It was unsuccessful, as the knights' horses got tangled in the besiegers' tent ropes and the riders fell from their horses and were slain. Eighteen knights, including both Templar and Frankish knights, were killed in the failed mission.[47] Abū al-Fidā, who was an eyewitness to the fall of Acre, gives an account of the sortie, including the horrific fate of one knight who 'fell into the latrine trench of the amīr's detachment and was killed'.[48]

The defenders' spirits were lifted on 4 May when King Henry arrived with reinforcements. They found the city in a dire situation, with the outer wall mined and the Tower of the King destroyed. After the king's arrival, there was a temporary ceasefire and two knights, Sir William de Villiers and William of Caffan (from the household of the Templar grand master), negotiated with the sultan.

The extent of the terms offered by the sultan was the evacuation of the city and the inhabitants given safe passage along with their goods. Unfortunately for the population of Acre, the terms were not acceptable to the Frankish nobility as they feared surrendering the city, thinking that the Europeans would see them as traitors.[49] The messengers could not reach a satisfactory agreement and the fighting continued.

The Mamluks launched a massive assault on the city, entering it by the gate of the destroyed tower and St Anthony's Gate. The assault began with the deafening sound of drums, alerting Templar Grand Master Guillaume de Beaujeu, who hastily mustered ten or twelve Templar knights and raced to St Anthony's Gate. En route they passed the Hospitaller quarter and were joined by the Hospitaller grand master, a mixture of Frankish knights, Hospitallers and footmen. The two masters led the hastily organised forces to attack the Mamluk troops at St Anthony's Gate.[50]

Despite the efforts of the combined orders, the Mamluk forces were too great, and they pelted the knights with Greek fire and javelins. In the hopeless struggle, the Templar grand master was struck by a javelin, which slipped through his light armour and struck him in his armpit. In the haste to engage, Guillaume de Beaujeu had not donned his full armour and was thus mortally wounded. His men carried him to the Templar fortress, where he succumbed to his injury and died, becoming the last Templar grand master to be killed fighting in the Holy Land.[51]

Unable to rout the Saracens, the Franks began to abandon their posts. While the Templar grand master lay dying, Otto de Grandson and Jean de Grailly attempted to defend the tower of the legate along with the French regiment originally established by King Louis IX. However, Jean de Grailly was wounded and vastly outnumbered, so they abandoned their position and fled.

King Henry and the Hospitallers agreed that the situation was hopeless and decided to leave Acre in their ships, abandoning the city to its fate.[52] Those who were unable to board ships were killed or captured by the sultan's forces. Thousands of desperate people fled to the Templar compound for refuge. Although temporarily safe, the citizens behind its walls could only watch as the last ships sailed out of Acre. *The Templar of Tyre* describes that those left behind 'gave a great cry' as the ships headed to Cyprus. The city of Tyre, which had single-handedly held out against Saladin and was the beachhead that enabled the Third Crusade, was abandoned by its lord and knights. In 1291 there was no Conrad of Montferrat to lead the defence, but a knight called Adam of Caffan, who abandoned Tyre and its population on 19 May at the sight of the ships leaving Acre.[53]

The remaining senior Templar knight left in Acre was the Templar Marshal Peter of Sevrey, who, after holding out for ten days, held talks with the sultan's representatives. It was agreed that the lives of those inside the Templar compound would be spared, and the sultan gave them his standard to place atop their battlements. However, after the Templars opened the gates, several of the sultan's soldiers began to pillage and lay hands on the women and children, forcing the Templars to defend them. The Franks shut the gate and killed the Mamluk troops inside.[54]

The sultan once again sent messengers to convince the Templars to surrender, and the Templar marshal trusted the sultan's word and opened the gates again. When he had the Templars in his power, he had the marshal and the other men beheaded. When those still inside, which included the wounded, heard the fate of the Templar marshal, they attempted to hold out in the tower. The Mamluks mined the structure, and it collapsed, killing those inside.

The city of Acre was captured on 18 May with the final defenders holding out for another ten days in the Templar compound.[55] So terrible was the massacre of the Christians at Acre by the Mamluks, that contemporary historian and eyewitness Abu al-Mahasin justified the slaughter by using Richard the Lionheart's execution of Muslim prisoners in 1191 as a comparison.[56]

The loss of Acre in 1291 effectively ended the Crusader states, and the few remaining territories were soon abandoned. After the death of Guillaume de Beaujeu, the Commander of the Land of Jerusalem, Theobald Gaudin, sailed for Sidon with several Templars. He was elected as grand master by the few Templars with him, and he began his time by fleeing Sidon for Cyprus. When those who remained in Sidon learned that the grand master was not sending any aid, they abandoned Sidon and slipped away under cover of darkness.[57]

With no relief from Europe on the way, the remaining territories soon surrendered. Tyre succumbed on 19 May and Sidon towards the end of June. Beirut capitulated on 31 July, and the Templar castles of Tortosa and the Castle of the Pilgrims were abandoned on 3 and 14 August. Once the Mamluks captured the last Frankish territories, they destroyed them to ensure the Franks could never return.[58]

The Crusader states, first established in 1098, lasted until 1291, with only the Kingdom of Cyprus still in the hands of the Franks. The Knights Templar were created to police the roads of Jerusalem before becoming a premier fighting force for the Franks with a vast array of castles and holdings in the Holy Land. However, with all the land of Outremer lost, the Templars retreated to Cyprus, where a new grand master would be elected to lead the them and find purpose now that Outremer was lost beyond recovery.

16

THE LAST GRAND MASTER

THE ISLAND OF RUAD

The Crusader states had been destroyed, and the Franks were driven from the Holy Land by Sultan al-Malik al-Ashraf. Although al-Malik al-Ashraf had finished the campaign begun by Rukn al-Dīn Baybars, the Crusader states had never truly recovered from the disaster at Hattin 100 years prior at the hands of Saladin.

The Mamluks had total mastery of the Holy Land, while the Franks retreated to Cyprus, but al-Malik al-Ashraf did not rule his new territory for long. The sultan was assassinated in December 1293 by a group of emirs, including Badr al-Dīn Baydarā, who, when out riding, brutally set upon al-Malik al-Ashraf and 'swords took him from every angle, cutting him up, until he became a pile of meat'. Baydarā succeeded al-Malik al-Ashraf as sultan but was himself murdered one day later.[1]

After the death of Guillaume de Beaujeu at Acre, Theobald Gaudin hastily became the new Templar grand master and oversaw the evacuation of the remaining Templar castles. Gaudin's reign was short as he died in 1292, which left the task of rebuilding the Templar order to another.

The leading candidates to be elevated to grand master were Hugues de Pairaud and Jacques de Molay. Most of the council preferred de Pairaud, but de Molay was able to outmanoeuvre his opponent and pressure the electoral council to make him grand master in 1292.

Jacques de Molay was from Burgundian lineage, born between 1240 and 1250, and joined the Knights Templar as a young man in 1265.[2] As grand master he was now tasked with defending Cyprus and Armenia and winning support from the senior Christian nobles to attempt to retake the lost territories in the Holy Land.[3]

In 1294, de Molay travelled to Europe and met with Pope Boniface VIII in Rome and King Edward I in England, where he received encouraging support to rebuild the Templars' military strength.[4] Hopes of recapturing the lost Crusader states soared when news came in that Ghazan, the Mongol Il-Khan of Persia, was about to attack the Mamluks with a huge army. Jacques de Molay wrote to King James II of Aragon in 1301 to inform him of the alliance between the Kingdom of Cyprus, the Armenians and the Mongols.

For their part in the invasion, the Templars, Hospitallers and forces from the Kingdom of Cyprus used the small rocky island of Ruad, which the Templars still held after the evacuation of Outremer, to attack and hold Tortosa to await the Mongol army. The Christian forces landed at Tortosa in December 1300, where they pillaged and destroyed the surrounding villages and towns, planning to join up with Ghazan's army. After twenty-five days of laying waste to Mamluk territory, the Christian forces returned to Ruad.

In February 1301, they received word from the Armenians that Ghazan was not about to attack the Mamluks. In the wake of the news, the Cypriot knights, along with the Hospitallers, returned to Cyprus while the Templars remained on the island to defend it.[5] Ruad was held by the Templars as a beachhead from which they could attempt the recapture of the lost Crusader states, and despite the failed invasion of 1300, hope remained that the Mongol army would appear.

Jacques de Molay wrote to King James II of Aragon, optimistic that the planned alliance would come to fruition:

> The king of Armenia sent his ambassadors to the king of Cyprus to tell him that the lord king of Amenia had learned that Ghazan was now on the point of entering the lands of the sultan with a horde of Tartars. As we knew this, we are now en route for the island of Tortosa, where our convent has maintained horses and arms the whole of this year.[6]

While waiting for the Mongol army, the Templars fortified the island and launched several raids on the mainland.

Ghazan's army did not appear, and the Templars found themselves again under siege. In September 1302, Ruad was attacked by a Mamluk fleet of sixteen ships.[7] It was defended by 120 knights, 500 archers and 400 servants serving under Templar Marshal Bartholomew.[8]

Despite the large number of defenders, the Templars were unable to drive the Mamluk forces from the island and instead entered negotiations for surrender. The Mamluks gave their word that the defenders' lives would be spared and allowed passage to a Christian territory of their choice. The Templars trusted the conditions would be met and surrendered.

Unfortunately, as with the Templar compound at Acre, the Mamluks went back on their word and beheaded the Syrian archers and took the Templars as prisoners to be sold as slaves.[9]

FRIDAY THE 13TH

The reputation of the Knights Templar was built on the order defending the Holy Land, and in that regard they had utterly failed. The Templars had amassed vast riches, land and political power to support the Franks' efforts in the Crusader states, but with Outremer lost, the order appeared redundant and vulnerable to criticism.

The events of the Templars' downfall began to be set in motion with the election of Pope Clement V, a Frenchman who, as Pope, never set foot in Rome and instead set up court at Avignon and packed the college with French cardinals. Although not directly under the control of the French King Philip IV, Clement needed the support of the French monarch for a grand new Crusade, having taken the cross in December 1305.[10]

The French king was burdened with significant debt, which he had inherited from his father's failed Crusade against Aragon, worsened by the recent wars with England and France. To ease his financial problems, Philip IV moved against groups within his power, such as the Italian bankers in 1291 and the Jews in 1306, seizing their property and assets and then expelling them from the kingdom. These financial gains helped the king in the short term, but to ease his debt, Philip IV looked to the riches of the Knights Templar. However, as historian Malcolm Barber asserts, even though the king moved to profit from the Templars' riches, it doesn't rule out that he believed the Templars guilty of the crimes accused and may have felt duty-bound to take action.[11]

A poem written by Rostan Berenguier of Marseilles addressed the criticism of the Templars:

> Why the Pope continues to tolerate them; tell me why he permits them to misuse the riches which are offered them for God's service on dishonourable and even criminal ends. They waste this money which intended for the recovery of the Holy Sepulchre on cutting a fine figure in this world; they deceive people with their idle trumpery, and offend God.[12]

After the loss of Ruad, there was much appetite for the merging of the Knights Templar and the Knights Hospitaller, but this was not supported by Jacques de Molay, arguing that the Hospitallers were founded for healing while the Templars were founded for war.[13]

In 1307, Jacques de Molay and the senior Templars were in France negotiating the future of Crusading with Pope Clement V and King Philip IV. On Friday, 13 October 1307, the king's officers arrested every known Templar in France, which was around 2,000. It wasn't just the senior Templars and knights but also the agricultural workers and household servants. Most of the Templars arrested were unarmed and unable to resist.

Aside from the Paris Temple, the Templar houses weren't fortified and their forces were stationed in Cyprus. Although the Paris Temple was a fortified stronghold, the unsuspecting Templars allowed the agents of the French king to walk in and seize it by force. The arrested Templars were brought to the temple to be imprisoned, questioned and tortured.

The French king seized the wealth contained in the Paris Temple, but it's worth noting that this was not the first time a European king had raided a Templar bank to solve their immediate financial problems. In June 1263, Prince Edward (the future King Edward I of England) stole £10,000 of the barons' money from the Templar treasury when the kingdom was split by the conflict between the Crown and Simon de Montfort and the barons.

In July 1307, King Edward II of England and Piers Gaveston stole money and jewels worth £50,000 from the London Temple.[14] While debt-ridden monarchs raiding the temple for money wasn't uniquely shocking, the sudden arrest of the Templars in France and the nature of the charges against the order shocked Europe.

The detention of the Templars on Friday, 13 October, was months in the planning by Philip IV and the king's accusations were discussed in a letter sent by Pope Clement V to Philip on 24 August 1307. In it, Clement reveals that the king and his representatives discussed their concerns back in 1305, which was only three years after the Templars lost the island of Ruad. Clement's letter speaks of initial shock at the accusations, stating, 'We were hardly able to bring our mind to believe what was being said at the time, since it seemed almost totally incredible and impossible.' However, he reveals that other voices later shared concerns about the Templars, 'We have heard several strange and unheard-of rumours about them, and so are obliged to harbour doubts; not without great bitterness, sorrow and turmoil in our heart we are forced to act on the foregoing, doing whatever reason demands.' At the letter's conclusion, the Pope declares, 'We propose to bring an enquiry of careful investigation of this matter in a few days.'[15]

Clement's comments demonstrate how widespread the negative perception of the Templars was at the time, and also show that while Jacques de Molay was negotiating the future of the order, a conspiracy to bring down the Templars was under way. Philip IV had issued an order for the arrests of the Templars a month earlier, on 14 September. The shocking charges against the Templars were outlined in the order, and included blasphemy, sodomy and heresy. The order included the king's horror at the Templars' crimes, stating that it was 'a bitter thing, a lamentable thing, a thing horrible to contemplate, terrible to hear, a heinous crime, an execrable evil, an abominable deed, a hateful disgrace, a completely inhuman thing, indeed remote from all humanity'.

Philip compares the Templars to 'stupid beasts' and describes the warrior monks as 'wolves in sheep's clothing'.[16] The dramatic language used may add to the assertion mentioned earlier by Barber that although the king profited financially from his persecution of the Templars, Philip may have truly believed the Templars were guilty.

The first of the three charges levied at the order was denying Christ upon initiation. According to the Order for Arrests, 'When they [initiates] enter the Order and make their profession, they are confronted with His image, and their miserable or rather pitiful blindness makes them deny Him three times and spit in His face three times.' After the Templar initiates deny and spit on the image of Christ, the document describes how the initiate is stripped naked and then kisses the receiving Templar official in three places. The Order for Arrests details these as 'the lower part of the dorsal spine', 'the navel', and 'on the mouth, in accordance with the profane rite of their Order'. The accusation of homosexual acts does not end at the initiation; according to the document, after the initiate is received into the Templar order, 'they are unequivocably [*sic*] bound to accept the request of another to perform the vice of that horrible, dreadful intercourse'.[17]

The final accusation was of heresy and the worship of false idols; the contradicting nature of these idols was further identified under the duress of torture. The accusation of heresy has associated the Templars with the occult for centuries and played a significant part in the Templars' fantastical perception.

HERESY AND TORTURE

The number of Templar knights arrested in France was particularly low as only fourteen knights were among the 138 members of the Templars heard by the Grand Inquisitor and only eighteen among the 546 defendants.[18] Some Templars managed to escape arrest on Friday the 13th, officially recorded as twelve, and the most prominent was the former grand master of France, Gérard de Villiers, who abandoned the order's mantle and shaved off his beard but was soon recognised and captured. John of Chali and Peter of Modies attempted to escape arrest by disguising themselves in striped clothes but were quickly caught. The Preceptor of Auvergne, Imbert Blanke, was able to flee to England before being apprehended, and one Templar was found begging in the streets of Paris.[19]

However, those imprisoned in the Paris Temple were questioned and tortured. The Order for Arrests gave instructions to the commissioners tasked with carrying out Philip's assault on the Templars. They were to obtain the truth using torture. The most sinister instruction was that those who confessed to guilt should be pardoned; otherwise, they would be sentenced to death.[20]

In captivity, the Templars were deprived of sleep, given only bread and water and shackled with iron chains. The Templar Ponsard de Gizy described how his hands were tied behind his back so tightly that blood ran down his fingernails, and he was left in a pit, unable to take more than a step for three months.[21] The Templars who did not confess to their crimes were subjected to horrific torture, such as the rack and the strappado. Those subjected to the strappado had their hands tied behind their back and were then suspended in the air via a rope by their tied hands. They were then dropped from a height and the rope was jerked just above the ground. Sometimes weights were added to the victim's feet or genitals to inflict greater pain. Gerard of Pasagio testified that he was brutally tortured this way with weights attached to his genitals and other parts.

Another horrific method involved rubbing fat on the prisoner's feet, which were then secured before a fire. The priest Bernard of Vaho suffered so greatly during this torture that after a few days the bones fell away from his feet.[22] It's not surprising that under these horrific conditions, almost all the Templars confessed to some or all of the crimes they were accused of. Out of the 138 Templars questioned in Paris, 134 confessed to some or all of the charges.[23]

Although the commissioners acted on the king's orders, Guillaume de Nogaret was credited with being the chief architect of the Templars' arrest and interrogation. He was the king's minister and had previously been involved in King Philip's conflict with Pope Boniface VIII and completed a dossier in 1307 accusing him of being an unbeliever and a magician who worshipped and conversed with demons.[24] Pope Boniface VIII died in 1303, shortly after being released from months of imprisonment at the hands of King Philip. He wasn't the only person de Nogaret charged as a heretic: Guichard, the Bishop of Troyes, was accused of magical practices and plotting to murder Queen Joan of France. De Nogaret added additional charges of sodomy and spitting on the cross, which draws a close comparison to the charges against Pope Boniface and the Templar order.[25]

Guillaume de Nogaret was heavily involved with the interrogation of the Templars and questioned Grand Master Jacques de Molay personally. He unexpectedly interrupted the inquisitors to accuse the order of paying homage to Saladin.[26]

Under torture, de Molay confessed to some of the charges, and his deposition was recorded on 24 October 1307. In his first confession, he admitted to denying Christ, but when asked to spit on an image of him, he said he had spat on the floor instead. Although Molay denied homosexual acts, he also claimed that those receiving initiatives 'should do to them and order them to do what had been done to him' and 'after receiving them he told some of those present to take them aside and do to them what was necessary'.[27]

The deposition of Geoffroi de Charney (21 October) mirrors that of the grand master, but although he was asked to deny Christ at the initiation, he could not remember being asked to spit on the image of Christ. Geoffroi said that during the initiation he was required to kiss the master on the navel and the Preceptor of Auvergne had said 'it was better to have sex between brothers of the Order than to assuage their lust with women'. However, Geoffroi denied doing this himself or being specifically asked to do it.[28] Hugues de Pairaud's deposition (9 November) reiterated the rejection of Christ at the initiation and the encouragement of homosexual acts but also gave details of the Templars' worship of false idols. He describes worshipping a head with two feet under its face and two behind it and having held and stroked the head at a chapter in Montpellier.[29]

Very few of the Templars questioned had any knowledge of the mysterious head idol, and only nine admitted to knowing about it. They gave very different accounts – Hugues de Pairaud described a head with feet, while others referred to it as having a beard, being painted on a beam and made of wood, silver and gold leaf. Others claimed to have worshipped an idol of Baphomet and a bearded head called Yalla. Jean de Cassagne admits to worshipping the idol then being shown the image of Christ before denying him and spitting on the image.[30] The association with these false idols and Baphomet would haunt the order's legacy for centuries. The origin and identity of the idol Baphomet are somewhat mysterious, however, it's most likely a corruption of the name Mohammed.[31]

JUDGEMENT AND EXECUTION

Following the investigation by Guillaume de Nogaret and the inquisitors, on 22 November 1307 Pope Clement issued the bull *Pastoralis Praeeminentiae*, which called all the kings and leaders of Christendom to arrest the Templars and hold their lands for the Church. Following this proclamation, investigations against the Templars began in England, Germany, Portugal, Spain, Italy and Cyprus.[32]

In December, two cardinals were sent to Paris to question Jacques de Molay and other senior Templars, which resulted in a struggle for dominion over the seized Templars. Eventually, the cardinals were given access, and Jacques de Molay showed his wounds to demonstrate the torture inflicted upon him, retracted his confession and claimed the Templar order was innocent of all charges.

In February 1308, Pope Clement suspended the investigation of the inquisitors and declared that he was in charge of dealing with the Templars.[33] King Philip attempted to bring the situation back under his control by trying to intimidate Clement through propaganda, slander and the threat of deposition, but the Pope refused to back down, and Clement and Philip agreed to set up two inquiries, one by the papal commission to look at the Templar organisation as a whole and a series of investigations headed by bishops to ascertain the guilt of individual Templars. As part of the agreement, Philip agreed to hand over seventy-two Templar prisoners to the custody of the Pope, but kept hold of Jacques de Molay and other high officers, claiming that they were too ill to travel.

From 28 June to 1 July at Poitiers, a commission of cardinals and the Pope heard from the seventy-two Templars. On 2 July, the Pope granted absolution to those who confessed and asked for forgiveness.[34] Curiously the Pope also gave clemency to Jacques de Molay and the other senior Templars held at Chinon Castle. Molay's absolution was not known until a historic document known as the Chinon Parchment was discovered in the Vatican Archives in 2001. The Parchment shows that, once again, Molay confessed to denying Christ. Michael Haag provides a rough translation of the Pope's absolution of the Templar grand master, 'We have decided to extend the mercy of absolution for these acts to brother Jacques de Molay, grand master of the said order'.[35]

This suggests that Clement was trying to save the Templars and salvage what he could of the order. However, the Knights Templar could not be saved so easily. In the face of opposition and defiance from many Templars, who defended the order and renounced their earlier confessions during the papal commission, in May 1310, the Archbishop of Sens had them burnt at the stake in Paris as relapsed heretics.

To settle the fate of the Templars and the control of their many assets, Pope Clement V held a council in Vienne to address the evidence against them in October 1311, four years after the Friday the 13th arrests. Clement invited the kings and leading nobles from Europe, but the only king to attend was Philip, who was personally invested in the fate of the Knights Templar. Clement had formally invited the Templars to attend the council to defend the order and, to his surprise, nine appeared to protest their innocence and claimed to speak for over 2,000 Templars. Their appearance was detrimental to the absolution Clement had previously granted, and they were swiftly arrested.

No decision had been made on the fate of the Templars by March 1312, and King Philip, with his brothers and a large force, arrived at Vienne to apply pressure on Pope Clement. On 22 March, Clement held a consistory in secret to decide whether the Knights Templar should be abolished or saved. He put the decision to a vote, with four-fifths voting to suppress the Templar order. The decision was made public on 3 April in the bull *Vox in excelso*, dated 22 March:

> Considering therefore the infamy, suspicion, noisy insinuation and the other things above which have been brought against the Order, and the secret and clandestine reception of the brothers of this Order [...] who have lapsed into the sin of wicked apostasy against the Lord Jesus Christ himself, the crime of detestable idolatry, the execrable outrage of the sodomites [...] not without bitterness and sadness of heart, not by the way of judicial sentence, but by the way of provision or apostolic ordinance, we abolish the aforesaid Order of Temple and its constitution, habit and name by an irrevocable and perpetually valid decree, and we subject it to perpetual prohibition with the approval of the Holy Council, strictly forbidding anyone to presume to enter the said Order in the future, or to receive or wear its habit, or to act as a Templar.[36]

The Order of the Knights Templar was officially dissolved, and on 2 May 1312, Clement issued the bull *Ad providam*, which granted all land and property in the possession of the order in October 1307 to be transferred to the Knights Hospitaller as all lands had originally been given to the Templars in aid of the Christian cause in the Holy Land. However, this did not include the Templar property in Castile, Aragon, Portugal and Majorca. King Philip only granted the French Templar property to the Hospitallers once they had agreed to pay 200,000 *livres tournois* as compensation for the Crown maintaining the properties.[37]

The Knights Templar were no more, and the secular authorities were required to hand out judgement on the former Templars. Most were sent to monasteries to continue living by their monastic vows. Those who were in France were now at the mercy of the French Crown, and many were sentenced to prison.[38] Jacques de Molay, who had hoped that papal absolution would save him, had to wait until 18 March 1314, when a council of cardinals (including the Archbishop of Sens) in Paris passed judgement on the last grand master and other senior former Templars – Hugues de Pairaud, Geoffroi de Gonneville and Geoffroi de Charney.

The cardinals decreed that due to their confessions, the four former Templars were to be incarcerated indefinitely. They had endured torture and years of imprisonment in King Philip's dungeon, and the harsh sentence forced the elderly Jacques de Molay and former Master of Normandy, Geoffroi de Charney to renounce their confessions and declare their innocence.

The late defiance of Jacques de Molay, now in his seventies and weak from years of imprisonment, sealed his fate. He and Geoffroi de Charney were sentenced to be burnt at the stake as relapsed heretics. They were taken to the Isle of Javiaux in the River Seine and executed. According to the verse of Geoffrey of Paris,' the last grand master gave a speech on the pyre:

> Gentlemen, at least
> Let me join my hands a little
> And make a prayer to God
> For now the time is fitting.
> Here I see my judgement
> When death freely suits me;
> God knows who is in the wrong and has sinned.
> Soon misfortune will come
> To those who have wrongly condemned us:

'God will avenge our death.'
'Gentlemen,' he said, 'make no mistake,
'All those who are against us
'Will have to suffer because of us.
'In that belief I wish to die.'

Jacques de Molay, the last Grand Master of the Templars, was burnt at the stake on 18 March 1314, almost two years after the Order of the Knights Templar was dissolved. Geoffrey of Paris is the only witness who mentions de Molay's last words, however, it paints a picture of a defiant man who cursed his enemies.

Geoffrey's verse may be a dramatic retelling, but neither Philip IV nor Pope Clement V would survive the year. Pope Clement died a month later on 20 April, and Philip IV died in a hunting accident on 29 November 1314. This created the legend that they died because of the curse inflicted upon them by Jacques de Molay.

THE END OF THE TEMPLAR ORDER

The Templar order existed for almost 200 years and was created to fill a specific need: to protect travellers on the roads when the king's forces could not. Over time, the Templars became the premier fighting force for the Franks in the Holy Land and amassed a vast amount of wealth, property and influence. However, following the loss of the Holy Land, their revolutionary form of knighthood no longer served a purpose and they became politically weak. The order established by the first Grand Master Hugues de Paynes in 1119, which defeated Saladin at the Battle of Montgisard in 1177 and fought with Richard the Lionheart in the Third Crusade, ended with its members tortured and incarcerated, its property seized, and its last grand master, an elderly, broken man, burnt at the stake.

However, as utterly destroyed as they were, the fall of the Templars was not the end of the story. Although the war in the Holy Land was lost, the war on the Iberian Peninsula was ongoing and still needed the strength of the military orders. In 1317, Pope John XXII granted the Templar properties to be given to two new military orders: the Order of Christ in Portugal and the Order of Montesa in Valencia. The Order of Montesa was created in July 1319 when King James II of Aragon gave it the castle of Montesa. The Order of Christ was created in 1319 by King Diniz of Portugal.[39]

These new orders performed the military roles of the Templars, but they were no longer under the authority of the Pope but of the kings who started each order. Both played a significant role in the Spanish *Reconquista*, which ended with the capture of Granada in 1492. Following this, the Order of Christ was involved in the exploration activities of Portuguese princes, such as Prince Henry the Navigator, who became the administrator of the order in 1420 and used its resources for exploration and colonising, which he defined as 'Crusading'.[40] The Order of Christ still exists in the twenty-first century as a Portuguese merit for outstanding service.[41]

Although the successors of the Templars continued on the Iberian Peninsula, the Knights Templar only existed within popular imagination when their international power and then sudden demise spawned myths and legends that still feature in the twenty-first century. The crimes attributed to the Templars and their confessions under torture associated them with witchcraft and the occult and influenced their popular perception.

The story of the Templars was kept alive by the persistence of fantastical myths that have inspired artists from the thirteenth right up to the twenty-first century. The story of the Knights Templar spans 900 years, continuing after their fall across a range of media, including literature, computer games and even Hollywood films such as *Star Wars*.

PART 4

TEMPLAR MYTHS AND HOLLYWOOD

17

THE GRAIL AND THE TEMPLARS

THE GUARDIANS OF THE GRAIL

The Holy Grail is a creation of medieval poets and has been featured in popular culture right up to the twenty-first century – from the 1975 cult comedy *Monty Python and the Holy Grail* to the MacGuffin of Steven Spielberg's 1989 adventure film *Indiana Jones and the Last Crusade*. The Holy Grail was also used as a metaphor in Dan Brown's 2003 novel *The Da Vinci Code*, where it is reimagined as the continuation of the bloodline of Jesus Christ. This idea of the grail representing Christ's lineage is based on pseudohistory and is not a theory entertained by serious scholars. However, all these prominent fictional tales include the Knights Templar because the Holy Grail became synonymous with the order of warrior monks. It is also important to mention that the Holy Grail wasn't originally associated with Christianity and was known initially as the Grail.

The Grail has appeared in popular culture since the end of the twelfth century. Chrétien de Troyes' Arthurian romance, 'The Story of the Grail' is one of a series of romantic poems, of which the first was 'Erec and Enide'. It was written around 1170 and tells the story of Arthurian knight Erec and his beloved Enide and their trials and adventures. The second Arthurian poem, 'Cligès', is dated to the mid-1170s and tells the story of Alexander, who travels from Greece to England to become a Knight of the Round Table. He has a son named Cligès, and after his father dies, the poem tells of his knightly valour and love for Fenice, his uncle's wife.

The third Arthurian poem is 'Lancelot, The Knight of the Cart', dated towards the end of the 1170s.[1] It has Lancelot and Guinevere as its main protagonists. It tells of Guinevere's abduction by the wicked Maleagant and her rescue by Lancelot. He is one of Arthur's most eminent knights, yet he betrays his king by entering into a passionate affair with Queen Guinevere.

The forbidden love of Lancelot and Guinevere became a common trope in Arthurian adaptations. In 1995, *The Knight of the Cart* was adapted by Hollywood in the Jerry Zucker-directed movie *First Knight*. The film stars Sean Connery as King Arthur, Richard Gere as Lancelot, Julia Ormond as Guinevere and Ben Cross as the villainous Maleagant.

The fourth of Chrétien's Arthurian poems was 'The Knight with the Lion', dated around 1180, where its protagonist, Yvain, rescues a lion from a serpent, and the lion becomes the knight's faithful companion.[2] While Yvain's character does not have the notoriety of Lancelot, 'The Knight with the Lion' was adapted into several languages, including the fourteenth-century Middle English poem 'Ywain and Gawain'.[3]

Chrétien de Troyes' final Arthurian poem, 'The Story of the Grail', was left unfinished by Chrétien, who died close to the end of the twelfth century. The poem tells the story of young Perceval becoming a knight at King Arthur's court and encountering the injured Fisher King. It is in the presence of the Fisher King that Percival first sees the Grail. However, it was not initially envisioned as the chalice that is featured in later adaptations. Chrétien details the Grail's introduction:

> Accompanying the attendants was a beautiful, gracious, and elegantly attired young lady holding between her two hands a bowl. When she entered holding this serving bowl, such brilliant illumination appeared that the candles lost their brightness just as stars and the moon do with the appearance of the sun.

Chrétien further describes the magnanimity of the Grail, adding, 'The bowl which came first, was of fine pure gold, adorned with many kinds of precious jewels, the richest and most costly found on sea or land, those on the bowl undoubtedly more valuable than any others.'[4] The original description of the Grail is far from the plain wooden cup depicted in Spielberg's *Indiana Jones and the Last Crusade*.

Despite being associated with a chalice, the word 'grail' initially referred to a serving bowl for fish.[5] Chrétien's inspiration for the fantastical grail of his poem may have been inspired by the cornucopia, also known as the horn of plenty from Celtic myth.[6] The Grail in Chrétien's poem was part of a procession of wondrous items that Percival witnessed, which included a shining, bleeding lance; a pair of candelabra that each held ten candles that lost their brightness when the Grail appeared; and finally a silver tray that concluded the procession. The Grail procession was in the castle of the Fisher King, a place that Percival had stumbled across when travelling to see his mother. While struggling to find a place to cross the river, a fisherman offered the young knight lodging and gave him directions to his home.

After a short trip, Perceval discovered that the home was, in fact, a castle. Chrétien described it as 'constructed of grey stone, it was square and flanked by turrets. The great hall stood in front of the tower, and the living quarters in front of the hall', and that 'from here to Beirut could be found no tower so beautiful or so well situated.'[7] Inside the castle, Perceval sat beside the Fisher King, who suffered from a crippling injury caused by a spear. When he awoke the following day, Perceval found himself alone and saw or heard no one until he saw the castle's drawbridge rise after he had exited the Fisher King's residence. Unknown to Perceval, he had failed a test that would have cured the Fisher King.

During the Grail procession, Perceval wanted to ask why the spear bled and who was served from the Grail, but he dared not speak as he had been cautioned by his mentor in knightly etiquette that he should refrain from talking too much. So, Perceval 'feared that if he asked a question, he would be taken for a peasant', and did not ask about the lance or grail.[8] Once he had left the castle, he encountered a woman who informed him that had Perceval asked about the Grail, the Fisher King would have been healed and would have once more been able to govern his land.

Perceval never cured the Fisher King in Chrétien's Grail poem, and the work was unfinished. However, several poets did add continuations to Chrétien's grail story, which ended with Perceval crowned as the Grail King.[9]

While some poets were working to continue Chrétien's grail story, two adapted Chrétien's work into their own. Burgundian poet Robert de Boron finished his own version of the grail story towards the end of the twelfth century, while Wolfram von Eschenbach finished his adaption *Parzival* in the early thirteenth. Both de Boron and von Eschenbach's poems built upon Chrétien's and added new aspects that would become synonymous with the Grail and feature in fiction up to the twenty-first century. It was Robert de Boron who associated the Grail with Jesus Christ and made it the cup from the Last Supper, which was also used to collect Christ's blood by Joseph of Arimathea.[10] The relationship between the Grail and the blood of Jesus Christ would be a major theme in Dan Brown's bestseller, *The Da Vinci Code*.

Wolfram von Eschenbach's Grail narrative *Parzival* dwarfed Chrétien's unfinished 9,000-line poem with his 25,000-line complete one. Wolfram expanded the Fisher King character by naming him King Anfortas, giving a detailed family history and making Anfortas Perceval's uncle.[11] Wolfram's grail differed greatly from Chrétien's bowl and Robert de Boron's cup, as it was reimagined as a stone called Lapsit exillis, which came to earth when Lucifer was cast down from heaven.[12] This divine stone, also known as 'The Gral', grants long-lasting life to those who gaze upon it, thus sustaining the life of those who reside within the Grail Castle. However, like the Fisher King of Chrétien's poem, King Anfortas is crippled by his wound and can only be healed by Perceval asking him about the grail, which he fails to do.

In Wolfrom's grail castle, Perceval also witnesses the procession of other wonderous items, such as the bleeding lance and the pair of candelabra, before the grail is brought forth and described as 'paradisal, transcending all earthly perfection'.[13] Unlike Chrétien's version, Wolfram names the lady carrying the Grail Repanse de Schoye, the sister of King Anfortas.

In addition to expanding the characters around the Grail King, Wolfram added a company of knights called Templars to the Grail Castle. These Grail guardians are keen warriors, and Perceval is warned of the danger. He's told that 'no ruse of war would help against their sorties. Till now any who rode against them took a perilous turning, for they stake their lives against others' and give no quarter. Such penance they are given for their sins'.[14]

Wolfram's Templars guarded the Grail with selfless wrath that connotes the Hugues de Paynes Templar knights guarding pilgrims travelling through the Kingdom of Jerusalem. Wolfram may have witnessed the martial abilities of the Knights Templar when he visited the Holy Land around 1200.[15] His inclusion of Templar guardians in his Grail narrative started the popular association of the Knights Templar and the Grail. However, it was Robert de Boron's version that associated the Grail with Christ and rebranded it as the Holy Grail.

The Knights Templar are still associated with the Holy Grail in popular culture, such as the 2017–19 historical TV series *Knightfall*, which follows the final years of the Knights Templar and Master of the Paris Temple, Landry de Lauzon's (played by Tom Cullen) quest to find the Holy Grail. The link between the Templars and the Grail is seen across other media formats, such as the 2011 computer game *The First Templar*, where players can play as Templar knight Celian d'Arestide in his quest to find the relic. Even though the game was not as successful as its 2007 predecessor, Ubisoft's *Assassin's Creed* (where the Templars are the villains), it demonstrates the continuation of the thirteenth-century association between the Grail and the Templars.

Iconic science fiction filmmakers George Lucas and Steven Spielberg also included the Knights Templar in their 1989 adventure film *Indiana Jones and the Last Crusade*. The Lucas-produced and Spielberg-directed blockbuster incorporates a Templar Grail guardian archetype who is renamed as a Knight of the Cruciform Sword with slightly tweaked Templar iconography. The symbol of the Knights of the Cruciform sword is similar to the infamous Templar red cross on a white background with two additional red bars added, one above the central part of the cross and one below. The top bar curves as a semicircle to connote the lip, and the other is a smaller straight line to depict the foot of the Grail cup. However, this symbol is set upon a white tabard, which the Knight of the Cruciform Sword wears atop a suit of armour, closely following the expected depictions of Templar knights.

In Jeffrey Boam's original screenplay for the film, this Templar-esque order were referred to as 'Grail Knights', with the Cruciform Sword aspect being added in Tom Stoppard's rewrites to add the Brotherhood of Cruciform Sword as an additional obstacle for Indiana Jones' Grail quest.[16] Although the Grail guardian knight was always part of the plan, the Templar-like order with similar iconography wasn't added until a later draft.

In a 2008 interview for *Entertainment Weekly*, Spielberg admitted that he didn't think the film would work because the Holy Grail had been cemented in popular culture by the 1975 film *Monty Python and the Holy Grail.*[17] The cult comedy subverts Arthurian themes and parodies the Grail story; however, the film doesn't feature the Templars directly, although it includes the Templar iconography of a red cross on a white background in the costume Sir Galahad (played by Michael Palin) wore.

Although strongly associated with the Grail story, the Knights Templar aren't always featured in prominent Grail fiction. John Boorman's 1981 film *Excalibur* features the quest for the Holy Grail in his adaptation of the fifteenth-century work *Le Morte de Arthur* but doesn't feature any Templar knights or Grail guardians.

However, the Templars' association with the Holy Grail would be further cemented in popular culture with the 2003 Dan Brown novel, *The Da Vinci Code.*

SANG REAL AND THE DA VINCI CODE

The Da Vinci Code is an international best-selling novel that sold over 80 million copies, and a film version was released in 2006, making $758,239,851 at the box office.[18] The novel and Ron Howard-directed film introduced the Grail myth to a new audience and further established the Knights Templars' association with the Grail that came from Wolfram von Eschenbach's *Parzival*. Like Wolfram and Robert de Boron, Brown also reimagines the Grail by proposing that the Holy Grail is a symbolic rather than physical item. In *The Da Vinci Code*, the Grail is a metaphor to represent the lineage of Jesus Christ through his marriage to Mary Magdalene. Simply put, in Brown's novel, the Grail is the continuation of the bloodline of Jesus Christ. This fantastical theory presented in the novel is underpinned by the notion of a linguistic error where the Spanish '*san greal*' should have been recorded as '*sang real*', which translates to 'royal blood'. However, this clever wordplay only works in modern Spanish, and no medieval language can be so easily manipulated to mean royal blood.[19]

Setting aside the validity of the theory, the royal blood theory was not the invention of Dan Brown but a concept published in the 1982 quasi-history book *The Holy Blood and the Holy Grail*. The theories featured so prominently in *The Da Vinci Code* that its authors, Michael Baigent, Richard Leigh and Henry Lincoln, unsuccessfully sued *The Da Vinci Code*'s publishers, Random House, for plagiarism. In the case of *Baigent and Leigh vs Random House*, the court concluded, 'There is no copyrights on ideas expressed in a work which claims to be a book of history' and the authors could 'not monopolise historical research or knowledge'.[20] Essentially, the books were different genres, one being presented as historical, the other a novel inspired by these fantastical theories.

Although a work of fiction, Brown still portrays the fantastical theories as historical facts. At the start of the novel, before the prologue, the book states:

> Fact: The Priory of Sion – a European secret society founded in 1099 – is a real organization. In 1975 Paris's Bibliothéque Nationale discovered parchments known as Les Dossiers Secrets, identifying numerous members of the Priory of Sion, including Sir Isaac Newton, Sandro Botticelli, Victor Hugo and Leonardo Da Vinci.[21]

Brown's claim of historical fact is disputed by the Master of the London Temple Robin Griffith-Jones, who details that the Priory of Sion was created by Pierre Plantard, a French fraudster, in the 1950s. Before the war, Plantard had been involved with right-wing groups that sought to re-establish the monarchy. After the war, he was imprisoned for fraud and embezzlement, but after his release, he resumed his political agenda and founded the Priory of Sion. It's important to note that the order was originally named after Mont Sion, close to the French town Annemasse, and the claim of association with Mont Sion in Jerusalem came later.[22]

Pierre Plantard wanted to use the Priory of Sion as a means to push for the re-establishment of the French monarchy and claimed that he was the true heir to the throne of France. To press Plantard's fantasy, he, with the help of associates, typed up a document of the Priory of Sion's history, which Plantard named *Les Dossiers Secrets*, and placed them in the Bibliothéque Nationale, the national library of France. It was these documents that were featured in the Lincoln, Baigent and Leigh book, *The Holy Blood and the Holy Grail*. Brown's claim of fact regarding the Priory of Sion is problematic as the organisation itself was started by a convicted fraudster, and the *Les Dossiers Secrets* were typed. However, Robin Griffith-Jones proposes that Brown did not believe Plantard's fantasy but playfully included it within his story – the novel's antagonist, Sir Leigh Teabing includes a direct name of one of *The Holy Blood and the Holy Grail* authors and Teabing is an anagram of another, Baigent.[23]

Although the Knights Templar were not originally associated with the Priory of Sion, *The Holy Blood and The Holy Grail* reimagined the Knights Templar as the military arm of the Priory of Sion, and this idea is carried over into *The Da Vinci Code*, where the Templars are dedicated to protecting the truth around the bloodline of Christ. In the novel, the Templars assume their literary Grail guardian role, but instead of a wonderous item, the Grail is the tomb of Mary Magdalene.

The novel presents an alternative history for the Knights Templar, which proposes that their founding mission to protect pilgrims on the road was just a façade. According to Robert Langdon, the esteemed professor and protagonist of Brown's novel, the Templars were created by the Priory of Sion to retrieve the documents buried beneath the Temple of Solomon. Langdon dismisses the historical reality of the Templars' origin by explaining that their actual role is 'a common misconception. The idea of protection of pilgrims was the guise under which the Templars ran their mission. Their true goal in the Holy Land was to retrieve the documents from beneath the ruins of the temple.'[24]

The book further ties into Templar conspiracies by claiming that they didn't grow rich and powerful from the many generous monetary gifts and land donations but by blackmailing the Catholic Church. Instead of French King Philip IV arresting the Templars because of accusations of heresy, Langdon claims the Templars were brought down to stop them from revealing the truth.

In *The Da Vinci Code*, Langdon discovers that the Templars had hidden the sarcophagus of Mary Magdalene within the crypts of Rosslyn Chapel in Scotland. The chapel had long been associated with the Templars, possibly dating back to Sir Walter Scott's reference to the Lords of Rosslyn in the nineteenth-century poem, 'The Lay of the Last Minstrel'.[25] It was constructed in 1446 by Sir William St Clair, notably over 100 years after the Templar Order was dissolved and the last grand master executed.

Despite no real connection between Rosslyn Chapel and the historical Templars, its unique architecture has become associated with deeper meanings that symbolise Templar and Masonic connotations (the link between the Freemasons and Templars will be explored in the next chapter). In having the Templars guard the symbolic Grail in the form of the bloodline of Jesus Christ, Brown draws a direct link from the medieval Grail literature to the Rosslyn Chapel heritage site.

Despite having no basis in historical reality, the Rosslyn Trust is keen to promote the relationship between Rosslyn Chapel, the Knights Templar and the Holy Grail. In fact, tourism to Rosslyn Chapel boomed following the release of Brown's novel, with 120,000 visitors in 2005 compared to 38,000 in 2003.[26] The popular association between the fantastical royal blood theory, *The Da Vinci Code* and the chapel are actively promoted and the chapel's gift shop sells copies of *The Da Vinci Code* and *The Holy Blood and the Holy Grail*.[27] The Rosslyn Chapel Trust preserves this heritage site, and due to the increase in tourism from Brown's fiction, the fantastical royal blood theory has played a significant part in the preservation of history as the increased revenue has contributed to the maintenance of the historic chapel.

Robin Griffiths-Jones proposes that Dan Brown is an heir to the medieval poetry of Chrétien de Troyes, Robert de Boron and Wolfram von Eschenbach, and his Grail story draws from similar themes.[28] Brown's novel incorporates the themes of personal growth through the journey, reconnecting with family and the quest for the wonderous item. However, unlike a divine bowl or celestial stone, Brown's Grail symbolises Christ's historical legacy. Brown incorporates aspects of Robert de Boron's story by associating the Grail with Christ. He also borrows from Wolfram von Eschenbach's story, including the Knights Templar as guardians of the Grail. It is through the interpretations and imagination of the medieval Grail poetry that the historical Knights Templar are still associated with the fictional grail to this day.

18

TEMPLAR OCCULT AND THE FREEMASONS

WITCHES AND THE OCCULT

The perception of the disgraced Templar order following its destruction varied across Europe. Some of the French chroniclers were swayed by the behaviour of Jacques de Molay and Geoffroi de Charney at the stake, which they perceived as that of condemned innocent men. Influential Italian writer Dante Alighieri addressed the Templars' fall in his 1321 poem, the *Divine Comedy*. In the poem, the founder of the French Capet Dynasty accuses Philip IV of greed and he 'lawlessly brought his greedy sails into the very Temple itself'.[1]

In the late fifteenth century, Felix Fabri of the Dominican Order wrote of the Templars' sins and rightful punishment:

> Albeit their own beginning was holy and full of virtue, yet afterwards they degenerated from their forerunners after they waxed fat and were spread about throughout the earth. Wherefore in the reign of Clement V, forasmuch as it became known to our people that they had gone over to the Saracens, and had fallen into many vices because of their great wealth [...] they were destroyed by Philip, King of France, with the consent of the sovereign pontiff of Rome, since they were leading exceedingly disgraceful lives.[2]

His verdict of the Templars turning away from their original mission mirrors that of the English opinion of the event, where chroniclers perceived that the Templars became complacent and self-indulgent and were thus destroyed by the French king.[3] Unlike the Hospitallers, who re-established themselves on the Island of Rhodes with a navy, the Knights Templar leadership were focused on launching another Crusade but were tarnished by failing to hold Acre in 1291 when protecting Christians in the Holy Land was their reason for existence.

The view of the Templars following the fall was not that of Devil-worshippers but of a failed order brought down by their greed and turning from their original mission. The associations with the occult, Baphomet and false idols did not come into the wider popular perception until the sixteenth century. In 1531, Heinrich Agrippa revisited those claims in his book *De Occulta Philosophia*, which raised the distant memory of the failed Templar order and placed the warrior monks within the context of witchcraft. Agrippa only briefly mentions the Templars but places them alongside witches, 'The detestable heresy of old Churchmen, and like to these are manifest in witches and mischievous women, which wickedness the foolish dotage of women is subject to fall into.'[4] In the sixteenth century, witch hunting was common practice, and by placing the Knights Templar alongside witches, Agrippa launched the Templars' association with the mystical and occult, which is still prevalent in the twenty-first century.

Another Renaissance writer, Guillaume Paradin, also addressed the Templars' mystical associations in his 1552 *Chronicle of Savoy*. He described how initiates to the Templar order were brought to a cave to worship an image covered with human skin that had two glowing carbuncles as eyes. He also added to the accusation of denying Christ and spitting on the cross by writing that following this, an orgy took place with women. He explained that this initiation mirrored the ceremonies of Bacchanals in Ancient Rome.[5]

Not all Renaissance writers weaved the Knights Templar memory into witchcraft. French writer Jean Bodin believed that the Templars were innocent and persecuted by Philip IV. Bodin asserted that the German chroniclers demonstrated the Templars were persecuted so that the French king could steal their properties and wealth.[6]

The Renaissance viewed the Templars as wicked heretics or oppressed victims, but at the end of the sixteenth century another nostalgic view of the Templars appeared in the guise of the romantic chivalric hero (see Chapter 19).[7]

The salacious occult imagining of the Templars was still apparent in popular culture during the twentieth century and into the twenty-first. The Spanish/Portuguese horror films of Amando de Ossorio used the dark occult practices of the Knights Templar to inspire the monsters of his 1972 film *Tombs of the Blind Dead*. The film features an evil order of medieval knights who carry out a blood ritual on a female sacrifice by tying her to a cross and then two knights on horses slash the victim with their swords before drinking the sacrifice's blood, which recalls the Renaissance Templar occult depiction. Much of the film is set in the twentieth century, and these knights are blind zombies who rise from their tombs to hunt on foot or via horseback for a group of teenagers to feast upon. The original version refers to them as 'Knights from the East', but in the English dub they are referred to as 'Templars'. The villainous knights are also dressed in white habits with a red, slightly reworked cross to depict Templars.[8] The fantastical horror plot proved successful and three sequel films were released: *Return of the Evil Dead* (1973), *The Ghost Galleon* (1974) and *Night of the Seagulls* (1975).

The Templars' association with the undead continued in the horror franchise, and the symbol of the Templars was used in 1996 for the logo of the evil Umbrella Corporation in the franchise-launching computer game *Resident Evil* by Capcom. The symbol is that of the top of an umbrella with eight triangular sections that alternate both red and white, creating the appearance of a red cross on a white background, the infamous symbol of the Knights Templar.

In the game, the Umbrella Corporation is a shadowy, worldwide company that created a virus that creates undead monsters. It coincides the image of the Knights Templar as a shadowy international organisation that became associated with the occult and, thanks to the work of Amando de Ossorio, the undead. In 2017, the *Resident Evil* film adaptations alone generated nearly $1 billion, demonstrating how successful the franchise, which also consists of computer games and TV shows, has been.[9] It further established the myth that the Knights Templar were engaged in occult and ungodly practices.

The Templar undead associations resurfaced again in the 2017 film *The Mummy*, starring Tom Cruise with Sofia Boutella as the mummy. In this version of the classic horror, the Egyptian mummy, Ahmanet, raises the Templars from their graves to act as her minions.[10] *The Mummy* demonstrates how influential the tortured Templar prisoners' accounts of false idols and Baphomet have been in influencing the legacy of the warrior monks.

THE TEMPLARS AS FREEMASONS

The sixteenth century imagined the Knights Templar as either evil magicians or oppressed victims, but the eighteenth century saw the warrior monks reinvented within the new fraternity known as Freemasonry. Freemasonry was inspired by the medieval guilds, where crafts were learnt and regulated, but the Freemasons grew out of the Masons Guild. The guilds were intended for those engaging in the trade, but in the seventeenth century, the Scottish Masonry Guild attracted a lot of interest from the upper classes wishing to join lodges.[11]

The Templar association came about in the eighteenth century when Masonry had spread to France. In 1736, a Scottish knight, Andrew Jacob Ramsey, who was a supporter of Bonnie Prince Charlie and receiver of a knighthood in the Order of Saint Lazare, addressed a group of French Freemasons, raised the Freemasons' origin above mere stonemasons and gave them a Crusading pedigree. The Knights Templar were still seen as controversial in France, so originally Ramsey claimed that the Knights Hospitaller were the ancestors of the Freemasons.

However, the Knights Hospitaller were still in operation, and by the eighteenth century, they were based in Malta and had been reinvented as the Knights of Malta. So, the origin was changed to include the Knights Templar as there were no Templars to dispute it.[12] Essentially, the Templars became associated with the Freemasons as a way to market the organisation to the French upper classes. Templar lodges appeared in the United States in 1769 and in England by 1778, but it was the German aristocracy that propelled the Templar form of masonry. Karl Von Hund, a wealthy landowner in Saxony, pushed the new style of Templar lodge. Hund was a Templar fanatic and, when he died in 1776, he was buried in the Templar costume he created.[13] The Templar association spread through European lodges, with German Masons adding to the tale that the Knights Templar had learnt secret wisdom and power when they occupied their headquarters atop the Temple of Solomon in Jerusalem. Jacques de Molay then passed this secret knowledge to his heirs before his execution, and now the Freemasons were the heirs to the Templar secrets.[14]

The Templar secrets varied from knowledge to treasure, which, according to the unidentified author of *De la Maconnerie Parmi Les Chretiens*, included a shroud containing the secrets of the order, the crown of the last King of Jerusalem, a candelabra from the Jerusalem Temple and four golden statues of the Evangelists from the Holy Sepulchre. This treasure was said by the unidentified author to have been retrieved from its hiding place inside two hollow pillars in the Parisian mausoleum by the Count of Beaujeu, the nephew of Jacques de Molay, the night before the latter was burnt at the stake.[15] This notion of a Templar secret still prevails in popular culture today and involves the Templars heading to America via Scotland and taking their treasure with them to bury under New York City to await the founding of the United States.[16]

The idea that the Knights Templars survived in secret in Scotland is an invention by Scottish Freemasons to further romanticise the association of the Templars with Freemasonry. In 1843, the Order of the Knights Templar in Scotland published a version of Templar history, which included their noble origin. The account, *Historical Notice of the Order*, proposes that it is an agreed fact that the Knights Templar fought alongside Robert the Bruce and helped defeat Edward II at the Battle of Bannockburn in 1314, months after the last Templar grand master, Jacques de Moley was burnt at the stake. The nineteenth-century account claims that the Knights Templar helped defeat the English, and in gratitude Robert the Bruce spared those Templars who would eventually become the Freemasons.

The romantic notion is not mentioned by any contemporary chroniclers and is also perplexing because before the Templars' arrest, the Templar soldiers were stationed in Cyprus and the Iberian Peninsula, while it was the non-combative administrators and agricultural workers that maintained the order's vast estates in Europe.[17]

The myth of the Templar treasure and the role of Freemason Ben Franklin tenuously linked the Knights Templar to American history. The perceived evidence of the Templars' pre-Columbus visit to America is proposed to be depicted in the carvings of Rosslyn Chapel. The chapel is rich with artistic carvings and is believed to feature carvings of two plants native to North America . One is supposedly of maize, a plant unknown in Britain when the chapel was built in 1456. Of course, the intention of the carvings is open to interpretation, and historian Michael Haag proposes that, despite the chapel's date of construction, they were added later. He argues that the carvings throughout the chapel are not part of the original stonework but were attached afterwards, and there are no reliable dates for their origin.[18] Also, the Freemasons, who claimed to be the descendants of the Knights Templar, played very little role in the founding of the United States. Although Benjamin Franklin was one of the five individuals who drew up the Declaration of Independence, this is more coincidence than Freemason plot because the declaration was mainly written by Thomas Jefferson, who was not a Freemason.[19]

Although created in the eighteenth century, the Knights Templars' link to Freemasonry and links to the Founding Fathers were further embedded in popular culture through the twenty-first-century Disney film series *National Treasure*. The first was released in 2004, starring Nicholas Cage as treasure hunter Benjamin Franklin Gates, the heir to the secrets of the Templars and Freemasons. The film grossed $347,512,318 at the box office, which spawned a sequel in 2007.[20] It drew heavily on the myths of the Knights Templar and Freemasons and grounded them within an idealised view of American history.

To present the Templar myths with some historical legitimacy in the film's opening, a young Ben Gates is taught by his grandfather that the Freemasons inserted symbols into the dollar bill to show their influence. Gates' grandfather claims the unfinished pyramid and the all-seeing eye on the reverse of the note are symbols of the Knights Templar. The All-Seeing Eye, otherwise known as the Eye of Providence, and the unfinished pyramid, connotes God watching over the United States as it continues its unfinished mission. These symbols evoke the puritanical beliefs that the United States was founded upon, not a Templar Masonic fantasy.[21]

In the opening scene, the young Benjamin Gates is sworn in by his grandad to continue the duties of the Templars, Freemasons and the Gates family as they are heirs to a clue to the secret Templar treasure. The other clues are hidden among landmarks of the War of Independence, such as the Hall of Independence. Benjamin is made a knight by his grandfather, and so the Templar myth of a secret treasure and Templars heading to America becomes associated with geographical reality and the founding of the United States.

The 2005 best-selling novel *The Last Templar* by Raymond Khoury also used the long-lost Templar treasure as the MacGuffin. The book sees archaeologist Tess Chaykin on a quest to retrace the steps of the last Templar and find the lost Templar treasure. The book was adapted into a TV mini-series in 2009, and unlike *National Treasure*, which featured a physical treasure, *The Last Templar* includes as the treasure the myth of a Templar secret that will shake modern Christendom.[22]

The Templar myths are also featured in Umberto Eco's 1988 novel *Foucault's Pendulum*, a satirical take on conspiracy theories and shadowy organisations. The story tells of three editors at a vanity publisher specialising in alternate history and theories, who create their own conspiracy theory by examining multiple occult manuscripts and alternative histories and fitting them together with a computer to create their own secret history called 'The Plan'. The Plan has its origins in the pseudo-history of the Knights Templar. One of the editors, Casaubon, an academic expert on the Knights Templar, crafts how the secret of the Templars has been passed on throughout history via different organisations to the present day. The Plan includes the myths of the Templars in Scotland and the Holy Grail, with Casaubon noting that 'The Templars have something to do with everything.'[23] Misfortune follows the creators of The Plan as they become obsessed and start to believe their creation to be true. They underestimate the impact of conspiracy theories and myth, while other occult obsessives also believe the false history and seek to ascertain the truth of The Plan, which ends in violence.

The Knights Templar are the perfect catalyst to instil history with myth, as the long-gone warrior monks are unable to challenge this false legacy. However, the examples of *National Treasure* and best-selling novel *The Last Templar* demonstrate how Ramsey and the Freemasons' reworking of history has influenced perceptions of the warrior monks. The works of fiction incorporate Templar myths to provide a link to a false past and depiction of the Templars. In the same way as the Renaissance writers propelled the association of the Templars with the occult, the Freemasons added a sense of legitimacy to the fantastical notions that the Knights Templar were the keepers of a great treasure and tremendous secrets.

19

HOLLYWOOD TEMPLARS AND JEDI KNIGHTS

THE VILLAINOUS TEMPLAR KNIGHT

The Knights Templar have been featured in fiction dating back as far as the thirteenth-century Arthurian Grail romances as the guardians of the Grail, but they were reintroduced to popular culture as a knightly archetype in the nineteenth-century novels of Sir Walter Scott. Scott's 1820 novel *Ivanhoe* featured Brian de Bois-Guilbert, a Templar knight, as the antagonist, while Sir Ivanhoe, the returning Crusader and loyal knight for Richard the Lionheart, is its titular hero. In the novel, Brian de Bois-Guilbert and the Templar grand master accuse the innocent Rebecca, the daughter of Jewish banker Issac of York, of witchcraft, blaming her for de Bois-Guilbert's unwanted advances and putting her on trial. Ivanhoe is Rebecca's champion in her trial by combat and he kills de Bois-Guilbert.

Ivanhoe features two types of Crusaders: the heroic and chivalrous Ivanhoe and the villainous Templar de Bois-Guilbert. Scott's Crusade literature was extremely popular, selling over 2 million books by 1840. Although previously seen as a shameful failure, the theme of Crusading captured the imagination of nineteenth-century Europe, which saw the expansion of European power to the east, as the Ottoman Empire declined, and the colonial exploits of European nations in North Africa. The European colonisation was reminiscent of the medieval colonisations of the Holy Land and the novels of Sir Walter Scott captured the European nostalgia for the Crusades.[1]

Scott was a Calvinist, which suggests that he featured the Knights Templar as the villains of his Crusade novels because they represented a disgraced relic of the Catholic Church who answered only to the Pope.[2]

Scott's Brian de Bois-Guilbert became the first Templar villain in what would be a medieval character archetype. *Ivanhoe* has been adapted by film and television since, beginning with two silent films, one British and one American, released in 1913.

Arguably, the most significant is the 1952 MGM production directed by Richard Thorpe, which stars Robert Taylor as Ivanhoe, Elizabeth Taylor as Rebecca and George Sanders as de Bois-Guilbert. Although Thorpe's version included the villainous actions of Brian de Bois-Guilbert, it downplayed his role as a Templar by not including the iconography, giving him blue stripes across his white mantle and replacing the role of the Templar grand master with Prince John overseeing Rebbecca's trial for witchcraft. The Templars' presence in the story was downplayed because Thorpe used the film to address the anxieties in Hollywood towards McCarthyism and the HUAC (House Committee on Un-American Activities), so Rebecca's witchcraft trial became a political one.[3] An adaptation of Scott's 1825 novel *The Talisman* was released in 1954, titled *King Richard and The Crusaders*, although it was not as well received as Thorpe's *Ivanhoe*.

As well as the horror movies of Amando de Ossorio, the remainder of the twentieth century saw the Templars feature in lower-budget releases such as the 1998 film *The Minion*, starring Dolph Lundgren as Lukas Sadorov, a Templar knight wielding a spiked gauntlet, who is charged with finding the key that opens the gates of hell before the shape-shifting Minion.[4]

Hollywood would revisit the villainous Templar knight in the twenty-first century with the release of Sir Ridley Scott's 2005 film *Kingdom of Heaven*, which depicts the political instability of the Kingdom of Jerusalem and the eventual loss of Jerusalem to Saladin (played by Ghassan Massoud). Scott's historical epic did not feature either side of the war as the villains but chose to include the Knights Templar as a third radical faction that can be blamed for the film's events.

To put the Knights Templar at the centre of the film's story, *Kingdom of Heaven* reimagines historical figures of the late twelfth century as Templars. Scott's film depicts the King of Jerusalem, Guy de Lusignan (played by Marton Csokas), and the former Prince of Antioch, Reynald de Châtillon (Brendan Gleeson), as Templars who are to blame for the war with Saladin that leads to the eventual loss of Jerusalem at the film's climax. In reality, although Reynald de Châtillon's actions provoked Saladin by breaking the truce to attack caravans (see Chapter 7), he and Guy were not members of the Templar Order but Frankish nobility.

The film's writer, William Monahan, justified his adaptation of the Crusades' history by explaining, 'You use what plays, or can be made to play, and you don't use what doesn't.'[5] In this way, the film was able to use the Templars' infamous iconography of the red cross on a white background to dress Guy de Lusignan and Reynald de Châtillon, so they are immediately recognisable as a separate faction. The other faction are dressed in light blue, which visually distinguishes them from the Templars. It is headed by Tiberias (played by Jeremy Irons), who appears to be based on Guy's rival, Count Raymond of Tripoli, who once allied with Saladin against Guy. The other prominent member is Balian of Ibelin (played by Orlando Bloom), who leads the defences and, in Scott's film, begins the film as a blacksmith in France. In splitting the Kingdom of Jerusalem into two factions, the film echoes the two types of Crusaders featured in Sir Walter Scott's novel with the heroic Balian de Ibelin and the villainous Guy de Lusignan.

A Crusades film released so close to the events of 9/11 and during President George W. Bush's war with Iraq was always going to be controversial, but Scott's *Kingdom of Heaven* had a positive reception, most notably from the Council on American-Islamic Relations (CAIR), who, after a private screening in April 2005, gave the film their approval.[6] In an interview with the *Guardian*, Sir Ridley Scott stated that he had received 'many letters from Islamic groups and societies thanking me for a very understanding film about Muslims'.[7] *Kingdom of Heaven* incorporated the villainous Templar archetype of Sir Walter Scott's novels to distance the film's Christian characters from the violent atrocities caused by the film's radical Templar faction. The film features Guy and Reynald and a company of Templar knights slaughtering a Muslim caravan, which then justifies Saladin's invasion of the Kingdom of Jerusalem.

The year 2007 saw the release of Ubisoft's video game *Assassin's Creed*, an open-world action game set during the Third Crusade, which would eventually become a global franchise. The player controls a member of the Assassins called Altaïr Ibn-La'Ahad, who fights against the villainous Knights Templar, who are seeking the mystical Apple of Eden, while the Christians and Muslims are at war during the Third Crusade. The game includes the Assassins as a third faction in the war, which the creative director Patrice Desilets explained in a 2007 interview that to ensure that the game doesn't take sides, 'you start by choosing a third party – this is what the Assassins are'.[8] To further distance the player from the conflict of the Third Crusade, the game incorporates a Knights Templar faction as the antagonists, who are violent and tyrannical to both Christians and Muslims.

Although *Assassin's Creed* incorporates the villainous Templar archetype as an antagonist faction as in Scott's *Kingdom of Heaven*, the game's Templar evokes the occult associations of the sixteenth century (see Chapter 18). Not only does the game have the Templars seeking to use the power of the mystical Apple of Eden to dominate the world, but it also removes the warrior monks' Christianity. One of the game's Templars tells Altaïr that he knows there is no afterlife and their treasure is the proof.[9]

The Templars' use of violence to oppress coincides with the villainous archetype, but the game extends it by infusing the depiction with the occult association of Renaissance writers. Although the Templars in the game are fantastical, the conflict between the Assassins and the Knights Templar in *Assassin's Creed* does have some basis in historical reality – in 1173, Abdallah, an Assassin envoy, was killed by a group of Knights Templar to prevent an alliance between the Franks and the Assassins (see Chapter 5).

The villainous Templar character from the novels of Sir Walter Scott has established itself in Hollywood and within popular culture through the adaptions of Scott's work. However, the notion that the Knights Templar were the worst of the Crusaders is not supported by the chroniclers and is contradicted by Islamic accounts of the time, such as Ibn al-Athīr's, which explained that Saladin's advisors described the Templars as religious men who could be trusted. The association of the Templars as the worst of the Crusaders can be traced to the blame they received following the loss of Outremer, the accusations of heresy and occult practices and the Templar villain from the romantic, medieval-set novels of Sir Walter Scott.

HEROIC TEMPLARS

While many Renaissance writers depicted the Templars as heretics or innocent victims, others incorporated the romantic theme of chivalry within their work, such as Italian poet Torquato Tasso's writing of heroic Crusaders in his epic sixteenth-century poem, *Jerusalem Delivered*.[10] Edmund Spenser included the heroic Redcrosse Knight as his hero in the 1596 poem, 'The Faerie Queene'. In this Arthurian-inspired poem, Redcrosse bears the red cross associated with the Templars on his armour, but it is later revealed that this is the cross of St George. Redcrosse bears further resemblance to the Knights Templar as he is a holy warrior, but his weakness is the sin of lust, which he shares with the fictional heroic Templar characters from the twentieth and twenty-first centuries.[11]

Jan Guillou's 1998 novel *The Road to Jerusalem*, which was adapted into the film *Arn: The Knight Templar* in 2007, has misfortune befall its hero, Arn Magnusson (played by Joakim Nätterqvist), who is seduced by his lover's sister, which causes him to be banished. Likewise, the 2011 English film *Ironclad* has a Templar hero, Thomas Marshall (played by James Purefoy), who, while on guard duty, sleeps with Lady Isabel (played by Kate Mara) and allows the besiegers to storm the castle.

The inclusion of a Templar hero in *Ironclad* and *Arn: The Knight Templar* has more similarity to Edmund Spenser's Redcrosse than Sir Walter Scott's Templar. *Ironclad* is set in England during the Barons' Revolt of the thirteenth century, and fictional Templar Thomas Marshall and a small force hold Rochester Castle against the army of King John to wait for relief from a French army.

The inclusion of a Templar knight to defend Rochester Castle bears little resemblance to reality. The film may have drawn inspiration from William Marshall, a nobleman involved in the conflict who became a Templar on his deathbed; however, he fought on the king's side. He was a hero of the English monarchy, led the royal forces and defeated the French prince and rebel barons at the Second Battle of Lincoln in 1217, which secured the future of the infant King Henry III.[12]

The Knights Templar were not involved with the siege of Rochester Castle, and the actual defence was led by William d'Aubigny (played by Brian Cox), who in the film is a supporting character to the Templar hero. While *Ironclad* pushed the Templars' involvement in the Barons' Revolt, in reality, they remained neutral and provided manor houses to be used for negotiations. *Ironclad*'s Templar hero evokes St George as he defends England dressed in Templar garb that also connotes the English national flag. The nationalistic imagery of *Ironclad* is parallel to an underlying pro-European theme as the hero struggles against the tyranny of the English monarch awaiting liberation from the French forces.[13]

Scholar Elizabeth Heale proposes that Redcrosse is used as a device to comment on the political climate at the time of *The Faerie Queene*'s publication, most notably Redcrosse's rescue of Lady Una and the slaying of a dragon. She suggests that St George's rescue of Una and her restoration to her kingdom refers to the restoration of a pure reformed Church after the country's misguided following of Roman Catholicism.[14] Heale's theory would coincide with the notion that *Ironclad* includes a Templar hero to signify a pro-European theme with nationalistic imagery.

Like Redcrosse, the Templar hero of the *Arn* series is also used as a device to underpin the theme of multiculturalism. Set in the twelfth century, *Arn: The Knight Templar* (2007) and *Arn: The Kingdom at Road's End* (2008), adapted from Jan Guillou's *Crusades Trilogy* (1998–2000), tell the story of young Swedish noble Arn Magnusson, who is forced to serve a twenty-year penance as a Templar knight for having premarital relations with Cecilia Algotsdotter (played by Sofia Helin), who is sentenced to twenty years' penance in a convent. In the Holy Land, Arn begins an unlikely friendship with Saladin (played by Milind Soman) after saving the sultan from armed bandits. This friendship pays dividends at the Battle of Hattin when Arn's life is spared from the slaughter by Saladin, who allows his Templar friend to return home, bringing a multicultural group of craftsmen to build a technologically sophisticated estate.

The film adaption of the novel drew criticism for its portrayal of Arn as a hero, such as Gwlady Fouché's review for *The Guardian*, titled 'Revisionism on a Grand Scale', where she argued that '*Arn* is trying to make a hero out of someone who wasn't' and criticises the depiction that 'Arn is a tolerant and multicultural-friendly crusader'. Aside from the film's Templar hero character, the reviewer chastises the film for Arn's relationship with Saladin, suggesting that 'his [Arn's] first reflex upon seeing a Saracen is to defend him rather than slaughter him, and he becomes buddies with Saladin'.[15]

While the idea of Saladin being friends with a Templar knight is fantastical, the idea that a Templar knight would not defend a Muslim is contradicted by a personal anecdote by the twelfth-century Muslim writer Usama ibn Munqidh. Usama described an incident in Jerusalem when he was assaulted by a European Christian when praying. Usama wrote, 'A Frank threw himself on me from behind, lifted me up and turned me so that I was facing east.' A group of Templars, who Usama described as 'friends of mine', intervened and removed the violent Christian. Usama adds that the Templars apologised and explained, 'He is a foreigner who has just arrived today from his homeland in the north, and has never seen anyone pray facing any other direction than east.'[16] Usama's personal experience contradicts the notion that the Knights Templar were the worst of the Christian knights, and the monstrous perception perhaps relates to depictions in the fiction of Sir Walter Scott and later in the film *Kingdom of Heaven*.

Jan Guillou alludes to conflicts in the Middle East, explaining that in the Arn series, 'The story is about the world today, our conflicts; but taking place 800 years back in time.'[17] Guillou is known for his pro-Palestinian views and criticises the 'War on Terror' and the vilification of Muslims, comparing it to the First Crusade.[18]

Similar to Edmund Spenser's Redcrosse, Arn is a holy warrior, who is susceptible to the charms of women and is a device to comment on the political climate of the time. Bo Tao Michaëlis, a Danish literary critic, explains that Jan Guillou's intention for the *Crusades Trilogy* was to show that Scandinavia is a product of encounters with other cultures, such as Islam and Judaism.[19]

Guillou incorporated a Templar hero who respects other cultures and embraces multiculturalism, while the fiction of Sir Walter Scott depicted the Templar knight as the worst of the European Crusaders. The Templars of *Kingdom of Heaven* evoked a fanatical nationalism, while in the same way as Thomas Marshall in *Ironclad*, Arn Magnusson signifies themes of nationalism – but removed from the radical depictions of Sir Ridley Scott – and instead champions other cultures and stands as a knight who represents a multicultural Sweden.

TEMPLARS IN SPACE

The Knights Templar have been featured in fiction dating back as far as the thirteenth-century Arthurian literature, in film as both heroes and villains and in computer games. They also influenced one of the most successful franchises in history, *Star Wars*.

The story of *Star Wars* came from a two-page synopsis written in 1973 by creator George Lucas, titled 'The Journal of the Whills'. However, before the short synopsis, the saga truly began when Lucas drew up lists of potential character names, which included Emperor Ford Xerxes XII, Xenos, Thorpe, Roland, Monroe, Lars, Kane, Hayden, Crispin, Leila, Zena, Owen, Mace, Wan, Star, Bail, Biggs, Bligh, Cain, Clegg, Fleet and Valorum. The list of characters was followed by a list of planet names, which included Alderaan, Anchorhead, Bestine, Starbuck, Lundee, Yavin, Kissel and Herald Square.[20] Fans of *Star Wars* will undoubtedly recognise several of these character names and places featured within the *Star Wars* universe.

From the list of names, Lucas then wrote 'The Journal of the Whills' synopsis, which told 'the Story of Mace Windy, a revered Jedi-Bendu of Ophuchi, as related to us by C.J. Thorpe, a padawan learner to the famed Jedi'. The synopsis explains that 16-year-old Chuiee Two Thorpe (C.J. Thorpe) enters the 'exalted Intersystems Academy to train as a potential Jedi-Templer [*sic*]'.[21]

The significance of the synopsis is that it mentions the Templars in relation to this early version of the Jedi. Although the word was dropped and became Jedi Knight in later versions, it is clear that the infamous Knights Templar partly inspired the Jedi of *Star Wars*. Mark Hamill, who played the original Jedi hero, Luke Skywalker, commented on the influence of the Templars on the Jedi in an interview for *The Wrap*, 'He [Lucas] was probably thinking more of King Arthur and the Knights of the Round Table, because it was more idealised and glamorous, certainly, than the Templar knights. But there's no question that his inspiration was rooted partially in this mythology.' The Arthurian inspiration for the Jedi is apparent in the original 1977 *Star Wars* film, including the Arthurian trope of a commoner (Luke Skywalker) being given a magic sword by an old wizard (Obi-Wan Kenobi).

The audience knew very little about the Jedi Knights from the original *Star Wars Trilogy* (1977–83) as, like the Templars in the setting of those films, the Jedi were no more. The Jedi were introduced by Obi-Wan Kenobi (played by Sir Alec Guinness), who explained to Luke, 'For over a thousand generations, the Jedi Knights were the guardians of peace and justice in the old Republic, before the dark times, before the Empire.' Obi-Wan then reveals what happened to the Jedi, 'A young Jedi named Darth Vader, who was a pupil of mine until he turned to evil, helped the Empire hunt down and destroy the Jedi Knights. He betrayed and murdered your father. Now the Jedi are all but extinct.'[22] It wasn't until the *Prequel Trilogy* (1999–2005) that the Jedi were depicted as a monastic order similar to the Knights Templar, and while the Templars' had an international presence, the Jedi Knights operated across the galaxy.

The prequel films revealed that the similarity between the Jedi and Templars is more than a throwaway word in an old synopsis. Both of these orders of knights operated independently from their government, and both lived by a strict set of rules. The Templars lived by the monastic rule bestowed upon them as the Primitive Rule in 1129 (see Chapter 1), while the Jedi lived by the Jedi Code. The Templar rule comprised of almost 700 clauses that informed the Templar knights how to live as warrior monks, while very little of the Jedi Code is revealed in the *Prequel Trilogy*. However, comparisons between the rule and the code can be drawn, such as the perils of attachment, which the Jedi Master Yoda explains, 'Attachment leads to jealousy; the shadow of greed that is'.[23] This notion is found within the Templar Rule, such as Clause 34, which states, 'Let no brother have a lockable purse or bag'. Attachment is also the subject of Clause 35, 'The master may give to whomsoever he pleases the horse and armour and whatever he likes of another brother, and the brother to whom the given thing belongs should not become vexed or angry: for be certain that if he becomes angry he will go against God.' The essence of Clause 35 relates closely to Yoda's warning of greed: both orders live as monks and, in the case of the Templars, are not allowed to have personal property as all remain under the control of the House Commander.[24]

During their early years, the Knights Templars' sole purpose was to patrol the roads of the Holy Land and protect travellers, which resembles the role of the Jedi Knights as the galaxy's guardians of peace and justice. However, following the death of the First Templar grand master, they moved away from this to become a standing army and a major military force in the Crusades, which is replicated in the *Prequel Trilogy* when the Jedi Knights play a significant role in the Republic Army during the Clone Wars.

The orders would also meet a similar end as both are brought down by an insidious conspiracy. The Knights Templar are accused of heresy by King Philip IV of France, while the Jedi are accused of treason by Emperor Palpatine. Both orders also feature an attack on their Temple headquarters – King Philip's soldiers raided the French Temple, while Palpatine sent Darth Vader to massacre all the Jedi at the Jedi Temple. While the few surviving Jedi, which included Yoda and Obi-Wan (played by Ewan McGregor), went into exile, the Knights Templar continued via two newly created knightly orders in Portugal and Spain (see Chapter 16).

The influence the Knights Templar had on Lucas' Jedi Order demonstrates how they have continued to capture imaginations as far back as the thirteenth-century grail poem *Parzival*, through novels, film, computer games and even influencing one of the greatest entertainment franchises of all time. Although the Templars were dissolved in 1312, they didn't just live on in the successive orders of the Order of Christ and the Order of Montesa, but their legacy continued through the emergence of the myths that were established during the Renaissance and further embellished by the Freemasons. These fuelled artistic imaginations and further embedded myths of the Grail, the occult, the Freemasons and even the romantic perception of the warrior monks into popular culture works that continue to influence the perception of the long-gone Order of the Knights Templar.

CONCLUSION

THE LEGACY OF THE KNIGHTS TEMPLAR

The Knights Templar were born from the blood and suffering of the First Crusade and created to police the roads of Outremer. They were a revolutionary form of knighthood founded on Christmas Day 1119, where knights lived a dual life as both warriors and monks. The First Grand Master Hugues de Paynes secured the monastic rule for the knights to live by, known as the Primitive Rule, at the Council of Troyes in 1129.

The revolutionary order was popular among the European lords, and donations of wealth and land were received to support the Templars in providing additional manpower to protect travellers in the Holy Land. However, following the death of Hugues de Paynes in 1136, the order expanded its influence within the Crusader states and became a premier fighting force of the Frankish Christians.

For almost 200 years, the Templar knights fought the Crusader cause in the Holy Land, amassing vast amounts of land and castles in Outremer to support the Frankish nobility in wars against Egypt and Syria. The Templars were highly influential in the military successes of the Crusader states, such as the Battle of Montgisard in 1177 and the surprise attack led by Templar Gilbert de Lacy on Nūr ad-Dīn in 1163, which forced the sultan to flee with what remained of his army.

However, for all the victories, the Templars strongly featured in some of the Christians' heaviest defeats. In 1187, at the Springs of Cresson, the Templar Grand Master Gérard de Ridefort launched an unwise attack on a far larger army, leading to the massacre of his knights. Later that year, he urged King Guy to abandon their camp's strong position and march on Saladin's army, which led to the annihilation of the Kingdom of Jerusalem's army at the Battle of Hattin.

In 1291, Mamluk Sultan al-Malik al-Ashraf conquered Acre and effectively ended the Crusader states almost 200 years after the First Crusaders had captured Jerusalem, forcing the Templars to relocate to Cyprus to plan a new Crusade, which never happened. The Templars were blamed for the loss of Acre as they had been granted enormous wealth to protect the Crusader states; however, there was little they could have done against the strength and resources of the Mamluks. After all, the Mamluks defeated the Mongols, who had been seen as invincible prior to the Battle of Ain Jalut in 1260.

Without the Crusader states, the Templars were considered redundant, making them politically weak. On Friday, 13 October 1307, King Philip IV arrested the Templars and seized their property, accusing the order of blasphemy, sodomy and heresy. Whether the king believed the charges is open to debate, but as he was struggling financially, he had previously seized the wealth of the Italian Bankers in 1291 and the Jews in 1306. The last Grand Master Jacques de Molay was burnt at the stake in 1314, and the Order of the Knights Templar was abolished.

So, what is the legacy of the Knights Templar? These warrior monks are seen in several guises, as chivalric knights, occultists and the worst of the Crusaders. The sixteenth century saw the associations of the Templars with the occult drawn from their confessions under torture, one that is still echoed today through media such as the 2017 Hollywood film *The Mummy*. The Templars became related to the fictional Holy Grail in the thirteenth century, a link that still captures the perception and connects them to popular culture within the realm of the fantastical, as exemplified in Dan Brown's novel *The Da Vinci Code*.

While the nineteenth-century novels of Sir Walter Scott portrayed the Templars to be the worst of the Crusaders, they were also reimagined romantically within the pseudohistory of the Freemasons and the novels of Swedish writer Jan Guillou. This romantic perception of the Templars inspired George Lucas when creating the Jedi Knights of the *Star Wars* universe, which is contrasted by their fantastical villainy in the *Assassin's Creed* franchise.

The Templars' sudden arrests shocked Europe, and their downfall fuelled imaginations and fantastical theories. However, with the order abolished, there was no one to safeguard their legacy, which is how the Freemasons came to claim them as their ancestors. The original inspiration for this book came from the desire to tackle the misappropriation of Templar history, which ranges from fantastical theories at best to fanatical extremism at worst.

The Order of the Knights Templar has captivated popular culture since its emergence in the early twelfth century; today, the Templars are used in media as a vehicle to incorporate contrasting themes of villainy, chivalry, the occult, the quest for the Grail and shadowy conspiracies. Despite being officially abolished by the Pope in 1312, the Knights Templar legacy reaches far beyond its role in the Crusades, becoming an infamous historical phenomenon whose story has been rewritten again and again over the centuries, ensuring that the long-gone warrior monks are not forgotten.

NOTES

Introduction

1 Michael Haag, *The Tragedy of the Templars: The Rise and Fall of the Crusader States* (London: Profile Books Ltd, 2014), pp. 24–25.
2 Thomas Ashbridge, *The Crusades: The War for the Holy Land* (London: Simon & Schuster, 2012), p. 19.
3 Ibid., pp. 19–20.
4 Ibid., p. 21.
5 Haag, *The Tragedy of the Templars*, p. 60.
6 Ashbridge, *The Crusades*, pp. 21–22.
7 Ibid., p. 22.
8 Ibid., pp. 34–35.
9 Fulcher of Chartres, in Patrick J. Geary (ed.), *Readings in Medieval History* (New York: Broadview Press Ltd, 1989), p. 427.
10 Ashbridge, *The Crusades*, p. 40.
11 Ibid., p. 42.
12 Ibid., p. 41.
13 Thomas Ashbridge, *The First Crusade: A New History* (London, Simon & Schuster, 2005), p. 84.
14 Solomon Bar Simson, in Geary (ed.), *Readings in Medieval History*, p. 437.
15 Ibid., p. 440.
16 Ibid., p. 438.
17 Ibid., pp. 441–42.
18 Hans Eberhard Mayer, *The Crusades* (Oxford: Oxford University Press,1990), p. 41.
19 Ashbridge, *The First Crusade*, pp. 102–03.
20 Mayer, *The Crusades*, p. 46.
21 Stephen, Count of Blois, to his wife Adela (June 1097) in Malcolm Barber & Keith Bate (trans.), *Letters from the East: Crusaders, Pilgrims and Settlers in the 12th–13th centuries* (Farnham: Ashgate Publishing Limited, 2013), p. 48.
22 Fulcher of Chartres, in Geary (ed.), *Readings in Medieval History*, p. 431.
23 Ibn al-Athīr, in Francesco Gabrieli (ed.), *Arab Historians of the Crusades* (London: Routledge, 1969), p. 8.
24 Ashbridge, *The First Crusade*, p. 240.
25 Haag, *The Tragedy of the Templars*, pp. 112–13.
26 Ashbridge, *The First Crusade*, p. 305.
27 Fulcher of Chartres, in Geary (ed.), *Readings in Medieval History*, p. 435.
28 Ibid.

Chapter 1

1 Ashbridge, *The Crusades*, p. 115.
2 Ibid., pp. 118–19.
3 Ibid., p. 119.
4 Jonathan Riley-Smith, *The Atlas of the Crusades* (London: Guild Publishing, 1991), p. 40.
5 Ibid., p. 36.
6 Ashbridge, *The First Crusade*, p. 151.
7 Saewulf, in John Wilkinson, Joyce Hill & William F. Ryan (eds) *Jerusalem Pilgrimage, 1099–1185* (United Kingdom: Taylor & Francis Group, 1988), pp. 100–01.
8 Daniel the Abbot, in Ibid., p. 156.
9 Haag, *The Tragedy of the Templars*, p. 124.
10 Ashbridge, *The Crusades*, p. 163.
11 Mayer, *The Crusades*, p. 73.
12 Sharan Newman, *The Real History Behind the Templars* (New York: The Berkley Publishing Group, 2007), p. 5.
13 Haag, *The Tragedy of the Templars*, p. 126.
14 James Wasserman, *The Templars and the Assassins: The Militia of Heaven* (Rochester: Inner Traditions International, 2001), p. 284.
15 Mayer, *The Crusades*, p. 82.
16 Haag, *The Tragedy of the Templars*, p. 136.
17 Ibid., p. 138.
18 J.M. Upton-Ward, *The Rule of the Templars* (Woodbridge: The Boydell Press, 2002), pp. 35–36.
19 Ibid., pp. 24–25.
20 Ibid., p. 32.
21 Ibid., p. 28.
22 Ibid., p. 30.
23 Newman, *The Real History Behind the Templars*, p. 39.
24 Upton-Ward, *The Rule of the Templars*, pp. 25–27.
25 Wasserman, *The Templars and the Assassins*, p. 164.
26 Ibid., p. 278.
27 Ibid., p. 279.
28 Ibid., p. 280.
29 Ibid., p. 283.
30 Upton-Ward, *The Rule of the Templars*, p. 49.
31 Ibid., p. 13.
32 Ibid., p. 51
33 Wasserman, *The Templars and the Assassins*, pp. 165–66.

Chapter 2

1 Ibn al-Qalānisi, in Gabrieli, *Arab Historians*, p. 40.
2 Mayer, *The Crusades*, p. 82.
3 Ibid., p. 83.
4 Ibid.
5 Ibid., p. 84.
6 Ibn al-Athīr, in Gabrieli, *Arab Historians*, p. 53.
7 Ibid., p. 55.
8 Ibid., p. 42.

9 Ibid., p. 43.
10 Ashbridge, *The Crusades*, p. 192.
11 Ibid., p. 193.
12 Ibn al-Athīr, in Gabrieli, *Arab Historians*, p. 51.
13 Ibn al-Qalānisi, in Ibid., p. 49.
14 Ashbridge, *The Crusades*, p. 194.
15 Ibn al-Qalānisi in Gabrieli, *Arab Historians*, p. 50.
16 Haag, *The Tragedy of the Templars*, p. 169.
17 Ibid., p. 174.
18 Ashbridge, *The Crusades*, p. 204.
19 Mayer, *The Crusades*, pp. 93–94.
20 Jonathan Riley-Smith, *The Crusades: A History* (London: Continuum International Publishing Group Ltd, 2010), p. 121.
21 Haag, *The Tragedy of the Templars*, p. 176.
22 Mayer, *The Crusades*, pp. 96–97.
23 Ibid., p. 98.
24 Haag, *The Tragedy of the Templars*, p. 177.
25 Jonathan Phillips, *The Second Crusade: Extending the Frontiers of Christendom* (New Haven & London: Yale University, 2010), p. 171.
26 Ashbridge, *The Crusades*, p. 220.
27 Odo of Deuil, *De Profectione Ludovici VII In Orientem* [*The Journey of Louis VII to the East*] (New York: W.W. Norton, 1948), pp. 63–65.
28 Ibid., p. 65.
29 Ibid., p. 67.
30 Ibid., p. 89.
31 Mayer, pp. 101.
32 Odo of Deuil, *De Profectione Ludovici VII In Orientem*, p. 117.
33 Phillips, *The Second Crusade*, p. 200.
34 Odo of Deuil, *De Profectione Ludovici VII In Orientem*, pp. 119–21.
35 Ibid., p. 121.
36 William of Tyre, translated as *A History of Deeds Done Beyond the Sea. Volume Two*, tr. A Babcock & A.C Krey (New York: Columbia University Press, 1948), pp. 176–77.
37 William of Tyre, *A History of Deeds Vol 2*, p. 177.
38 Odo of Deuil, *De Profectione Ludovici VII In Orientem*, p. 125.
39 Phillips, *The Second Crusade*, p. 202.
40 Ibid.
41 Odo of Deuil, *De Profectione Ludovici VII In Orientem*, p. 127.
42 Ibid., p. 141.

Chapter 3

1 Louis VI, King of France, letter to the Archbishop of Reims, Sugar, the Abbot of St Denis, and Count Ralph of Vermandois in Barber & Bate (eds), *Letters from the East*, p. 46.
2 Michael the Syrian, *The Syriac Chronicle of Michael Rabo (The Great) A Universal History from the Creation*, translated by Matti Moosa (New Jersey: Beth Antioch Press, 2014), p. 670.
3 Ibid., p. 671.
4 Ibid.
5 Majorie Chibnall (ed. and trans.), *The Historia Pontificalis of John of Salisbury* (Clarendon Press: Oxford, 1986), pp. 52–53.

6 William of Tyre, *A History of Deeds Vol 2*,p. 184.
7 Ibid., p. 185.
8 Mayer, The Crusades, p. 106.
9 Phillips, *The Second Crusade*, p. 217.
10 William of Tyre, *A History of Deeds Vol 2*, p. 187.
11 Ibn al-Qalānisi, in Gabrieli (ed.), *Arab Historians of the Crusades*, p. 57.
12 Ibid., p. 57.
13 William of Tyre, *A History of Deeds Vol 2*, p. 187–188.
14 Ibid., p. 191.
15 Ibn al-Athīr, in Gabrieli (ed.), *Arab Historians of the Crusades*, p. 60.
16 Ibn al-Qalānisi, in Gabrieli (ed.), *Arab Historians of the Crusades*, p. 59.
17 William of Tyre, *A History of Deeds Vol 2*, p. 195.
18 Phillips, *The Second Crusade*, p. 140.
19 Chibnall (ed. and trans.), *The Historia Pontificalis of John of Salisbury*, p. 57.
20 Conrad III letter to Wibald, Abbot of Stavelot, and Corvey, in Barber & Bate (trans.), *Letters from the East*, p. 47.

Chapter 4

1 William of Tyre, *A History of Deeds Vol 2*, p. 197.
2 Ashbridge, *The Crusades*, p. 241.
3 William of Tyre, *A History of Deeds Vol 2*, p. 198–199.
4 Ibid., p. 199.
5 Andrew of Montbard to Everard des Barres, late 1149 or early 1150, in Barber & Bate (trans.), *Letters from the East*, p. 48.
6 Ashbridge, *The Crusades*, p. 243.
7 Haag, *The Tragedy of the Templars*, pp. 194–95.
8 Mayer, *The Crusades*, p. 107.
9 Ibn al-Athīr, in Gabrieli (ed.), *Arab Historians of the Crusades*, pp. 71–72.
10 Katherine Pangonis, *Queens of Jerusalem: The Women Who Dared to Rule* (London: Weidenfeld & Nicolson, 2022), p. 159.
11 William of Tyre, *A History of Deeds Vol 2*, p. 213.
12 Ibid., p. 204.
13 Mayer, *The Crusades*, pp. 108–09.
14 William of Tyre, *A History of Deeds Vol 2*, pp. 205–07
15 Malcolm Barber, *The New Knighthood* (Cambridge: University Printing House, 2021), p. 73.
16 William of Tyre, *A History of Deeds Vol 2*, p. 202.
17 Ibid., p. 203.
18 Ibid., p. 220.
19 Ibid., pp. 227–28.
20 H.A.R. Gibb, *Damascus Chronicle of the Crusades: Extracted and Translated from the Chronicle of Ibn al-Qalānisi* (London: Luzac & Co., 1932), p. 316.
21 Malcolm Barber, *The New Knighthood*, p. 75.
22 Bahā' al-Dīn, in Gabrieli (ed.), *Arab Historians of the Crusades*, p. 112.
23 William of Tyre, *A History of Deeds Vol 2*, p. 235.
24 Mayer, *The Crusades*, p. 112.
25 Ibid., p. 114.
26 Ashbridge, *The Crusades*, pp. 247–48.

Chapter 5

1 William of Tyre, *A History of Deeds Vol 2*, p. 255.
2 Ibid., pp. 255–56.
3 Ibid., p. 260.
4 Ibn al-Qalānisi, in Gabrieli (ed.), *Arab Historians of the Crusades*, p. 67.
5 William of Tyre, *A History of Deeds Vol 2*, p. 261.
6 Malcolm Barber, *The New Knighthood*, p. 95.
7 Katherine Pangonis, *Queens of Jerusalem*, p. 171.
8 William of Tyre, *A History of Deeds Vol 2*, pp. 296–98.
9 Mayer, *The Crusades*, p. 117.
10 Barber, *The New Knighthood*, pp. 75–76.
11 Ashbridge, *The Crusades*, p. 267.
12 William of Tyre, *A History of Deeds Vol 2*, p. 303.
13 Ibid., p. 305.
14 Ibid., p. 306.
15 Ibid., p. 307.
16 Ibid., p. 308.
17 Barber, *The New Knighthood*, p. 97.
18 Amalric, King of Jerusalem, to Louis VII, King of France (12 January 1165), Antioch in Barber & Bate (trans.), *Letters from the East*, p. 62.
19 William of Tyre, *A History of Deeds Vol 2*, p. 310.
20 Bahā' al-Dīn Ibn Shaddād, *The Rare and Excellent History of Saladin*, translated by D.S. Richard (Oxon: Routledge, 2016), p. 42.
21 William of Tyre, *A History of Deeds Vol 2*, p. 321.
22 Ashbridge, *The Crusades*, p. 270.
23 William of Tyre, *A History of Deeds Vol 2*, p. 331.
24 Ibid., p. 332.
25 Ibid., p. 336.
26 Ibid., p. 342.
27 Ashbridge, *The Crusades*, p. 271.
28 Barber, *The New Knighthood*, p. 97.
29 William of Tyre, *A History of Deeds Vol 2*, p. 312.
30 Barber, *The New Knighthood*, p. 100.
31 William of Tyre, *A History of Deeds Vol 2*, p. 391.
32 Ibid., p. 392.
33 Ibid., p. 393.
34 Barber, *The New Knighthood*, p. 101.
35 Mayer, *The Crusades*, p. 120.
36 Bahā' al-Dīn Ibn Shaddād, *The Rare and Excellent History of Saladin*, p. 44.
37 William of Tyre, *A History of Deeds Vol 2*, p. 357.
38 Bahā' al-Dīn Ibn Shaddād, *The Rare and Excellent History of Saladin*, p. 45.

Chapter 6

1 Ashbridge, *The Crusades*, p. 275.
2 Bahā' al-Dīn Ibn Shaddād, *The Rare and Excellent History of Saladin*, p. 26.
3 Ibid., p. 18.
4 Ibid., pp. 22–23.
5 Ibid., p. 28.

6 Ibid., p. 25.
7 Ibid., p. 35.
8 William of Tyre, *A History of Deeds Vol 2*, p. 363.
9 Ibid., p. 364.
10 Bahā' al-Dīn Ibn Shaddād, *The Rare and Excellent History of Saladin*, p. 46.
11 William of Tyre, *A History of Deeds Vol 2*, p. 364.
12 Ashbridge, *The Crusades*, p. 281.
13 Ibid., p. 282.
14 Ibn al-Athīr, in Gabrieli (ed.), *Arab Historians of the Crusades*, p. 69.
15 William of Tyre, *A History of Deeds Vol 2*, p. 394.
16 Ibn al-Athīr, in Gabrieli (ed.), *Arab Historians of the Crusades*, pp. 70–71.
17 William of Tyre, *A History of Deeds Vol 2*, p. 395.
18 Bahā' al-Dīn Ibn Shaddād, *The Rare and Excellent History of Saladin*, p. 51.
19 Ibn al-Athīr, *The Chronicle of Ibn al-Athir for the Crusading Period from al-Kamil fi'l-Ta'rikh*, Part 2, translated by D.S. Richard (Oxon: Routledge, 2016), p. 233.
20 Ibn al-Athīr, *The Chronicle of Ibn al-Athir for the Crusading Period from al-Kamil fi'l-Ta'rikh*, Part 2, pp. 233–34.
21 Ashbridge, *The Crusades*, p. 287.
22 Wasserman, *The Templars and the Assassins*, p. 135.
23 William of Tyre, *A History of Deeds Vol 2*, p. 398.
24 Ibid.
25 Ashbridge, *The Crusades*, pp. 301–02.
26 Katherine Pangonis, *Queens of Jerusalem*, p. 173.
27 William of Tyre, *A History of Deeds Vol 2*, p. 426.
28 Ashbridge, *The Crusades*, pp. 306–07.
29 Ibn al-Athīr, *The Chronicle of Ibn al-Athir*, Part 2, p. 253.
30 Raymond, Brother of the Hospital, to the Christian faithful (1178), Jerusalem, in Barber & Bale (trans.), *Letters from the East*, p. 72.
31 Haag, *The Tragedy of the Templars*, p. 255.
32 Helen Nicholson, *The Knights Templar: A New History* (Stroud: Sutton Publishing, 2001), p. 66.
33 Haag, *The Tragedy of the Templars*, pp. 255–56.
34 Ibn al-Athīr, *The Chronicle of Ibn al-Athir for the Crusading Period from al-Kamil fi'l-Ta'rikh*, Part 2, p. 254.
35 Ashbridge, *The Crusades*, p. 311.
36 Ibn al-Athīr, *The Chronicle of Ibn al-Athir for the Crusading Period from al-Kamil fi'l-Ta'rikh*, Part 2, p. 266.
37 William of Tyre, *A History of Deeds Vol 2*, p. 443.
38 Haag, *The Tragedy of the Templars*, p. 259.
39 Ibn al-Athīr, *The Chronicle of Ibn al-Athir for the Crusading Period from al-Kamil fi'l-Ta'rikh*, Part 2, p. 265.
40 Ibid., pp. 265–66.
41 Haag, *The Tragedy of the Templars*, p. 259.
42 Malcolm Barber, *The New Knighthood*, p. 86.
43 Haag, *The Tragedy of the Templars*, pp. 259–60.

Chapter 7

1 Bahā' al-Dīn Ibn Shaddād, *The Rare and Excellent History of Saladin*, pp. 57–58.
2 Ibid., pp. 59–60.

3 Ashbridge, *The Crusades*, p. 319.
4 Bahā' al-Dīn Ibn Shaddād, *The Rare and Excellent History of Saladin*, p. 68.
5 Ibn al-Athīr, *The Chronicle of Ibn al-Athir for the Crusading Period from al-Kamil fi'l-Ta'rikh*, Part 2, p. 308.
6 William of Tyre, *A History of Deeds Vol 2*, p. 492.
7 Ibid., p. 416.
8 Peter W. Edbury, *The Conquest of Jerusalem and The Third Crusade: Sources in Translation* (Aldershot: Ashgate Publishing Limited, 2007), pp. 151–53.
9 William of Tyre, *A History of Deeds Vol 2*, p. 446.
10 Edbury, *The Conquest of Jerusalem*, pp. 150–51.
11 Mayer, *The Crusades*, p. 131.
12 Ibid., p. 132.
13 Edbury, *The Conquest of Jerusalem*, pp. 14–15.
14 Ibid., pp. 38–39.
15 Ibid., p. 26.
16 Ibid., pp. 154–55.
17 Ibn al-Athīr, *The Chronicle of Ibn al-Athir for the Crusading Period from al-Kamil fi'l-Ta'rikh*, Part 2, p. 315.
18 Ibid., p. 316.
19 William of Tyre, *A History of Deeds Vol 2*, p. 505.
20 Edbury, *The Conquest of Jerusalem*, p. 30.
21 Bahā' al-Dīn Ibn Shaddād, *The Rare and Excellent History of Saladin*, p. 37.
22 Ibn al-Athīr, *The Chronicle of Ibn al-Athir for the Crusading Period from al-Kamil fi'l-Ta'rikh*, Part 2, p. 316.
23 Bahā' al-Dīn Ibn Shaddād, *The Rare and Excellent History of Saladin*, p. 37.
24 Edbury, *The Conquest of Jerusalem*, pp. 31–32.
25 Ibid., pp. 31–32.
26 Ibid., pp. 156–57.
27 Ibid., p. 32.
28 Princes and Ecclesiastics Beyond the Sea to Emperor Frederick Barbarossa (July 1187), in Barber & Bate (trans.) *Letters from the East*, p. 76.
29 Edbury, *The Conquest of Jerusalem*, pp. 32–33.
30 Ibn al-Athīr, in Gabrieli (ed.), *Arab Historians of the Crusades*, p. 118.

Chapter 8

1 Ashbridge, The Crusades, p. 345.
2 Mayer, *The Crusades*, pp. 134–35.
3 Ashbridge, *The Crusades*, p. 343.
4 Edbury, *The Conquest of Jerusalem*, p. 39.
5 Mayer, *The Crusades*, p. 135.
6 Imād al-Dīn, in Gabrieli (ed.), *Arab Historians of the Crusades*, p. 130.
7 Bahā' al-Dīn Ibn Shaddād, *The Rare and Excellent History of Saladin*, p. 73.
8 Ibn al-Athīr, *The Chronicle of Ibn al-Athir*, Part 2, p. 322.
9 Edbury, *The Conquest of Jerusalem*, p. 46.
10 Ibn al-Athīr, *The Chronicle of Ibn al-Athir*, Part 2, p. 322.
11 Edbury, *The Conquest of Jerusalem*, p. 47.
12 Ibid., p. 161.
13 Terricus, Grand Preceptor of the Temple, to All Preceptors and Brethren of the Temple in the West (between 10 July and 6 August 1187), in Barber & Bate (trans.), *Letters from the East*, p. 78.

14 Barber, *The New Knighthood*, p. 93.
15 Ibid., p. 95.
16 Ibn al-Athīr, *The Chronicle of Ibn al-Athir*, Part 2, p. 322.
17 Ibid., p. 323.
18 Imād al-Dīn, in Gabrieli (ed.), *Arab Historians of the Crusades*, p. 135.
19 Edbury, *The Conquest of Jerusalem*, p. 161.
20 Bahā' al-Dīn Ibn Shaddād, *The Rare and Excellent History of Saladin*, p. 75.
21 Ibn al-Athīr, *The Chronicle of Ibn al-Athir*, Part 2, p. 324.
22 Imād al-Dīn, in Gabrieli (ed.), *Arab Historians of the Crusades*, p. 75.
23 Ibn al-Athīr, *The Chronicle of Ibn al-Athir*, Part 2, p. 324.
24 Imād al-Dīn, in Gabrieli (ed.), *Arab Historians of the Crusades*, p. 138.
25 Ibn al-Athīr, *The Chronicle of Ibn al-Athir*, Part 2, p. 324.

Chapter 9

1 Edbury, *The Conquest of Jerusalem*, p. 49.
2 Ibn al-Athīr, *The Chronicle of Ibn al-Athir*, Part 2, p. 326.
3 Ibid., pp. 327–30.
4 Ibid., p. 331.
5 Bahā' al-Dīn Ibn Shaddād, *The Rare and Excellent History of Saladin*, p. 77.
6 Ibn al-Athīr, *The Chronicle of Ibn al-Athir*, Part 2, p. 331.
7 Edbury, *The Conquest of Jerusalem*, pp. 56–57.
8 Ibn al-Athīr, *The Chronicle of Ibn al-Athir*, Part 2, p. 332.
9 Imād al-Dīn, in Gabrieli (ed.), *Arab Historians of the Crusades*, p. 158.
10 Edbury, *The Conquest of Jerusalem*, p. 62.
11 Imād al-Dīn, in Gabrieli (ed.), *Arab Historians of the Crusades*, p. 158.
12 Ashbridge, *The Crusades*, pp. 360–61.
13 Ibid., p. 361.
14 Ibn al-Athīr, *The Chronicle of Ibn al-Athir*, Part 2, p. 334.
15 Imād al-Dīn, in Gabrieli (ed.), *Arab Historians of the Crusades*, p. 175.
16 Mayer, *The Crusades*, p. 139.
17 Eraclius, Patriarch of Jerusalem, to Pope Urban III (September 1187), in Barber & Bate (trans.), *Letters from the East*, p. 81.
18 Ibn al-Athīr, *The Chronicle of Ibn al-Athir*, Part 2, pp. 328–29.
19 Ibid., p. 335.
20 Ibid., p. 336.
21 Ashbridge, *The Crusades*, p. 394.
22 Terricus, former Grand Preceptor of the Temple at Jerusalem, to Henry II, King of England (January 1188), in Barber & Bate (trans.), *Letters from the East*, p. 84.
23 Ibn al-Athīr, *The Chronicle of Ibn al-Athir*, Part 2, p. 337.
24 Ibid., p. 356.
25 Mayer, *The Crusades*, p. 136.
26 Ashbridge, *The Crusades*, p. 371.
27 Jessalynn Bird, Edward Peters & James M. Powell (eds), *Crusade and Christendom: Annotated Documents in Translation from Innocent III to the Fall of Acre, 1187–1291* (Philadelphia: University of Pennsylvania Press, 2013), p. 6.
28 Ibid., p. 7.
29 Ibid., p. 8.
30 Ashbridge, *The Crusades*, p. 378.
31 Mayer, *The Crusades*, p. 139.

32 Ibid.
33 Barber, *The New Knighthood*, p. 278.
34 Mayer, *The Crusades*, p. 140.
35 Helen J. Nicholson, Chronicle of the Third Crusade: A Translation of the Itinerarium Pereginorum et Gesta Regis Ricardi (Oxon: Routledge, 2016), p. 146.
36 Ibid., p. 145.
37 Edbury, *The Conquest of Jerusalem*, p. 80.
38 Ibid.
39 Ibid., pp. 80–81.
40 Bahā' al-Dīn Ibn Shaddād, *The Rare and Excellent History of Saladin*, p. 97.
41 Edbury, *The Conquest of Jerusalem*, p. 81.
42 Bahā' al-Dīn Ibn Shaddād, *The Rare and Excellent History of Saladin*, pp. 98–99.
43 Edbury, *The Conquest of Jerusalem*, p. 170.
44 Ashbridge, *The Crusades*, p. 405.
45 Edbury, *The Conquest of Jerusalem*, p. 170.
46 Ibid.
47 Bahā' al-Dīn Ibn Shaddād, *The Rare and Excellent History of Saladin*, p. 102.
48 Ibn al-Athīr, *The Chronicle of Ibn al-Athir*, Part 2, p. 368.
49 Bahā' al-Dīn Ibn Shaddād, *The Rare and Excellent History of Saladin*, p. 104.
50 Edbury, *The Conquest of Jerusalem*, p. 170.
51 Ibid., p. 83.
52 Ibn al-Athīr, *The Chronicle of Ibn al-Athir*, Part 2, p. 368.
53 Nicholson, *Chronicle of the Third Crusade*, p. 79.
54 Ibid., p. 79.
55 Ibn al-Athīr, *The Chronicle of Ibn al-Athir*, Part 2, p. 370.

Chapter 10

1 Nicholson, *Chronicle of the Third Crusade*, pp. 88–89.
2 Ibn al-Athīr, *The Chronicle of Ibn al-Athir*, Part 2, p. 374.
3 Ibid., p. 372.
4 Nicholson, *Chronicle of the Third Crusade*, p. 91.
5 Ibid., p. 99.
6 Ibid., pp. 94–96.
7 Mayer, *The Crusades*, p. 141.
8 Ibn al-Athīr, *The Chronicle of Ibn al-Athir*, Part 2, p. 375.
9 Nicholson, *Chronicle of the Third Crusade*, pp. 67–68.
10 Bahā' al-Dīn Ibn Shaddād, *The Rare and Excellent History of Saladin*, p. 104.
11 Nicholson, *Chronicle of the Third Crusade*, pp. 98–99.
12 Ibid., p. 129.
13 Bahā' al-Dīn Ibn Shaddād, *The Rare and Excellent History of Saladin*, p. 104.
14 Edbury, *The Conquest of Jerusalem*, p. 173.
15 Ibid., p. 96.
16 Bahā' al-Dīn Ibn Shaddād, *The Rare and Excellent History of Saladin*, p. 145.
17 Ibn al-Athīr, *The Chronicle of Ibn al-Athir*, Part 2, p. 386.
18 Richard I, King of England, to William Longchamps, Bishop of Ely and Chancellor (6 August 1191), Acre, in Barber & Bate (trans.), *Letters from the East*, p. 90.
19 Bahā' al-Dīn Ibn Shaddād, *The Rare and Excellent History of Saladin*, p. 150.
20 Malcolm Barber, *The New Knighthood* (Cambridge: University Printing House, 2021). p. 119.

21 Bahā' al-Dīn Ibn Shaddād, *The Rare and Excellent History of Saladin*, p. 146.
22 Nicholson, p. 204.
23 Ibid, p. 188.
24 Ibid, p. 205.
25 Bahā' al-Dīn Ibn Shaddād, *The Rare and Excellent History of Saladin*,p. 155.
26 Nicholson, *Chronicle of the Third Crusade*, p. 207.
27 Mayer, *The Crusades*, p. 146.
28 Bahā' al-Dīn Ibn Shaddād, *The Rare and Excellent History of Saladin*, p. 161.
29 Nicholson, *Chronicle of the Third Crusade*, p. 221.
30 Ibid., p. 222.
31 Mayer, *The Crusades*, p. 146.
32 Ashbridge, *The Crusades*, p. 445.
33 Ibn al-Athīr, *The Chronicle of Ibn al-Athir*, Part 2, p. 389.
34 Nicholson, *Chronicle of the Third Crusade*, p. 229.
35 Bahā' al-Dīn Ibn Shaddād, *The Rare and Excellent History of Saladin*, p. 165.
36 Edbury, *The Conquest of Jerusalem*, p. 180.
37 Mayer, *The Crusades*, p. 146.
38 Bahā' al-Dīn Ibn Shaddād, *The Rare and Excellent History of Saladin*, p. 165.
39 Nicholson, *Chronicle of the Third Crusade*, p. 231.
40 Ashbridge, *The Crusades*, p. 452.
41 Riley-Smith, *The Atlas of the Crusades*, p. 64.
42 Mayer, *The Crusades*, p. 147.
43 Nicholson, *Chronicle of the Third Crusade*, p. 244.
44 Ibid., pp. 245–48.
45 Richard I, King of England, to N. (1 October 1191), Jaffa, in Barber & Bate (trans.), *Letters from the East*, p. 91.
46 Nicholson, *Chronicle of the Third Crusade*, pp. 246–47.
47 Ibid., p. 248.
48 Ibid., pp. 252–53.
49 Ibid., p. 253.
50 Ibn al-Athīr, *The Chronicle of Ibn al-Athir*, Part 2, p. 391.
51 Mayer, *The Crusades*, p. 145.

Chapter 11

1 Ibn al-Athīr, *The Chronicle of Ibn al-Athir*, Part 2, p. 391.
2 Nicholson, *Chronicle of the Third Crusade*, p. 264.
3 Ibn al-Athīr, *The Chronicle of Ibn al-Athir*, Part 2, p. 392.
4 Ashbridge, *The Crusades*, p. 479.
5 Nicholson, *Chronicle of the Third Crusade*, p. 266.
6 Ibn al-Athīr, *The Chronicle of Ibn al-Athir*, Part 2, p. 393.
7 Nicholson, *Chronicle of the Third Crusade*, p. 280.
8 Ibid., p. 291.
9 Ibid., p. 304.
10 Bahā' al-Dīn Ibn Shaddād, *The Rare and Excellent History of Saladin*, p. 194.
11 Nicholson, *Chronicle of the Third Crusade*, p. 304.
12 Ibid., p. 300.
13 Ibid., pp. 302–03.
14 Edbury, *The Conquest of Jerusalem*, pp. 112–13.
15 Ibid., p. 114.

16 Bahā' al-Dīn Ibn Shaddād, *The Rare and Excellent History of Saladin*, pp. 200–01.
17 Ibn al-Athīr, *The Chronicle of Ibn al-Athir*, Part 2, p. 396.
18 Edbury, *The Conquest of Jerusalem*, p. 115.
19 Nicholson, *Chronicle of the Third Crusade*, p. 272.
20 Ibid., pp. 336–37.
21 Bahā' al-Dīn Ibn Shaddād, *The Rare and Excellent History of Saladin*, pp. 215–16.
22 Ibid., pp. 219–20.
23 Nicholson, *Chronicle of the Third Crusade*, p. 353.
24 Bahā' al-Dīn Ibn Shaddād, *The Rare and Excellent History of Saladin*, pp. 221–22.
25 Nicholson, *Chronicle of the Third Crusade*, p. 355.
26 Bahā' al-Dīn Ibn Shaddād, *The Rare and Excellent History of Saladin*, p. 222.
27 Nicholson, *Chronicle of the Third Crusade*, p. 355.
28 Bahā' al-Dīn Ibn Shaddād, *The Rare and Excellent History of Saladin*, pp. 222–23.
29 Nicholson, *Chronicle of the Third Crusade*, p. 371.
30 Bahā' al-Dīn Ibn Shaddād, *The Rare and Excellent History of Saladin*, p. 231.
31 Nicholson, *Chronicle of the Third Crusade*, p. 380.
32 Ibid., pp. 382–83.
33 Mayer, *The Crusades*, p. 149.
34 Bahā' al-Dīn Ibn Shaddād, *The Rare and Excellent History of Saladin*, p. 244.

Chapter 12

1 Ibn al-Athīr, *The Chronicle of Ibn al-Athir*, Part 3, pp. 25-26..
2 Ibid., p. 39.
3 Ibid., p. 42.
4 Ibid., p. 50.
5 Mayer, *The Crusades*, p. 247.
6 Ibid., p. 240.
7 Ibn al-Athīr, *The Chronicle of Ibn al-Athir*, Part 3, p. 29; Edbury, *The Conquest of Jerusalem*, p. 143.
8 Mayer, *The Crusades*, p. 249.
9 Ibid., p. 196.
10 Edward Peters (ed.), *Christian Society and the Crusades, 1198–1229: Sources in Translation* (Philadelphia: University of Pennsylvania Press, 1971), pp. 4–5.
11 Ashbridge, *The Crusades*, pp. 527–28.
12 Peters, *Christian Society and the Crusades*, p. 10.
13 Riley-Smith, *The Atlas of the Crusades*, p. 84.
14 Peters, *Christian Society and the Crusades*, p. 18.
15 Mayer, *The Crusades*, p. 203.
16 Ibid., p. 204.
17 Ibid., p. 217–18.
18 Ashbridge, *The Crusades*, p. 551.
19 Barber, *The New Knighthood*, p. 127.
20 Mayer, *The Crusades*, pp. 220–21.
21 Peters, *Christian Society and the Crusades*, p. 58.
22 Ibid., p. 88.
23 Ashbridge, *The Crusades*, p. 552.
24 James of Vitry, Bishop of Acre, to Pope Honorius III (August 1218), in Barber & Bate (trans.), *Letters from the East*, p. 110.

25 James of Vitry, Bishop of Acre, to Pope Honorius III (September 1218), Damietta, in Barner & Bate (trans.), *Letters from the East*, p. 113.
26 Ibid., p. 114.
27 Peters, *Christian Society and the Crusades*, p. 72.
28 Ibn al-Athīr, *The Chronicle of Ibn al-Athir*, Part 3, pp. 177–78.
29 Peters, *Christian Society and the Crusades*, pp. 85–86.
30 Ibid., p. 86.
31 Ibid., p. 88.
32 Barber, *The New Knighthood*, p. 129.
33 Ibid., p. 128.
34 Peters, *Christian Society and the Crusades*, p. 107.
35 Ibid., p. 111.
36 Peter of Montaigu, Master of the Temple, to Alan Martel, Preceptor of the Temple in England (Mid-September 1221), in Barber & Bate (trans.), *Letters from the East*, p. 124.
37 Ashbridge, *The Crusades*, p. 560.
38 Peters, *Christian Society and the Crusades*, p. 125.
39 Ibn al-Athīr, *The Chronicle of Ibn al-Athir*, Part 3, p. 180.
40 Peters, *Christian Society and the Crusades*, pp. 127–28.
41 Peter of Montaigu, Master of the Temple, to Alan Martel, Preceptor of the Temple in England (Mid-September 1221), in Barber & Bate (trans.), *Letters from the East*, p. 125.
42 Peters, *Christian Society and the Crusades*, p. 129.
43 Ibn Wāsil in Gabrieli (ed.), *Arab Historians of the Crusades*, p. 264.
44 Peters, *Christian Society and the Crusades*, p. 132.
45 Peter of Montaigu, Master of the Temple, to Alan Martel, Preceptor of the Temple in England (Mid-September 1221), in Barber & Bate (trans.), *Letters from the East*, p. 125.

Chapter 13

1 Barber, *The New Knighthood*, p. 131.
2 Ashbridge, *The Crusades*, p. 565.
3 Mayer, *The Crusades*, p. 233.
4 Ibid., p. 234.
5 Peters, *Christian Society and the Crusades*, p. 151.
6 Barber, *The New Knighthood*, p. 133.
7 Ibn al-Athīr, *The Chronicle of Ibn al-Athir*, Part 3, p. 293.
8 Peters, *Christian Society and the Crusades*, p. 163.
9 Ibn al-Athīr, *The Chronicle of Ibn al-Athir*, Part 3, p. 179.
10 Peters, *Christian Society and the Crusades*, pp. 163–64.
11 Ibn al-Athīr, *The Chronicle of Ibn al-Athir*, Part 3, p. 294.
12 Peters, *Christian Society and the Crusades*, p. 167.
13 Ibid., p. 160.
14 Sibt Ibn al-Jauzī in Gabrieli (ed.), *Arab Historians of the Crusades*, p. 264.
15 Peters, *Christian Society and the Crusades*, p. 160.
16 Barber, *The New Knighthood*, p. 133.
17 Ashbridge, *The Crusades*, p. 572.
18 Ibn Wāsil in Gabrieli (ed.), *Arab Historians of the Crusades*, p. 276.
19 Sibt Ibn al-Jauzī, in Ibid., p. 275.
20 Janet Shirley (ed.), *Crusader Syria in the Thirteenth Century: The Rothelin Continuation of the History of William of Tyre with Part of the Eracles or Acre Text* (Oxford: Taylor & Francis Group, 1999), p. 46.

21 Ibid., p. 51.
22 Ibid., p. 53.
23 Mayer, *The Crusades*, p. 257.
24 Barber, *The New Knighthood*, p. 139.
25 Shirley, *Crusader Syria in the Thirteenth Century*, pp. 57–58.
26 Ibid., p. 58.
27 Richard, Earl of Cornwall and Count of Poitou, to Baldwin of Reviers, Earl of Devon, the Abbot of Beaulieu, and Robert, clerk (July 1241), in Barber & Bate (trans.), *Letters from the East*, p. 138.
28 Shirley, *Crusader Syria in the Thirteenth Century*, p. 63.
29 Robert, Patriarch of Jerusalem and Papal Legate, and other Prelates in the Holy Land, to the Prelates of France and England (25 November 1244), Acre, in Barber & Bate (trans.), *Letters from the East*, pp. 143–44.
30 Barber, *The New Knighthood*, p. 145.
31 Robert, Patriarch of Jerusalem and Papal Legate, and other Prelates in the Holy Land, to the Prelates of France and England (25 November 1244), Acre, in Barber & Bate (trans.), *Letters from the East*, p. 144.
32 Ashbridge, *The Crusades*, p. 575.
33 Barber, *The New Knighthood*, p. 147.
34 Robert, Patriarch of Jerusalem and Papal Legate, and other Prelates in the Holy Land, to the Prelates of France and England (25 November 1244), Acre, in Barber & Bate (trans.), *Letters from the East*, p. 145.

Chapter 14

1 Mayer, *The Crusades*, p. 260.
2 Peter Jackson (ed.), *The Seventh Crusade, 1244–1254: Sources and Documents* (Aldershot: Ashgate Publishing Ltd, 2007), p. 50.
3 Shirley, *Crusader Syria in the Thirteenth Century*, p. 66.
4 Jackson, *The Seventh Crusade*, p. 17.
5 Mayer, *The Crusades*, p. 261.
6 Jackson, *The Seventh Crusade*, p. 63.
7 Shirley, *Crusader Syria in the Thirteenth Century*, p. 69.
8 Barber, *The New Knighthood*, p. 148.
9 Shirley, *Crusader Syria in the Thirteenth Century*, p. 86.
10 Jackson, *The Seventh Crusade*, p. 88.
11 Ibid., p. 91.
12 Ibn Wāsil in Gabrieli (ed.), *Arab Historians of the Crusades*, p. 286.
13 Shirley, *Crusader Syria in the Thirteenth Century*, p. 87.
14 Ashbridge, *The Crusades*, p. 593–94.
15 Jackson, *The Seventh Crusade*, p. 100.
16 Shirley, *Crusader Syria in the Thirteenth Century*, p. 95.
17 Ibid., pp. 95–96.
18 Ibn Wāsil in Gabrieli (ed.), *Arab Historians of the Crusades*, p. 294.
19 Shirley, *Crusader Syria in the Thirteenth Century*, p. 97.
20 Ashbridge, *The Crusades*, p. 597.
21 Barber, *The New Knighthood*, p. 151.
22 Shirley, *Crusader Syria in the Thirteenth Century*, p. 99.
23 Ibid., pp. 100–01.
24 Jackson, *The Seventh Crusade*, p. 102.

25 Ibid., p. 105.
26 Ashbridge, *The Crusades*, p. 604.
27 Shirley, *Crusader Syria in the Thirteenth Century*, pp. 102–03.
28 Jackson, *The Seventh Crusade*, p. 110.
29 Ashbridge, *The Crusades*, p. 606.
30 Riley-Smith, *The Atlas of the Crusades*, p. 96.

Chapter 15

1 Jackson, *The Seventh Crusade*, pp. 150–52.
2 Ibid., p. 153.
3 Ashbridge, *The Crusades*, p. 611.
4 Haag, *The Tragedy of the Templars*, p. 314.
5 Ashbridge, *The Crusades*, p. 612.
6 Mayer, *The Crusades*, p. 270.
7 Paul Crawford (trans.), *The Templar of Tyre: Part III of the 'Deeds of the Cypriots'* (Oxon: Ashgate Publishing, 2021), p. 37.
8 Mayer, *The Crusades*, p. 270.
9 Crawford, *The Templar of Tyre*, p. 38.
10 Ashbridge, *The Crusades*, pp. 630–31.
11 Crawford, *The Templar of Tyre*, p. 44.
12 Barber, *The New Knighthood*, p. 167.
13 Crawford, *The Templar of Tyre*, p. 50.
14 Barber, *The New Knighthood*, p. 166.
15 Ibid., p. 167.
16 Crawford, *The Templar of Tyre*, p. 51.
17 Mayer, *The Crusades*, p. 281.
18 Crawford, *The Templar of Tyre*, p. 59.
19 Ashbridge, *The Crusades*, pp. 636–37.
20 Crawford, *The Templar of Tyre*, p. 68.
21 Ashbridge, *The Crusades*, pp. 643–44.
22 Marc Morris, *A Great and Terrible King: Edward I and the Forging of Britain* (London: Windmill Books, 2009), p. 100.
23 Crawford, *The Templar of Tyre*, p. 69.
24 Ashbridge, *The Crusades*, p. 644.
25 Crawford, *The Templar of Tyre*, p. 77.
26 Mayer, *The Crusades*, pp. 283–84.
27 Barber, *The New Knighthood*, p. 173.
28 Ibid., pp. 173–74.
29 Crawford, *The Templar of Tyre*, p. 75.
30 Barber, *The New Knighthood*, p. 174.
31 Crawford, *The Templar of Tyre*, pp. 86–87.
32 Ibid., pp. 99–100.
33 David Cook (trans.), *Baybars' Successors: Ibn al-Furāt on Qalāwūn and al-Ashraf* (Oxon: Routledge, 2020), p. 203.
34 Crawford, *The Templar of Tyre*, pp. 100–01.
35 Cook, *Baybars' Successors*, p. 204.
36 Barber, *The New Knighthood*, p. 176.
37 Crawford, *The Templar of Tyre*, p. 102.
38 Cook, *Baybars' Successors*, p. 211.

39 Crawford, *The Templar of Tyre*, p. 102.
40 Mayer, *The Crusades*, pp. 285–86.
41 Cook, *Baybars' Successors*, p. 216.
42 Ibid., p. 220.
43 Crawford, *The Templar of Tyre*, p. 103.
44 Ibid., pp. 104–05.
45 Mayer, *The Crusades*, p. 286.
46 Alain Demurger, *The Last Templar: The Tragedy of Jacques de Molay* (London: Profile Books Lts, 2009), p. 55.
47 Crawford, *The Templar of Tyre*, p. 107.
48 Abu al-Fidā in Gabrieli (ed.), *Arab Historians of the Crusades*, p. 345.
49 Crawford, *The Templar of Tyre*, pp. 108–09.
50 Ibid., pp. 110–11.
51 Ibid., pp. 111–12.
52 Ibid., p. 113.
53 Ibid., pp. 115–16.
54 Abu al-Mahasin in Gabrieli (ed.), *Arab Historians of the Crusades*, p. 348.
55 Crawford, *The Templar of Tyre*, pp. 116–17.
56 Abu al-Mahasin in Gabrieli (ed.), *Arab Historians of the Crusades*, p. 349.
57 Crawford, *The Templar of Tyre*, p. 118.
58 Mayer, *The Crusades*, p. 286.

Chapter 16

1 Cook, *Baybars' Successors*, pp. 275–76.
2 Demurger, *The Last Templar*, p. 4.
3 Ibid., p. 73.
4 Haag, *The Tragedy of the Templars*, p. 335.
5 Demurger, *The Last Templar*, p. 102.
6 James of Molay, Master of the Temple, to King James II of Aragon (8 November 1301), Limassol, in Barber & Bate (trans.), *Letters from the East*, p. 168.
7 Demurger, *The Last Templar*, p. 107.
8 Barber, *The New Knighthood*, p. 294.
9 Crawford, *The Templar of Tyre*, p. 161.
10 Haag, *The Tragedy of the Templars*, pp. 339–40.
11 Barber, *The New Knighthood*, pp. 298–99.
12 Peter Partner, *The Murdered Magicians: The Templars and their Myth* (Wellingborough: Thorsons Publishing Group, 1987), p. 36.
13 Ibid., p. 37.
14 Barber, *The New Knighthood*, p. 278.
15 Letter of Clement V to Phillip IV (24 August 1307), in Barber & Bate (trans.), *The Templars: Selected Sources* (Manchester: Manchester University Press, 2002), pp. 243–44.
16 Order for Arrests (14 September 1307), in Barber & Bate (trans.), *The Templars*, pp. 244–45.
17 Ibid., p. 245.
18 Partner, *The Murdered Magicians*, p. 59.
19 Malcolm Barber, *The Trial of the Templars* (Cambridge: Cambridge University Press, 1994), p. 46.
20 Order for Arrests (14 September 1307), in Barber & Bate (trans.), *The Templars*, p. 248.

21 Deposition of Ponsard of Gizy (27 November 1309) in Barber & Bate (trans.), *The Templars*, p. 290.
22 Barber, *The Trial of the Templars*, p. 56.
23 Ibid., p. 58.
24 Partner, *The Murdered Magicians*, p. 52.
25 Ibid., p. 54.
26 Newman, *The Real History Behind the Templars*, p. 274.
27 Order for Arrests (14 September 1307), in Barber & Bate (trans.), *The Templars*, p. 253.
28 Ibid., p. 251.
29 Ibid., pp. 254–55.
30 Barber, *The Trial of the Templars*, pp. 61–62.
31 Newman, *The Real History Behind the Templars*, p. 338.
32 Ibid., p. 354.
33 Barber, *The Trial of the Templars*, pp. 77–78.
34 Haag, *The Tragedy of the Templars*, pp. 355–56.
35 Ibid., p. 361.
36 Barber, *The Trial of the Templars*, pp. 228–29.
37 Ibid., p. 231.
38 Haag, *The Tragedy of the Templars*, p. 366.
39 Helen Nicholson, *The Knights Templar: A New History* (Stroud: Sutton Publishing Limited, 2001), pp. 231–32.
40 Ibid., p. 236.
41 Michael Haag, *The Knights Templar: History & Myth* (London: Profile Books Ltd, 2009), p. 247.

Chapter 17

1 David Staines (trans.), *The Complete Romances of Chrétien de Troyes* (Bloomington: Indiana University Press, 2010), p. xii.
2 Ibid., p. xii.
3 Ibid., pp. xii–xxiii.
4 Ibid., p. 379.
5 Ibid., p. xxiv.
6 Rebecca A. & Samuel J. Umland, *The Use of Arthurian Legend in Hollywood Film: From Connecticut Yankees to Fisher Kings* (Westport: Greenwood Press, 1996), p. 13.
7 Staines, *The Complete Romances of Chrétien de Troyes*, p. 377.
8 Ibid., p. 379.
9 Ibid., p. xv.
10 Umland & Umland, *The Use of Arthurian Legend in Hollywood Film*, p. 13.
11 Patrick Masters, *The Knights Templar in Popular Culture: Film, Video Games and Fan Tourism* (Jefferson: McFarland & Company, Inc., 2022), pp. 107–08.
12 Wolfram Von Eschenbach, *Parzival*, translated by A.T. Hatto (London: Penguin Books Ltd, 2004), p. 240.
13 Ibid., p. 125.
14 Ibid., p. 250.
15 Haag, *The Knights Templar*, pp. 253–54.
16 Masters, *The Knights Templar in Popular Culture*, p. 119.
17 Daly, S., 'Spielberg and Lucas: The titans talk!', *Entertainment Weekly*, 18 April 2008.
18 Masters, *The Knights Templar in Popular Culture*, p. 124.

19 Newman, *The Real History Behind the Templars*, p. 365.
20 Susan Aronstein, 'The Da Vinci Code and the Myth of History' in K.J. Harty (ed.), *The Holy Grail on Film: Essays on the Cinematic Quest* (North Carolina: McFarland & Company, Inc., 2015), p. 112.
21 Dan Brown, *The Da Vinci Code* (New York: Double Day, 2016), p. 11.
22 Robin Griffith-Jones, *The Da Vinci Code and the Secrets of the Temple* (London: Canterbury Press Norwich, 2006), pp. 15–16.
23 Ibid., pp. 16–18.
24 Brown, *The Da Vinci Code*, p. 214.
25 Newman, *The Real History Behind the Templars*, p. 394.
26 David Martin-Jones, 'Film tourism as heritage tourism: Scotland, diaspora and The Da Vinci Code (2006)' in *New Reive of Film and Television Studies*, 12:2 (2014), p. 167.
27 Masters, *The Knights Templar in Popular Culture*, p. 156.
28 Griffith-Jones, *The Da Vinci Code and the Secrets of the Temple*, p. 65.

Chapter 18

1 Partner, *The Murdered Magicians*, p. 89.
2 Barber, *The New Knighthood*, p. 315.
3 Partner, *The Murdered Magicians*, p. 90.
4 Heinrich Cornelius Agrippa von Nettesheim in Donald Tyson (ed.) & James Freake (trans.), *Three Books of Occult Philosophy* (Woodbury: Llewellyn Publications, 2009), p. 114.
5 Partner, *The Murdered Magicians*, pp. 93–94.
6 Ibid., p. 95.
7 Ibid., p. 96.
8 Masters, *The Knights Templar in Popular Culture*, p. 186.
9 Tartaglione, O., '"Resident Evil: The Final Chapter" To Push Franchise Past $1B Global This Weekend', *Deadline*, 27 January 2017. Retrieved from https://deadline.com/2017/01/resident-evil-the-final-chapter-franchise-crossing-one-billion-dollars-global-box-office-1201895482
10 Masters, *The Knights Templar in Popular Culture*, p. 190.
11 Newman, *The Real History Behind the Templars*, p. 402.
12 Frank Sanello, *The Knights Templars: God's Warriors, the Devil's Bankers* (Maryland: Taylor Trade Publishing, 2003), pp. 221–22.
13 Partner, *The Murdered Magicians*, pp. 116–17.
14 Barber, *The New Knighthood*, p. 318.
15 Sanello, *The Knights Templars*, pp. 223–24.
16 Newman, *The Real History Behind the Templars*, p. 361.
17 Haag, *The Knights Templar: History & Myth*, pp. 268–69.
18 Ibid., pp. 270–71.
19 Ibid., pp. 270–73.
20 Masters, *The Murdered Magicians*, p. 124.
21 Ibid., p. 138.
22 Ibid., p. 189.
23 Barber, *The New Knighthood*, p. 334.

Chapter 19

1 Jonathan Phillips, 'The Crusades', *History Today*, 59 (11) (2009), p. 13.
2 Masters, *The Knights Templar in Popular Culture*, p. 40.
3 Ibid., pp. 41–42.

4 Ibid., p. 187.
5 Ibid., p. 43.
6 Nicholas Haydock, *Movie Medievalism: The Imaginary Middle Ages* (Jefferson: McFarland & Company, Inc., 2008), p. 48.
7 Irvine, L, '$225 Isn't bad I guess', *The Guardian*, 6 October 2005. Retrieved from www.theguardian.com/film/2005/oct/06/features.lindesayirvine
8 Stuart, K., 'Interviews with Assassins', *The Guardian*, 9 May 2007. Retrieved from www.theguardian.com/technology/gamesblog/2007/may/09/interviewswith
9 Masters, *The Knights Templar in Popular Culture*, p. 80.
10 Partner, *The Murdered Magicians*, p. 96.
11 Masters, *The Knights Templar in Popular Culture*, pp. 50–51.
12 Ibid., pp. 52–53.
13 Ibid., p. 54.
14 Elizabeth Heale, *The Faerie Queene: A Readers Guide* (2nd ed. Cambridge: Cambridge University Press, (1999), p. 42.
15 Fouché, G., 'Revisionism on a Grand Scale', *The Guardian*, 8 October 2008. Retrieved from www.theguardian.com/film/2008/oct/08/2
16 Usama in Gabrieli (ed.), *Arab Historians of the Crusades*, pp. 79–80.
17 Masters, *The Knights Templar in Popular Culture*, p. 56.
18 Erik Hedling, 'The Arn Franchise: Launching a Small Country Blockbuster', Film International, 35:6 (2008), p. 62.
19 Michaëlis, B.T., 'Guillou', January 2001. Retrieved from www.forfatterweb.dk/oversigt/guillou- jan/print_zguillou00
20 Jonathan W. Rinzler, *The Making of Star Wars: The Definitive Story Behind The Original Film* (London: Ebury Press, 2008), pp. 12–13.
21 Ibid., p. 13.
22 George Lucas (dir.), *Star Wars Episode IV: A New Hope* (Lucasfilm, 1977).
23 George Lucas (dir.), *Star Wars Episode III: Revenge of the Sith* (Lucasfilm, 2005).
24 Upton-Ward, *The Rule of the Templars*, p. 28.

BIBLIOGRAPHY

Aronstein, Susan, 'The Da Vinci Code and the Myth of History'. In K.J. Harty (ed.), *The Holy Grail on Film: Essays on the Cinematic Quest* (North Carolina: McFarland & Company, Inc., 2015).

Ashbridge, Thomas, *The First Crusade: A New History* (London, Simon & Schuster, 2005).

Ashbridge, Thomas, *The Crusades: The War for the Holy Land* (London: Simon & Schuster, 2012).

Bahā' al-Dīn Ibn Shaddād, *The Rare and Excellent History of Saladin*, translated by D.S. Richard (Oxon: Routledge, 2016).

Barber, Malcolm, *The Trial of the Templars* (Cambridge: Cambridge University Press, 1994).

Barber, Malcolm, *The New Knighthood* (Cambridge: University Printing House, 2021).

Barber, Malcolm, & Keith Bate (trans.), *The Templars: Selected Sources* (Manchester: Manchester University Press, 2002).

Barber, Malcolm, & Keith Bate (trans.), *Letters from the East: Crusaders, Pilgrims and Settlers in the 12th–13th centuries* (Farnham: Ashgate Publishing Limited, 2013).

Bird, Jessalynn, Edward Peters & James M. Powell (eds), *Crusade and Christendom: Annotated Documents in Translation from Innocent III to the Fall of Acre, 1187–1291* (Philadelphia: University of Pennsylvania Press, 2013).

Brown, Dan, *The Da Vinci Code* (New York: Double Day, 2016).

Chibnall, Majorie (trans. and ed.), *The Historia Pontificalis of John of Salisbury* (Clarendon Press: Oxford, 1986).

Cook, David (trans.), *Baybars' Successors: Ibn al-Furāt on Qalāwūn and al-Ashraf* (Oxon: Routledge, 2020).

Crawford, Paul (trans.), *The Templar of Tyre: Part III of the 'Deeds of the Cypriots'* (Oxon: Ashgate Publishing, 2021).

Daly, S., 'Spielberg and Lucas: The titans talk!', *Entertainment Weekly* (18 April 2008).

Demurger, Alain, *The Last Templar: The Tragedy of Jacques de Molay* (London: Profile Books Lts, 2009).

Edbury, Peter W. (ed.), *The Conquest of Jerusalem and the Third Crusade: Sources in Translation* (Aldershot: Ashgate Publishing Limited, 2007).

Eschenbach, Wolfram von, *Parzival*, translated by A.T. Hatto (London: Penguin Books Ltd, 2004).

Fouché, G., 'Revisionism on a Grand Scale', *The Guardian* 8 October 2008. Retrieved from www.theguardian.com/film/2008/oct/08/2

Gabrieli, Francesco (ed.), *Arab Historians of the Crusades* (London: Routledge, 1969).

Geary, Patrick J. (ed.), *Readings in Medieval History* (New York: Broadview Press Ltd,1989).

Gibb, H.A.R., *Damascus Chronicle of the Crusades: Extracted and Translated from the Chronicle of Ibn al-Qalanisi* (London: Luzac & Co., 1932).

Griffith-Jones, Robin, *The Da Vinci Code and the Secrets of the Temple* (London: Canterbury Press Norwich, 2006).
Haag, Michael, *The Knights Templar: History & Myth* (London: Profile Books Ltd, 2009).
Haag, Michael, *The Tragedy of the Templars: The Rise and Fall of the Crusader States* (London: Profile Books Ltd, 2014).
Haydock, Nicholas, *Movie Medievalism: The Imaginary Middle Ages* (Jefferson: McFarland & Company, Inc., 2008).
Heale, Elizabeth, *The Faerie Queene: A Readers Guide* (2nd ed. Cambridge: Cambridge University Press, 1999).
Hedling, Erik, 'The Arn Franchise: Launching a Small Country Blockbuster', *Film International*, 35:6 (2008).
Ibn al-Athīr, *The Chronicle of Ibn al-Athir for the Crusading Period from al-Kamil fi'l-Ta'rikh*, Part 2, translated by D.S. Richard (Oxon: Routledge, 2016).
Ibn al-Athīr, *The Chronicle of Ibn al-Athir for the Crusading Period from al-Kamil fi'l-Ta'rikh*, Part 3, translated by D.S. Richard (Oxon: Routledge, 2016).
Irvine, L., '$225 Isn't bad, I guess', *The Guardian*, 6 October 2005. Retrieved from www.theguardian.com/film/2005/oct/06/features.lindesayirvine
Jackson, Peter (ed.), *The Seventh Crusade, 1244–1254: Sources and Documents* (Aldershot: Ashgate Publishing Ltd, 2007).
Lucas, George (director), *Star Wars Episode IV: A New Hope* (Lucasfilm, 1977).
Lucas, George (director), *Star Wars Episode III: Revenge of the Sith* (Lucasfilm, 2005).
Martin-Jones, David, 'Film tourism as heritage tourism: Scotland, diaspora and *The Da Vinci Code* (2006)', *New Reive of Film and Television Studies*, 12:2 (2014).
Masters, Patrick, *The Knights Templar in Popular Culture: Film, Video Games and Fan Tourism* (Jefferson: McFarland & Company, Inc., 2022).
Mayer, Hans Eberhard, *The Crusades* (Oxford: Oxford University Press, 1990).
Michael the Syrian, *The Syriac Chronicle of Michael Rabo (The Great) A Universal History from the Creation*, translated by Matti Moosa (New Jersey: Beth Antioch Press, 2014).
Michaëlis, B.T., 'Guillou', January 2001. Retrieved from www.forfatterweb.dk/oversigt/guillou- jan/print_zguillou00
Morris, Marc, *A Great and Terrible King: Edward I and the Forging of Britain* (London: Windmill Books, 2009).
Newman, Sharan, *The Real History Behind the Templars* (New York: The Berkley Publishing Group, 2007).
Nicholson, Helen, *The Knights Templar: A New History* (Stroud: Sutton Publishing Limited, 2001).
Nicholson, Helen, *Chronicle of the Third Crusade: A Translation of the Itinerarium Pereginorum et Gesta Regis Ricardi* (Oxon: Routledge, 2016).
Odo of Deuil, *De Profectione Ludovici VII In Orientem* [*The Journey of Louis VII to the East*] (New York: W.W. Norton, 1948).
Pangonis, Katherine, *Queens of Jerusalem: The Women Who Dared to Rule* (London: Weidenfeld & Nicolson, 2022).
Partner, Peter, *The Murdered Magicians: The Templars and their Myth* (Wellingborough: Thorsons Publishing Group, 1987).
Peters, Edward (ed.), *Christian Society and the Crusades, 1198–1229 : Sources in Translation* (Philadelphia: University of Pennsylvania Press, 1971).
Phillips, Jonathan, 'The Crusades', *History Today*, 59(11) (2009).
Phillips, Jonathan, *The Second Crusade: Extending the Frontiers of Christendom* (New Haven & London: Yale University, 2010).

Riley-Smith, Jonathan, *The Atlas of the Crusades* (London: Guild Publishing, 1991).
Riley-Smith, Jonathan, *The Crusades: A History* (London: Continuum International Publishing Group Ltd, 2010).
Rinzler, Jonathan W., *The Making of Star Wars: The Definitive Story Behind The Original Film* (London: Ebury Press, 2008).
Sanello, Frank, *The Knights Templars: God's Warriors, the Devil's Bankers* (Maryland: Taylor Trade Publishing, 2003).
Shirley, Janet (ed.), *Crusader Syria in the Thirteenth Century: The Rothelin Continuation of the History of William of Tyre with Part of the Eracles or Acre Text* (Oxford: Taylor & Francis Group, 1999).
Staines, David (trans.), *The Complete Romances of Chrétien de Troyes* (Bloomington: Indiana University Press, 2010).
Stuart, K., 'Interviews with Assassins', *The Guardian*, 9 May 2007. Retrieved from www.theguardian.com/technology/gamesblog/2007/may/09/interviewswith
Tartaglione, O., '"Resident Evil: The Final Chapter" To Push Franchise Past $1B Global This Weekend', *Deadline*, 27 January 2017. Retrieved from https://deadline.com/2017/01/resident-evil-the-final-chapter-franchise-crossing-one-billion-dollars-global-box-office-1201895482
Tyson, Donald, (ed.) & James Freake (trans.), *Three Books of Occult Philosophy* (Woodbury: Llewellyn Publications, 2009).
Umland, Rebecca A., & Samuel J., *The Use of Arthurian Legend in Hollywood Film: From Connecticut Yankees to Fisher Kings* (Westport: Greenwood Press, 1996).
Upton-Ward ,J.M., *The Rule of the Templars* (Woodbridge: The Boydell Press, 2002).
Wasserman, James, *The Templars and the Assassins: The Militia of Heaven* (Rochester: Inner Traditions International, 2001).
Wilkinson, John, Joyce Hill & William F. Ryan (eds), *Jerusalem Pilgrimage, 1099–1185* (United Kingdom: Taylor & Francis Group,1988).
William of Tyre, translated as *A History of Deeds Done Beyond the Sea*, translated by A. Babcock & A.C. Krey (New York: Columbia University Press, 1948).

INDEX